THE DESIRE FOR SYRIA IN MEDIEVAL ENGLAND

In June 1458, two boats were cornered by pirates off the coast of Malta. Their captain – Robert Sturmy – proved no match for the notorious Genoese freebooter Giuliano Gattilusio and was summarily killed by him. The precious cargo for which Sturmy paid with his life contained stealable goods but also cultural significance. Sweet wines, spices, silks, jewels, and minerals – these alluring commodities gripped the medieval English imagination. E.K. Myerson utilises this dramatic incident of Mediterranean plunder to reveal the impact of Syrian imports on medieval art, language, and everyday life. They argue that the cultural category of 'Syriana' became a powerful tool, used to evoke both the sacred sites of the Holy Land and the global marketplaces of the Mamlūk Empire. Myerson's innovative book draws on their research into medieval archives, conceptual art, and postcolonial and queer theory, showing how medieval 'Syriana' transformed English society in ways which continue to resonate today.

E.K. MYERSON is an artist, writer, and curator, currently studying at the Royal College of Art. Their academic and creative writing has appeared in publications including *GLQ*, *The TLS*, *Wasafiri Magazine*, *New Medieval Literatures*, *postmedieval*, and *Wellcome Collection Stories*. They were a Genesis Jewish Book Week Emerging Writer in 2021–22. They received their PhD in medieval literature from Birkbeck College in 2022, and have held postdoctoral fellowships at the Wellcome Trust/ ISSF Fund, the Parker Library, and Emmanuel College, Cambridge. Their essay-film 'submerged reliquary of a Kentish saint', made with artist Sophie Mei Birkin at the Jarman Lab, was screened at the Birkbeck Institute of the Moving Image in 2022 and 2023.

'*The Desire for Syria in Medieval England* is an eloquent and original study of the internationalism of medieval Europe and the Near East. E.K. Myerson shows how the global marketplace of the later Middle Ages influenced English culture, as commerce and commodification went hand in hand with an ambivalent desire for the East. *The Desire for Syria in Medieval England* helps us to see the intersections of longing and power in a timely account of how medieval culture understood the wider world.'

Anthony Bale, Professor of Medieval and Renaissance English, University of Cambridge

'A startling work of scholarship, imagination, and defamiliarisation, this book is as exciting as it is original.'

Devorah Baum, Professor of English Literature, University of Southampton

'*The Desire for Syria in Medieval England* is an entrancing, exhilarating revelation of how the idea of Syria and the desire for the precious things emanating from it pervaded late medieval and early modern England. E.K. Myerson's book is arranged as a glittering inventory of the goods carried by merchant ships between the Levant and Europe, which allows them to riddle out with erudite delight the meanings – magical, medical, mercantile, alchemical, and sacramental – of commodities like sweet wine, spices, silk, jewels, and alum. Nor does Myerson let us forget how much of the desire for Syria persists in our present, which their particoloured history reflects back to itself in a medieval mirror.'

Steven Connor, Professor of English and Director of Research, Digital Futures Institute, King's College London

'A rich and timely book that explores the deep connections between European markets and the products of the Holy Land. The story of a shipwreck is the starting point for a fascinating analysis of medieval texts, from poetry to pilgrimage accounts. Myerson has a wonderful eye for detail and brings the objects and fantasies of the fifteenth century into sharp – and thought-provoking – focus.'

Marion Turner, J. R. R. Tolkien Professor of English Literature and Language, University of Oxford

'Like one of the medieval craftworkers who appear in these pages – jeweller, silk weaver, or glass engraver – E.K. Myerson has wrought a remarkable, intricate, and wonderful story of cultural entanglement. Scrupulously attentive to the unsaid and the unexamined, adventurous and imaginative in their approach, and ever thoughtful in their commentary, they complicate prevalent views of Muslim, Jewish, and Christian hostility. *The Desire for Syria in Medieval England* is an exciting and unusual study, packed with a rich cargo of treasures – in more ways than one.'

Marina Warner, author of Stranger Magic: Charmed States and the Arabian Nights

THE DESIRE FOR SYRIA IN MEDIEVAL ENGLAND

E.K. MYERSON
University of Cambridge

CAMBRIDGE
UNIVERSITY PRESS

CAMBRIDGE
UNIVERSITY PRESS

Shaftesbury Road, Cambridge CB2 8EA, United Kingdom

One Liberty Plaza, 20th Floor, New York, NY 10006, USA

477 Williamstown Road, Port Melbourne, VIC 3207, Australia

314–321, 3rd Floor, Plot 3, Splendor Forum, Jasola District Centre, New Delhi – 110025, India

103 Penang Road, #05–06/07, Visioncrest Commercial, Singapore 238467

Cambridge University Press is part of Cambridge University Press & Assessment, a department of the University of Cambridge.

We share the University's mission to contribute to society through the pursuit of education, learning and research at the highest international levels of excellence.

www.cambridge.org
Information on this title: www.cambridge.org/9781009426800

DOI: 10.1017/9781009426848

When citing this work, please include a reference to the DOI: 10.1017/9781009426848

First published 2026

Cover image: Trade on the seaports of the Levant. Photo: Lanmas / Alamy Stock Photo Printed

in the United Kingdom by TJ Books, Padstow, Cornwall

A catalogue record for this publication is available from the British Library

A Cataloging-in-Publication data record for this book is available from the Library of Congress

ISBN 978-1-009-42680-0 Hardback

Contents

Figures

Abbreviations

IJMES –	*International Journal of Middle East Studies*
JMEMS –	*Journal of Medieval and Early Modern Studies*
MED –	*Middle English Dictionary*, online edition (Ann Arbor, MI: University of Michigan Press, 2021) <https://quod.lib.umich.edu/m/middle-english-dictionary/dictionary>
MLN –	*Modern Language Notes*
OED –	*Oxford English Dictionary Online*, <oed.com>
PMLA –	*Publications of the Modern Language Association*
SAC –	*Studies in the Age of Chaucer*

Prologue: Robert Sturmy's Last Voyage

On Friday 9 June 1458, a pirate ship swerved and fired on two Bristolian trading boats as they passed the coast of Malta, on their return from the Levant. I found the event transcribed in a legal document of the fifteenth century.[1] I could see the inky vessels with their lost signatures, the *Katherine Sturmy* and the *Marie*, trapped in the footnotes of an unwritten narrative. These ships of the Bristol merchant Robert Sturmy contained over £18,000 worth of Syrian and Mediterranean goods – nearly £11.6 million in contemporary terms.[2] The cargo contained sweet wines, spices, jewels, silks, and the mineral alum. These were high-status commodities, with the potential to shift the fortunes of their traders and the city to which they were returning. This event, its protagonists, and their cargo belong to a history of cultural encounter, failure, and desire.

'Today, on the 18th June', wrote the Viceroy of Sicily in Latin, in a letter sent to King Henry VI of England, a man called John Heyton came 'to this Isle of Ghawdex'. Heyton was injured and grieving, recalling how, as he and Robert were sailing past Malta, a 'carvel of Genoa attacked . . . and chased them'. The attacking ships were captained by the notorious pirate Giuliano Gattilusio (1435–80). The survivors who returned to England described how they were 'horribly and *hevyously* without pity and compassion *murdred*, *slayne*, drowned and cast into the *see*'.[3] The chase lasted three days – before the pirates captured the ships and, in the words of the Viceroy of Sicily, 'placed the said John and the said Robert and others who after the harsh battle and cruel slaughter and bloodshed remained half-alive, on the Isle of Malta. And they sailed to Libya with the two ships.'[4]

I find myself unable to resist my own fantasies as I read these historical records – I can see Robert left bleeding on the beach, his shirt ripped, as John, his partner, tries to lift him – I can see the doctors and priests running towards them as Robert presses his lips to the other man's wet shirt and tastes the salt on his tongue which is the sea, and which is his own blood – John crying as Robert, his captain, begins to lose consciousness.

Snap out of it, I think – this is not a movie. Or is it? The medievalist Carlo Ginzburg asked rhetorically: 'Without cinema, without the close-up' would the critic 'have been able to speak of microhistory?'[5] In electing to structure my study around one specific historical journey, I was motivated by Michael Wintroub's study of the voyages taken by the humanist poet and sailor Jean Parmentier from France to Sumatra in 1529.[6] Like Wintroub, I see the voyage as a route into understanding the society which framed its departure.

On 11 June 1458, Sturmy died, leaving a widow in Bristol, Ellen (née Talbot). Gattilusio commandeered his ships with their precious cargo and steered them to Libya. Sturmy's business partner, John Heyton, survived and made his way home with the crew who survived.

The Trials of the Genoese

When he returned to England, Heyton brought a case before King Henry VI 'in his own name and that of Robert Sturmy'.[7] He argued that they deserved compensation for the value of the lost goods – and an additional £10,000 damages for 'the *hevyous affraye*, grievous *woundyng*, maiming and blood-letting of them done by the Genoese . . . and for their *lechecrafte* [medicines], costs and expenses done by them in . . . coming home by *straunge* countries'.[8] The pirate Gattilusio was out of reach in Libya. Instead, the Genoese residents in London and Southampton were rounded up on royal command, imprisoned and put on trial for the value of the lost goods. One chronicler wrote that 'the *Jannays* took *Stumyes* ship of *Bristow* . . . which had been in *hethenesse*. Wherefore the Genoese *beyng* in London were arrested and put into the Fleet, and were adjudged to pay for the *harmys* that their *nacion* had done.'[9] In the medieval period, the term *natio* was used to describe a person's place of birth and mother tongue.[10] The discourse and emergent structure of nationhood was already present in the Middle Ages, although the modern nation-state was not yet in operation.[11]

The trials of the Genoese took place between August and November 1458. The records give a sense of the status of the incident. A man called William Denys of Devonshire came forward to give evidence. He made his pilgrimage to Jerusalem in 1458, at the same time and along the same routes as Sturmy's trading vessels – their ships passed one another in the Mediterranean. Returning from Jerusalem, he reached Rhodes, where he learned of the Genoese ships 'which had robbed Robert Sturmy and John Heytone'. Denys learned that the same pirate ships were (apparently) on their way to capture the Earl of Worcester, a fellow passenger on his ship – and so the group travelled swiftly to Corfu in order to find new ships to avoid the attack. In Corfu, they were told that the Genoese still sailed with Sturmy's ships, which they were taking 'together with the merchandise of the English to be sold in another place'. From Corfu, Denys travelled through the Adriatic Sea to Poreč, where he was told that Sturmy's other ship, the *Marie*, had been sent away with all the merchandise, to be sold. From Poreč he crossed over to Venice, where the rumour was that the Genoese state had sent sailors to aid Gattilusio.[12] In each stop on his voyage, Denys learned news of the event – showing how reports moved around these connected locations. The goods on Sturmy's ships were significant and valuable enough that their loss was an international sensation.

Elizabeth Lambourn's microhistory of the twelfth-century Judeo-Arabic luggage list of the merchant Abraham Ben Yiju takes his inventory as a starting point for a portrait of twelfth-century trade across the Indian Ocean, opening up everyday experiences of premodern travel and exchange.[13] Setting off into the critical waters which Wintroub's and Lambourn's books have cleared, this book contains a cultural history of the Syrian and Mediterranean commodities on Sturmy's ships: sweet wine, spices, silks, jewels, and the mineral alum.

Voyaging between Histories

Sturmy's failure came at a critical moment in the history of English trade and global relations. Across the imagination of the scene hovers a grid, the lines of an undrawn map. Paul Gilroy writes that ships are 'cultural and political units'.[14] These premodern ships were the units of an unfixed culture and a changeable politics, hovering between these states: ownership, citizenship, relationship. Their status is hard to define. The financial scale of Sturmy's venture implies that his aim was to create a direct maritime link between Bristol and the Levant, cutting out the Italian intermediaries who monopolised the market. In 1458, merchants sailing back to Bristol were – what? The symbolism of these voyages is uneasy – trade, on the verge of colonialism, on the brink: the coastline of histories. As Cord Whitaker has argued, while 'modernity is where we expect to find race', the race-thinking of the Middle Ages had a direct influence on early modern colonialism.[15] But Sturmy travelled in the wake of ships which came before him, and was travelling towards an unconquerable global centre. Insofar as his ship inscribed English power that was a known fantasy, the futility of which was realised in the encounter with imperial command, in the marketplaces of the Mamlūk Empire.

If Sturmy had travelled towards Syria two centuries earlier, he would have been travelling towards European Christian settlements. From the eleventh to the thirteenth century, the Frankish crusaders had occupied select territories across Syria, following the call for holy war from Rome.[16] These were the crusader states: Edessa (1097–1150), Antioch (1098–1287), Tripoli (1102–1289), and Jerusalem (1099–1291).[17] Together these states were known in Europe as 'Syria' or 'Outremer' – the lands *outre-mer*, beyond the sea – and have been described as colonial-style settlements.[18] In 1187, Jerusalem was conquered. After that, Acre ['Akka/'Akko] was the capital of the Christian Kingdom of Jerusalem. The crusaders never captured Aleppo or Damascus: even at the peak of Christian rulership, major regions of Syria remained unattainable. From the mid thirteenth century, all of the Christian settlements were in steady decline.[19] In 1291, the Mamlūk Empire recaptured the last crusader settlement of Acre. The Mamlūk Empire (1250–1517) extended across Egypt and Syria, establishing these locations as global centres of trade and cultural production, which medieval Europeans could emulate, but could not surpass. By the time Sturmy arrived in the Mediterranean, these dynamics were well established.

As European trade with the Mamlūk Empire continued to grow, the likelihood of Christian settlement of Syria continued to decline. Janet Abu-Lughod has shown that medieval Europe was economically dependent on global networks.[20] Some scenes surrounding the objects on Sturmy's ships will foreshadow and record histories of European settlement and extraction – but they also witness the realities of an alternative premodern economic system. These commodities are ambivalent signifiers, containing foreboding but also remembering a moment when the British Empire was not inevitable.

Still, Sturmy has been seen as a precursor to the colonial traders who followed him. Evan Jones writes: 'Any analysis of why England – a relatively small and poor country – became Europe's premier economy has to begin with Sturmy.'[21] David Abulafia comments of Sturmy's conflict with the Genoese that: 'These were the violent beginnings of the ties between England and the Mediterranean that would transform the sea in later centuries.'[22] But seeing Sturmy's voyage as a 'beginning' is not entirely accurate. Sturmy was travelling along marine paths which had been crossed for at least 300 years, and all of the commodities on his ships were already circulating within well-established international networks.[23] Although the movement towards European colonialism had already begun elsewhere – the first shipment of African slaves had arrived in Portugal in 1444 – it did not begin with Sturmy. In 1497, the Bristol-based, Genoese-born John Cabot sailed out in search of the sources of spices, reaching North America, an action which has been seen as laying the foundations for British colonisation.[24] In the sixteenth century, the international trade routes from Bristol became the paths of the transatlantic slave trade, with Bristol becoming England's main port for the slave trade in the early eighteenth century.[25] These later voyages wash throughout the history which separates Sturmy from the present day. For example, several of the texts in this study survive in manuscripts donated to the British Library by Hans Sloane, who owned slaves and whose additional wealth was derived from his marriage to the widow of a plantation owner.[26] These realities shape the preservation, reception and aftermath of the narratives described in this project: but Sturmy's relationship to these histories is inconclusive. As Matthew X. Vernon writes: 'By turning our gaze to the medieval period we can see what might be called a pre-history to later patterns of desire and appropriation' which 'must be repeatedly reconsolidated with maneuvers that create the space for unexpected correspondences between identities'.[27]

In *Poetics of Relation*, the postcolonial theorist Édouard Glissant describes how 'Root identity . . . rooted the thought of self and of territory and set in motion the thought of the other and of Voyage.' The imperial ship transported a sense of self-centrality with it, constructing the Other as the inverse of that dominant subject. While the ship was moving, its captain – subjectively – was not. By contrast: Relation identity 'does not think of a land as a territory from which to project toward other territories . . .. Relation identity exults the thought of errantry.'[28] Instead of taking a Voyage in a single direction, the Relational subject wanders between places. As a trader, Sturmy's journey was not errant – but he was not an imperial captain either. I take these ambivalences and uncertainties as a starting point for analysis: a route into an unfixed cultural moment.

Robert Sturmy before the Voyage

Little is known of Robert Sturmy until the 1430s, at which point he began his career as a merchant-sailor. Like other Bristol merchants, he started by trading goods in Ireland and Gascony. By the mid 1440s, Sturmy had begun importing rare dyes, citrus fruits, and paper – and also began exporting English wool to Pisa, indicating that he had managed to create a network of professional connections in Italy.

In 1446, Sturmy made his first trading voyage beyond Europe.[29] A fifteenth-century notebook records 'the voyage of Robert Sturmy to Jerusalem 1446'. The author, William Worcester (1415–1482), was the secretary of the landowner Sir John Falstoff (1380–1459), and made his notes while travelling around South-Western England. He wrote: '*memorandum* that in the month of July . . . Robert *Sturmyn*, merchant of the town of Bristol, began his voyage of the port of Bristol from King Road to Jerusalem, with about 160 pilgrims'. It was common for merchants to fund their ventures by taking paying passengers. Worcester goes on to describe how returning from

> the port of Jaffa . . . by the island of Modon the ship, called the *Cog Anne*, was on the 23rd December by a sudden storm and strong wind arising in the dark and dead of night suddenly and without warning driven on a rock and ashore, and thirty-seven of the passengers and seamen were drowned, to the very great grief of their friends in Bristol, and of their wives.

The pilgrims were not on board – they had chosen to return home overland. At the island of Modon 'a certain devout bishop' buried the bodies of the thirty-seven dead and 'founded a holy chapel there to pray for their souls and for those of all the faithful departed'.[30]

That time Sturmy survived. When he returned to Bristol he refocused his ambitions on local government. In 1450, he became a town councillor. In 1451, he was made sheriff. In 1453, he rose to the position of mayor. During this period, he kept lodgings for foreign merchants – who, according to medieval law, typically needed an official host in order to be allowed residency in England.[31] He continued to put money in ships: in 1454 he funded the cost of 'a stately *vessell*, only for the *werre*'.[32]

And in 1457, ten years after his last traumatic attempt, Sturmy applied to King Henry VI for a new international trading licence. He was awarded a trading permit for £37,000 worth of tin, lead, cloth, and wool – England's premier exports – which he planned to exchange in the Levant for the goods recorded above: spices and silks, jewels and minerals. On 27 June 1457, Sturmy wrote his will. In June 1457, his ships were fitted out in Bristol. On 6 September 1457, Richard Benneyth

> with force and arms, namely swords, staves and knives, assaulted the same Robert in Bristol and beat, wounded and maimed him so that his life was despaired of, and arrested a certain ship of Robert's called the *Katerine* moored there and then kept that ship under arrest there for ten days following, for which reason the same Robert could not sail overseas with his goods in that ship, to the said Robert's loss of £200.[33]

Richard Benneyth was convicted, damages were awarded, and Sturmy left for his final voyage. The exact date of his departure is uncertain: he had definitely left before 19 April 1458, as on that date he is represented in absentia at the session of the King's Bench by his attorney John Beelle.[34]

Sturmy's Route

On his 1458 voyage, Sturmy travelled through Pisa, Naples, Rhodes, and Chios. The island of Chios was a Genoese trading settlement, off the coast of modern-day Turkey. It is likely that Sturmy bought the majority of his Syrian and Mediterranean goods from Chian marketplaces – as suggested by his purchase of alum. According to the terms of the Genoese monopoly, this mineral could only be bought at Chios.

Crusader Acre had been the main overseas Genoese trading base. After the Mamlūk Empire steadily took each one of the Christian states, the European settlers established trading-post settlements around the edges of the former territories, in order to maintain their trading connections.[35] The Genoese established settlements around the Aegean coast – turning to trade on the island of Chios in response to the collapse of the Christian crusader states. To a medieval European traveller, the island of Chios was tantalisingly proximate to the Holy Land. The groves of mastic trees wept a healing gum which was only available on this island. The Chian landscape, marketplaces, and Genoese fortifications could be read as reminders of the Christian presence in Greater Syria. At the north of the island a thirteenth/fourteenth-century church in the mountains marks the devotional site of the Agio Gala caves – 'agio gala' meaning milk, in recognition of the milky fluid which runs down from the stalactites, as though from the Virgin's breasts. Visiting Chios allowed medieval Europeans to come close to an imaginative and transactional experience of the Holy Land, via the island fantasies of the Genoese-run settlement. The marketplaces from which Sturmy's goods were bought were established through the desire for surrogate territories.

In the fifteenth century, Chios was the site of a major slave market: although Sturmy was not trafficking people, he bought his goods from a centre of the medieval slave trade. Hannah Barker has described the existence of a common culture of slavery between Christian and Muslim groups across the medieval Mediterranean, dominated by Genoese, Venetian, and Mamlūk states.[36] Slavery was fundamental to Mamlūk society: *mamlūk* literally translates as the term for a male slave. The Mamlūk rulers were freedmen, and their governance was upheld by a continued system of military and domestic slavery.[37] When the Burgundian traveller Bertrandon de la Brocquière (c. 1400–1459) came to Damascus he 'saw also, in a market-house, a lamentable sight – a public sale of Christians for slaves, both men and women' – and 'witnessed at Damascus the sale of a young black girl of not more than fifteen or sixteen years of age'.[38] In his account the child was brought along the streets nearly naked – a traumatic scene, recalled in grief. Sturmy and Heyton would have been witnesses to the trade in Chios – but their reaction goes unrecorded, and their investment in these networks was undeterred. On other ships the commodities which Sturmy bought did travel alongside enslaved people: in 1445, the Italian merchant Ieronimus Catanus arrived in Genoa, logging a cargo of thirty-six slaves, together with alum, cotton, rice, sugar, pepper, and ginger.[39] Looking past violence and exploitation towards his dream of profit, Sturmy came away from Chios with his cargo.

Chios was conquered by a Genoese joint-stock company in 1346. The Genoese settlers established a monopoly controlling the sale of the alum which they mined in Phokaia – modern-day Foça, on the Aegean coast, just across the sea, close enough to be visible from the shore.[40] And it was one of the investors in this settlement who observed and wanted to put a stop to Sturmy's venture.

The Pirate Gattilusio

Having traded in Chios, Sturmy went onwards to Crete, and started his return voyage from Heraklion in May 1458. He had been sailing home for less than a month when Gattilusio began his attack. Born on the island of Mitilini to a Genoese father and Greek mother, Giuliano Gattilusio was a member of an estranged branch of the powerful Gattilusio family. The Gattilusio lordships extended across Genoese territories. The family attempted to distance themselves from association with Giuliano as the reports of his piracy spread. In 1458, Gattilusio was at the height of his piratical career, active in the Mediterranean since 1450.[41] He had invested his wealth in a number of alum mines in Phokaia – and was the principal of the Maona di Scio, the association of Italian investors who managed the tax revenues from the island of Chios.[42] Sturmy's trip to Chios had drawn Gattilusio's attention – the goods on his ships seemed to be a threat, that amount of alum travelling back to England in a Bristolian cargo might be a challenge to Gattilusio's own profit network. As an investor and accountant, Gattilusio calculated that violence was the best solution to the potential disruption to the market. At the end of the battle this bureaucratic pirate was left with one less competitor.

Cargo Recollected

In this book, I have gathered together Sturmy's dispersed cargo in one place for the first time since the fateful attack of June 1458. I do not aim to reconstruct Sturmy's biography, identity, or intentions more than I have done already. The complex questions of premodern identity and power which Sturmy's voyage raises, however, will recur throughout the course of the book. The international reaction to Sturmy's failure shows the status of these objects in medieval economic and political spheres. These goods were desired by merchants, pirates, pilgrims, tailors, translators, doctors, knights, mystics, cooks, taverners, bookmakers, silk-women, alchemists, dyers, illuminators, poets, priests, and lovers.

Although other objects like those catalogued on Sturmy's ship did reach England, the inventory with which I begin is a list of absent goods. I take the loss of these artefacts as a starting point. Sturmy's cargo did arrive in England, as a cargo of the mind. Following Sturmy's missing merchandise led me through collections of real and fantasised goods which were kept in unexpected places. These written records take medieval objects out of the museum cabinet and return them to the moment of their consumption, theft, and veneration, getting close to objects as they were moved, used, and contaminated. While Sturmy's ships were sold off two thousand miles away from English shores, the desire for Syria was here, being unpacked and resold.

Introduction: De Sire, *the Origins of English Desire*

In medieval England, *de Sire* meant 'from Syria' and sounded like longing. The word 'desire' had recently entered Middle English from the Old French *desirrer*, deriving from the Latin *desidere*, originally meaning 'from the stars'. These celestial and earthly regions were out of reach, transcendent: the origins of desire. The English yearning for Syrian commodities was a movement upwards, reaching out towards what was already travelling outwards. This was the impulse which motivated Sturmy's voyage: all of the objects on his ships had once travelled *de Sire*. At the trials of the Genoese in 1458, Sturmy's partner John Heyton was a key witness, as were other survivors. Heyton submitted an inventory of their lost cargo, as evidence for the prosecution. These are the goods which were kept on Sturmy's lost ships:

> swete wynes as Tyer and Malvesies . . .
> alome foile and roche . . .
> dyvers spices . . .
> bowstavys . . .
> carpetys . . .
> grete chestes and coffers and mo stuffid with clothes of silke . . .
> purses, rynges and presious stonys . . .
> coyne and plate . . .
> mennes clothyng . . .
> Summa totalis of the seid 2 shippes with thapparailles, merchaundises and goodes as is aforesaid . . . £18,166 13s 4d.[1]

Labelled as Syrian in English marketplaces and imaginations, these goods gained commercial and spiritual credibility. Their value increased through association with the global marketplaces and sacred sites of Mamlūk Syria. These origins were sometimes real and sometimes fictive: 'Syriana' sold alongside authentic products. The objects on Sturmy's ship were gone by the time Heyton recorded them. But other ships did manage to bring these goods to medieval England – as well as bring the English to Syria.

Travelling to Syria, by Ship or in the Mind

As Robert Sturmy's ship was leaving England, other boats were setting sail in the same direction, carrying groups of pilgrims destined for the holy sites. The former bursar of Eton William Wey travelled to Jerusalem in 1458 as part of the same pilgrimage group as William Denys, who testified at the trials of the Genoese.[2] William Wey and Sturmy had crossed paths before: both men voyaged to Compostella in 1456, joining company at Plymouth.[3] Wey returned home to England, but was not called to testify in the trials. He wrote his own record of his journey, titled *The Matter of Jerusalem*, addressing other English pilgrims who were planning to go to the Holy Land.[4] He advises them to 'take no *Englysch* gold with *yow* from Brussels for *ye* shall lose in the exchange, and also for the most part of the way they will not exchange it'. The English gold coin, the noble, was seen as useless abroad – showing the failure of the English attempt to intervene in the gold standard.[5] Instead Wey recommends that:

> In *Surrey* you shall have *dremes* and *halfe dremes*; ii *dremes* be worth iii *Venyse grotes*. . . . *Doketys*, *grotys*, *grosettis*, and *soldys* of Venice, will go well in *Surrey*; that is to say in the *holy londe*, and none other, without great loss. Here ye may know diversity of moneys as from *Englond* unto *Surrey* in the *holy londe*.[6]

The label 'Surrey' refers not to the English county – it is the Middle English spelling for 'Syria', defined in relation to the Christian Holy Land. Here, as in many of the premodern texts which form the basis of this project, 'Syria' effectively acts as a premodern shorthand for Greater Syria, the region known as Bilad al-Sham, stretching across the eastern Mediterranean. As such, the desire for Syria contains within it the yearning for Palestine, Lebanon, Turkey, and Jordan. Discussing these sites through medieval quotations as 'Syrian' is not intended as an erasure of national identities, but as a way of paying attention to the historic modes of mapping which existed centuries before the 1916 Sykes–Picot Agreement. Wey's advice is practical, based on an up-to-date understanding of currency exchange. The 'dreme' refers to the Arabic dirham.[7] The Venetian ducat was the supreme international gold currency from the fourteenth century. English readers of Wey's text visualised 'Syria' as a sacred, but not an abstract location: this was a region at the intersection of the major devotional and trading networks.

Addressing curious readers, the English author John Trevisa's fourteenth-century translation of Bartholomaeus Anglicus' Latin encyclopaedia *On the*

Properties of Things includes a catalogue of nations. The entry '*De Siria*' describes a place which:

> is most *riche* of wax and *swete* spices and of metal, most *stronge* with cities and castles, *moyste* with most noble rivers, lakes and *pondes*; and hath noble *havens* of the sea . . . The men be stern and great warriors, and occupied in diverse countries and lands with *divers chaffare* and *marchaundyse*.[8]

Unlike Wey's, this description does not assume the desire to travel to Syria – static readers in England were also keen to know about the world. Trevisa's description does not focus on Syria as a sacred location but on its economic and military strength, its architecture of fortified cities, its landscape of rivers and coastal harbours, and its produce. The sweet spices and extracted metals travel through the 'havens', the seaside ports which brought these products to England – as Sturmy had intended to do.

Medieval English churchgoers, readers, and travellers would have had access to maps of the Holy Land, which were designed variously to be hung in chapels for contemplation, to be opened out at the beginnings of manuscripts, and to provide practical information.[9] From the mid thirteenth century onwards, medieval maps increasingly emphasised Jerusalem as a geographic as well as a spiritual centre.[10] These medieval English texts and images of Syria were based both on direct observations of the region, and on biblical, Classical, and crusader-era sources, which created the sense of a transhistorical connection forged across the Mediterranean. It was understood that travel across the seas between Syria and Europe was spiritually and practically essential – these routes had been retraced for centuries.[11]

The Benedictine monk, chronicler, and artist Matthew Paris wrote his *Chronica Maiora* [Great Chronicle] in St Albans between 1240 and 1259. These chronicles tell the history of the British Isles, situated in a global context. One manuscript of the text opens with a map of the journey to Jerusalem, with inserted parchment strips which the reader has to open in order to see the full route [Figure 0.1].[12] Jerusalem is shown as a square, walled city, containing three holy sites: the Dome of the Rock, 'Solomon's Temple', and the Holy Sepulchre. The book encourages a contemplative encounter with the space. To see the full map, the reader needs to open out the flap – a physical gesture that might aid the imagination of travel. A camel walks jauntily through the desert carrying merchandise. Matthew Paris had likely never visited the Holy Land – these details would have been based on the reports of returning travellers. At the time when Matthew Paris drew this map, the crusader settlement of Jerusalem

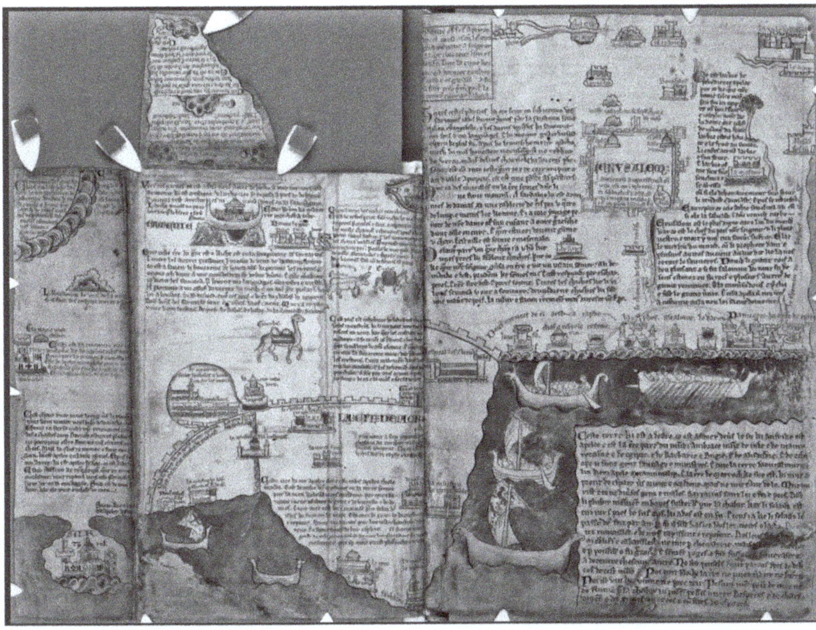

Figure 0.1 Map of the Holy Land. Source: Corpus Christi College, Cambridge. MS 26, fols. iii verso–recto. Printed with permission of the Parker Library.

was already lost: the capital of the Christian Kingdom was Acre. The ships travelling through the green Mediterranean look like they are heading towards Acre – an unfortified, wavy coast. Images like this map continued to preserve the idea of these sites as significant to Christian identity, long after the last crusader settlement had fallen too.

The 1291 conquest of Acre consolidated the region under Mamlūk rule: Syria was divided into seven *Mamlakas* [kingdoms]. The Mamlaka of Damascus was the largest and most powerful, containing modern-day central Syria and the majority of Palestine.[13] The city of Jerusalem was a subdistrict (*wilaya*), receiving administrative direction from Damascus.[14] Medieval texts – like Wey's – which describe the Holy City as being 'in Syria', recall both memories of the crusader settlements and contemporary Mamlūk administration. The Mamlūk rulers' extensive building programmes between 1260 and 1517 transformed the architectural landscape of Jerusalem, with new mosques, colleges, schools, hospitals, fountains, and pilgrim houses, often repurposing crusader structures and establishments.[15] When medieval English travellers visited and described Syria, they observed these Mamlūk projects: their traces are found throughout later medieval English images of arches and minarets, an iconography of Jerusalem with a distinctly Mamlūk style.

This study begins in 1291 and ends in 1516, before the Ottoman conquests of Egypt and Jerusalem, which signalled the end of Mamlūk rule over the Holy Land. In 1517, the shift to Ottoman command was immediately apparent to English travellers: the Norfolk parson Richard Torkington, who left Rye in March 1517 and arrived in the Holy Land in July, recorded that 'the *great Turke* having in Dominion All the *holi londe* ... we were received by the *Turkys* and *Sarasyns*'.[16] Torkington arrived at a transitional moment, describing being 'admitted by the *lordes*, *Turkes*, and *Mamolukes* of the *Citie*, to enter in to the Temple of the holy *Sepulcre*'.[17] The 'Turk' was an emergent racialised category in the Middle Ages, which – as the Ottoman Empire gained control of the Holy Land – became preeminent in early modern English discourses of Islam and the Orient.[18] The exchanges which took place between medieval English travellers and the Ottoman Empire are beyond the scope of this project, as are exchanges which occurred between the Mamlūk Empire, the Mongol Empire, and the Ming Dynasty, among other major global powers. The entangled histories which I have researched here reach out towards these other encounters – every project has a boundary line, and I hope that mine is porous enough to speak to other knowledge after its completion.

Chaucer's Syria

A group of Syrian merchants is central to the 'Man of Law's Tale', one of the narratives in the collection *The Canterbury Tales*, by Geoffrey Chaucer (d. 1400). The author was a clerk who used to rent a tenement house in the chapel gardens at Westminster Abbey. When he died, as a former tenant, Chaucer was entitled to be buried with a plain slab near the entrance to the south transept of St Benedict. In 1556 he was dug up and reburied inside the Abbey as the indifferent first resident of 'poet's corner', and unwittingly became known as 'the father of English literature'. In the General Prologue to the *Tales*, the narrator – also named Chaucer – joins a group of pilgrims in a tavern in Southwark. Intending to travel together to the shrine of Thomas Becket, in Canterbury, the Host suggests a game to make their journey less dull: a storytelling competition. The group includes a Knight back from the crusades, a Prioress, a Miller – and the Man of Law, who works in the London Inns of Court. The lawyer is dressed neatly, wearing a silk belt, with small stripes.[19] He waits patiently to tell his tale, and when he is called to speak, he first gives credit to his sources: 'O *riche marchauntz*' (II. 122), the 'fathers of *tidynges* | And tales' (II. 129–30). Working near the London docks, the lawyer has had plenty of opportunity to speak with traders, who brought back stories as well as goods from their travels. The tale which follows was, he says, taught to him by a merchant whom he met long ago (II. 132–33).

The lawyer's tale begins: '*In Surrye whilom dwelte a compaignye* | *Of chapmen riche*' – in Syria once dwelt a company of rich merchants – who were '*sadde and trewe*', trustworthy and honest (II. 134–5). These Syrian merchants '*wyde-where* sent their *spicerye*, | *Clothes of gold*, and *satyns* rich of hue' (II. 136–137). Based on a merchant's report, these Syrian traders are central both to the narrative and to the economic system within which they are placed. The goods which these merchants sell are those which were found on Sturmy's ships – they are realistic, proximate items. The merchants travel '*wyde-where*' – a word which conveys the scale of 'everywhere' but with an enhanced sense of marvel, evoking the globalised trading networks through which spices and silks travelled from Syria.[20] The angle at which the tale is positioned places England as part of the mysterious '*wyde-where*', and Syria at the known centre from which movement flows.

In Chaucer's tale, the Syrian merchants set the action in motion. Having travelled to Rome for business and pleasure, where they hear of the great beauty of the Christian Emperor's daughter, Custance, they go '*hoom* to *Surrey*' (II. 173) – home, to Syria. Their identity as a group is not specified; critics have typically assumed that these merchants were Muslim or Christian, but Jewish traders also moved around the Mediterranean.[21] Hearing that his favourite merchants are back, the Sultan – like Chaucer's lawyer – is keen to hear their 'tidynges' – their reports, their tales of wonder (II. 181). When they are summoned, they tell the Sultan about the beautiful Custance. Based on description alone, the Sultan decides he must marry her. He sends for his counsellors, who advise that if he wants to marry Custance he must convert to Christianity, which he does. Informed of the Sultan's conversion, the Emperor agrees to send his daughter to be wed. The report of a beautiful Christian girl is enough to cause Christianity to spread from Rome to Syria – the spontaneous conversion of the Muslim ruler drawing on enduring fantasies of the Christian recovery of the Holy Land.

Chaucer's tale illustrates the ways in which imagination and reality overlap and combine in medieval tales. The tale is supposedly set in the sixth century, when Syria was actually part of the Christian Byzantine

Empire – but the travelling merchants and the Muslim rulers evoke a context closer to the Mamlūk Empire, contemporary with Chaucer's composition. The past was not forgotten in the present, but it inflected the ways in which medieval travellers and readers continued to experience the world.

Post-Acre Melancholia

The objects on Sturmy's ship arrived in the aftermath of the collapse of the crusader settlements which – like the former territories of the British Empire today – were ambivalently remembered and preserved in medieval England. Late medieval trade took place along the same routes which had once led to and from the crusader states, via Venice and Rhodes. The commodities which became medieval Syriana had first been transported from the Frankish settlements. They were overlaid with the recollection of their original significance, as signifiers of Christian rulership in the Holy Land.

To understand the implications of these post-crusading contexts, I turned to Paul Gilroy's concept of postcolonial melancholia. Gilroy invokes the Freudian frameworks of Alexander and Margarete Mitscherlich, who diagnosed post-WWII German society with melancholia, prompted by the inability to mourn the national loss of moral legitimacy. In Gilroy's analysis of contemporary British society, melancholia describes a neurotic syndrome dating to the decline of the British Empire.[22] For Gilroy, this syndrome is characterised by the urge towards homogeneity – the refusal of cultural hybridity – combined with a love of exotica.[23] The refusal to process the traumas of the past leads to a nation-building ethnocentric fiction: a partial account of the present given false lineage by an equally partial account of history. After the Christian failures of the crusades, the sense of loss – of territory, of power, of status – resulted in a state of mind which, following Gilroy, I term post-Acre melancholia.

I define post-Acre melancholia as a neurotic syndrome dating to the decline of the Christian Kingdom of Jerusalem. As with its post-imperial equivalent, post-Acre melancholia creates a problem of time: forcing the fantasy of the past in front of the realities of the present. For Gilroy, the body of the 'postcolonial migrant' has become an 'anachronistic figure bound to the lost imperial past'.[24] That is: the refusal to include Empire and decolonisation in the narrative of British history creates a continued mist of imperial fantasy, which distorts the perception of lived experience.

The British Empire still lives in the imagination of many today; the Kingdom of Jerusalem lived in imaginations in late medieval England. Post-1291, many were unable to accept the irrecoverable loss of Acre as part of the narrative of Christian identity. An illusory narrative of history creates an unstable, illusory narrative of the present. In my study, the figures of Syrian merchants and English knights bring the lost settlements to life in late medieval texts. Further symptoms of post-Acre melancholia include hostility to immigrants and international traders, whose existence challenged the security of the nostalgic fantasy. As Aziz Atiya has shown, crusading remained central to European politics for over two-hundred years after the fall of Acre, both as an idea and as an active, albeit futile, political endeavour.[25] Critics have drawn attention to the genre of late medieval romance as a site in which the crusades were reimagined.[26] I build on these insights, showing how the produce of interfaith contact in Mediterranean marketplaces was reimagined as the loot of crusading conflicts, lending a material basis to fantasies of – and attempts at – resettlement and reconquest.

There was no specific English involvement in the 1291 battle of Acre, and the contribution of specifically English forces to the establishment and maintenance of the Crusader Kingdom was limited in comparison to – for example – French men-at-arms. As such post-Acre melancholia does not relate to an ideal of England so much as an ideal of Christendom – according to which, the failures of French forces are relevant to the English ego because they articulate the failure of common Christian desires. In that sense there is a dual process of denial in these melancholic English narratives, which deny the marginal role of English knights and commanders during the crusades, in addition to denying the failure of the Christian states. As it features in the medieval English imagination, post-Acre melancholia projects a fantasy of continued Christian power and a fantasy of English involvement in that collective power. The realities obscured are those of Christian failure and English impotence. Lauren Berlant describes melancholia as 'the subject's desire to temporize an experience of the loss of an object/scene with which she has invested her ego continuity'.[27] The word 'temporize', meaning 'to delay' as well as 'to evade', draws attention to the fact that post-Acre melancholia creates both a psychic and a temporal disjuncture.

The premodern experience of time was not linear: especially when navigating space in the Holy Land, biblical histories were experienced as simultaneous with present realities. In addition, objects and texts remained part of the current intellectual landscape for hundreds of years. A manuscript copied in the twelfth century could remain part of the university syllabus in the fifteenth century. In churches, generations of priests continued to repair and wear the same vestments for hundreds of years: the evidence of excavations shows that eleventh-century silks were still in use in Aldgate in the fourteenth century. Reflecting these habits of re-use, at times my analysis moves quickly between centuries, allowing chronologies to collapse through a long lens, or leaping between crusading, classical, biblical, and heavenly moments. In the minds of many medieval illuminators, surgeons, and labourers, history had gone nowhere, and the future had already begun. Throughout this book I keep an eye on historical events, situating texts, images, and objects in their specific contexts, aiming to balance an awareness of the impact of proximate historical events with a sense of the longer (historical and imaginative) traditions which shaped cultural production.

The medieval conception of the Holy Land as a self-evidently Christian territory had an enduring influence, with its residue in present-day borders. In 1917, the British conquest of Jerusalem was covered as a long-overdue 'victory' in the medieval struggle between Christendom and Islam: one cartoon in the magazine *Punch* showed (instead of General Allenby) the English crusader King Richard the Lionheart overlooking the city, and was captioned 'The Last Crusade'.[28] The establishment of the British Mandate of Palestine was the precondition for the establishment of the state of Israel, as contractually determined in the Balfour Declaration; in that sense a line could be traced from medieval imaginative geographies to the current occupation. The complex colonial afterlives of the medieval are not the subject of this text, which is focused on the premodern – although I remain aware of the fact that these histories are read in – and have implications for – the present.

For me, post-Acre melancholia describes how crusading continued to shape late medieval identity.[29] Affixing the 'post-' of 'postcolonial' to 'Acre' rather than 'colonial' in my study, I acknowledge both the historically contingent alterity of the medieval, and the influence of postcolonial theory on my work.[30] Post-Acre melancholia persisted in English imaginations throughout the period of my study, but never prevailed in active form, and could never erase the realities of cross-cultural contact against which the syndrome struggled. Reports from returning travellers and in translation brought knowledge which contradicted the melancholic narrative, reinforcing the historic truth of the loss of Christian settlements and creating desires which exceeded the single desire for the recovery of land. Across medieval England, alternative perspectives subverted the supposedly hegemonic desire for Christian supremacy.

The Arrival: Rakowitz's Lamassu

When I began working on this project in 2018, there was a bright sculpture on the Fourth Plinth in London's Trafalgar Square: a glittering recreation of a lost Assyrian Lamassu [Figures 0.2 and 0.3]. The flanks of the guardian deity were plastered with shining Arabic packaging: made from tins of Iraqi date syrup. The sculpture is part of artist Michael Rakowitz's project *The invisible enemy should not exist*, an ongoing series of recreations of Assyrian artefacts which have been stolen or destroyed.[31] The cleaned tins are sticky, politically: the ancient date plantations have been decimated during the Iraq wars, significant responsibility for which resides in the British Parliament at Westminster, a short distance from the square in which the Lamassu stood. This recent history of destruction interrupted the two-thousand-year-long global movement of Iraqi dates. Rakowitz's work brings out the dense entanglement of trade, conflict, consumption, dialogue, and human mobility.

Rakowitz is the descendant of Iraqi-Jewish date traders, a personal background which he interrogates in his practice. In the participatory

Figure 0.2 Michael Rakowitz, *The invisible enemy should not exist* (1). Source: author's own photograph.

Figure 0.3 Michael Rakowitz, *The invisible enemy should not exist* (2). Source: author's own photograph.

artwork *RETURN* (2004–), he reopened his grandfather's import business, Davidsons & Co., in New York.[32] The catalyst for the project was Rakowitz's realisation that Iraqi dates were already covertly entering America, in cans of Basra syrup labelled 'Made in Lebanon', repackaged to avoid UN sanctions on Iraq. Rakowitz made contact with Al Farez Co., a date export business based in Baghdad, who agreed to send a shipment. The dates were flown to Damascus airport, where they were held in transit, as customs officers demanded additional charges. To avoid the delay, the general manager of Al Farez Co. suggested that the dates be declared as 'product of Syria' – a suggestion which Rakowitz, after consultation, declined, in case the dissonance between the origins of the dates on the boxes and in the documents caused issues at US customs. The delayed cargo was abandoned in Damascus, and a new shipment was ordered.

Reconstructed from the durable cans of these perishable goods, Rakowitz's Lamassu pointed its noble features towards Nelson's Column [Figure 0.3]. These proximate monuments – one temporary, one fixed, for now – provide alternative models of transnational travel. The presence of the Lamassu in Trafalgar Square was both a distinct projection of its origins and a distinct statement of arrival, asking the viewer to recall the traumas of war and the vitality of dialogue. The Lamassu was not enclosed, like the many Assyrian sculptures in the British Museum collection, a short walk away. The solid walls of the museum were substituted for open air, the hazards of pigeons, and the sunlight and seasonal changes passing across its back. The sculpture haunted the postcolonial city. A proximate incarnation of that colonial past, the lions at the base of Nelson's statue (as Rakowitz points out) are made from reclaimed melted canons of ships captured at the battle of Trafalgar. Nelson gazes out in his plumed hat towards imperial waters, the imagined seascape of his victories. Beneath the anchored feet of the Lamassu, the plinth became a pier, a harbour.

My research project reconfigured itself in light of Rakowitz's tin-can Lamassu. Instead of the more straightforward literary study which I had planned, I restructured my research into a study of the mobile commodities – bought, stolen, and recreated – which travelled to England. In Rakowitz's Lamassu, the past and the present are brought into dissonant, complex contact within one apparently static object: the bright tin fused with the antique form. In his ongoing series *May the obdurate foe not be in good health* (2011–), Rakowitz applies the same practice of reconstruction to missing and endangered antiquities in Syria, in the era of civil war, plastering papier mâché votive statues and astrolabes with food wrappers.[33] These ostentatious forgeries speak through the materials of contemporary consumables. Alexander Nagel and Christopher Wood argue that Renaissance architecture and artworks are not merely passively anachronistic but actively 'anachronic', holding 'incompatible models in suspension without deciding'.[34] Rakowitz's artworks inhabit that same condition, of suspended incompatibility – their imitative skins draped over fragile histories, preserving and recreating statues. Taking the wrappers off their papier mâché moulds will not reveal the original: these ghosts have arrived in a new time and space, in a remade condition.

Syriana Reconstructed

In the Middle Ages, craftspeople based in Christian Europe were industriously employed in the imitation business. In medieval Lucca, Italian weavers were recorded as the producers of 'soriani' – knowingly imitating Syrian fabrics.[35] These medieval forgeries speak to Rakowitz's artworks – they hover between histories and places, without the option of return to their origins, given that the origin is fictive or half-remembered. The category of Syriana is not reliable: it includes faux-Mamlūk creations, pseudo-Syrian objects absorbed into medieval imaginations of the Holy Land. Syriana is hybrid, a melange of the authentic, the translated, and the mistranslated which speaks to the realities of cross-cultural contact and production. There was an appropriative, exoticising impulse in the aspirational European desire to become Syrian, to make Syriana – but an appropriative impulse developed in an alternative global system, in which English appropriation did not rest on imperial wealth. I see Syriana as the unstable fabrics from which English culture was constructed, a construction which undermined itself in its own making.

Using the category of 'Syriana', I have chosen to evade the critical concepts of the 'Orient' and the 'Islamicate world', tactically grouping together a disparate range of locations under a term which allows me to tell a different narrative. The category of Syriana, produced in economic conditions of European dependence on non-Christian networks, is a European category which seeks to become non-European, and a Christian category which seeks proximity to the non-Christian – desires which are often acknowledged ambivalently, uneasily, enviously.

Syriana is a collection of objects, a catalogue of surrogates which memorialise Christian 'Syria' – but which also remember alternative histories. Syriana came into existence in contact zones across the eastern Mediterranean.[36] In the fourteenth-century *Travels* of John Mandeville, Jerusalem is described as a '*myddes*': a space 'in the midst' of the world.[37] Kim Philips has proposed the development of 'precolonial studies' in parallel with the continuation of postcolonial approaches to the Middle Ages, based on themes of encounter.[38] While I share common ground with Philips, I do not use the terminology of the 'precolonial', since many of these cross-cultural encounters took place in the shadows of the expansionist missions of the crusades, in Mamlūk imperial territories and Italian trading colonies.[39] These are alternative but not straightforwardly de-territorial scenes, which occurred while English lordships were extending into Ireland, Wales, and Scotland.[40] The divergent elements in medieval English culture – ethnonationalist territorialism and an alternative reality of relational existence – create contradictions which I aim to sustain within my narrative, not flatten into false coherence.

Nagel and Wood write that: 'The institution of pilgrimage was a culture's way of acknowledging that it knew what authenticity really was, even if most of the time it chose to forget all that and make replicas.'[41] Across Europe, replicas of the Holy Sepulchre both affirmed the significance of sacred space, and deconstructed that concept through the devotional attachment to visibly constructed versions. I see this contradictory affirmation of and deconstruction of origins as the intellectual basis for the making of Syriana.

Physical artefacts did travel from Syria to medieval England. Now displayed in the Victoria & Albert Museum, the 'Luck of Edenhall' is an enamelled Mamlūk glass vessel. It was likely made in Syria c. 1350, and kept on arrival in Europe in a leather case embossed with 'IHS' [Jesus].[42] Embossed with the name of Christ, the cover repackages its contents, signalling the Christian appropriation of the object. Maria Georgopoulou writes: 'It was the Syrian/Levantine origin of these gilt enamelled beakers that made them precious relics of the Christian Holy Land, even if they were made by non-Christian hands in Muslim territories.'[43] As Esin Atil has argued, the Mamlūk period was a moment of artistic renaissance, with profits from global trade channelled into substantial patronage systems.[44] The production of new containers for these items was an act of reframing, but it was also a marker of esteem, both of the artistic merits and of the origins of the vessels. It was difficult to take these fragile vessels on long journeys – they had to be placed in expertly made woven baskets.[45] The leather case of the 'Luck' had a symbolic and practical function. Elsewhere in Europe the same practice of reframing is in evidence: in France, a Syrian enamelled cup known as the 'Cup of Charlemagne' was given a French gilded silver foot; Arabic-inscribed pilgrim flasks became Christian reliquaries.[46] The 'Luck' was treasured as a relic in England, becoming associated with narratives of magical power which gave rise to its name. Relabelled on arrival, the 'Luck' still shines in Mamlūk glass, a transparent reminder of the hands and tools which made it, carefully preserved by those who understood it differently. The meaning of the 'Luck' hovers between the frame and its contents. Imitative 'Syrian' objects aspired to be worshipped like the 'Luck', placed carefully in treasuries, becoming transcendent through the absorption of the sacred aura.

Rakowitz's artworks, as imitations, produce an aura gleaming in tin, not stone, which remembers the historic but is expressed in the new marvel of contemporary packaging: a bright and fragile surface which now cannot be discarded in the search for the rediscovery of the original object. These are precious forgeries, irreplaceable with the non-substitutable original, articulating a new kind of identity, asserting their position as a state of being in between: in between times and places. The objects and ideas which travelled out from Jerusalem passed through a series of islands and harbours across the Mediterranean, *al-Baḥr al-Abyaḍ al-Mutawassiṭ* – the white intermediate sea, containing within it the islands of the Aegean archipelago, an embayment of encounters and dangerous liasons.[47] In England, mixed and collaged replicas coexisted with attested originals – both the original and the imitation travelled through the same routes before arriving.

Reframing Muslims and Jews

The desire to Christianise extended to people, not just objects. In Chaucer's lawyer's tale, sorrowing for Custance's fate, the lawyer can only narrate, not control her journey: 'forth I let her *saille*' (II. 321), he says, as Custance sets out to Syria. Meanwhile, lamenting her son's conversion to Christianity, the Sultaness decries that he 'will leave his *olde sacrifices*' (II. 325). The misconception that Muslims, Jews, and pagans alike engaged in idolatry and sacrifice was common in medieval England – including among those who, like the lawyer, were in contact with those who lived and worked in cross-cultural communities. The distorted image of Islam simultaneously forgets and remembers the realities of Mamlūk Syria, reflecting its power and status at the same time as these are officially disparaged. Custance does not arrive alone: she comes in a company of Christians. But the Sultaness plots against her son, his new bride, and their companions: on her orders, they are '*al tohewe and stiked at the bord*', all hewn apart and stabbed, while they are sat at their table (II. 430). The action of the knives on the bodies of these guests brings cannibalism into association with the mass slaughter. The Syrian converts, including the Sultan, are killed – but are not eaten, their carved bodies lie bleeding out on the floor of the dining hall.

Patricia Clare Ingham and Michelle R. Warren have noted: 'If Conrad's novella [*Heart of Darkness*] is part of the "canon" of postcolonial scholarship on English modernism, Chaucer's "Man of Law's Tale" occupies a similar position in medieval English studies.'[48] These critiques have opened up into the field of premodern critical race studies. Suzanne Akbari has identified medieval Orientalism as a historically contingent representational discourse which emphasises the bodily and the religious alterity of the 'Saracen' and the 'Jew', from which modern Orientalism developed.[49] Geraldine Heng has interrogated the intersection between premodern trade and racialisation, arguing that cross-cultural trade resulted in a European religious-racial category which she describes as 'Saracens, Inc.'[50] The employees of this fictive enterprise were the means by which Syriana arrived in England. In this book I draw on the work of Akbari and Heng but move sideways, towards an understanding of the ways in which the lines of Muslim and Jewish identities became blurred, both in representations and reality.

The cultural theorist Ella Shohat has written of the need to restore forgotten histories of the 'Judeo-Muslim hyphen'.[51] Shohat's argument responds both to the Israeli state partition between Jews and Palestinians, and the American political and cultural landscape, in which her Arab-Jewish identity is seen as an impossible contradiction. As a religious-racial category, the 'Saracen' was imprecise: Jewish and Muslim merchants were often seen through the same lens. Following Shohat, I read this imprecision as a sign of community: assimilated Jews misread as 'Saracens' remember those who lived in transnational neighbourhoods. Reflecting the conditions of their lives, which were at once mobile and locally embedded, the lingua franca of Jews across the premodern Mediterranean was Judeo-Arabic: Arabic written in Hebrew letters. As Jessica Goldberg has shown, Jewish merchants operated across the Mediterranean, creating a transnational community which was the site of cultural – that is, not purely financial – exchange.[52] This Jewish presence has often fallen between the gaps in analysis of the relationship between the 'Latin West' and the 'Islamic World', as figured in medieval English texts.[53] But although the Jews had been expelled from England in 1290, medieval English travellers continued to encounter Jews across the eastern Mediterranean.

Excavating these fragmentary histories, these scenes arrive in the present as ambivalent artefacts. Since its inception, the modern state of Israel has used archaeological methods in order to justify the possession of land on the basis of the historic presence of Jewish communities, deploying the lithic as a literal foundation for ideology.[54] Israeli archaeological digs have often marginalised finds dating from the Mamlūk period, which are, in Eyal Weizman's words, 'dismissed . . . discarded . . . or simply left alone to rot and crumble'.[55]

Across the Mediterranean, travellers and immigrants adopted new idioms and bought new clothes, forgot to adhere to religious laws or began asserting their religion more intently. Jews living within the Mamlūk Empire were integrated into legal and social frameworks: they were not the rulers of the region, but neither were most of the Muslim population, the workers in the sugar factories, the silk-weavers. Retracing the arrival of Judeo-Muslim texts, material goods, and technologies in England, my work responds to Shirin Khanmohamadi's argument for the existence of a 'late medieval ethnographic poetics' characterised by 'a profound openness to alternative perspectives and voices'.[56] Following

Khanmohamadi's Bakhtinian attention to the dialogic elements of medieval works, I find that heterogeneous voices repeatedly interrupt and complicate Middle English texts, with figures speaking against and within their own misrepresentation.

Reading through the mask of the 'Saracen' to find the historical presence of these complex interwoven communities, I find these histories affirm Paul Gilroy's sense of 'the intercultural history of the diaspora concept'.[57] In the conclusion of his work *The Black Atlantic*, Gilroy turns to Jewish theorists – including Ella Shohat – in a gesture of intellectual solidarity, drawing a link between the concept of the Jewish diaspora and the diaspora as an articulation of Black identity. Reading Rakowitz, Shohat, and Gilroy backwards into the Middle Ages, I see the historic existence of Judeo-Muslim communities as the bedrock on which this intercultural concept was developed. That is: the diaspora becomes an intercultural concept because the diaspora has always been intercultural. Instead of trying to sort out and recategorise these layers, I stay with that original sedimentary entanglement. But instead of taking that entanglement as denying an identity-based analysis, I contend that the records of specific communities – Jewish, Muslim – can still be read from texts in which their lines are blurred. A non-essentialised reading of these hybrid histories returns the communities of the past to view in their historic state of undefinition.

I do not know what condition of the world this text will be received in, but I know that as I prepare to submit the final version of this manuscript, a genocide is unfolding in Gaza. The histories which I set out to remember – histories of interwoven Judeo-Muslim communities and a complex, intercultural diaspora – seem more out of touch than ever with present geopolitical relations. In a sense this collection has become an archive both of the premodern and of the recent past during which I completed my research: it is hard to say what book would have been written if I had started from the present moment. I am aware that the shadow of that event will fall over this text. I persist in thinking that complex, ambivalent narratives have a place even in these times.

Commodity Studies

In addition to blurring lines of identity, the category of medieval Syriana absorbs and confuses objects with variable functions: relics become saleable, souvenirs become worthy of veneration. Syriana is a property category which reveals a desire for the unpossessable – knowing that the object of desire always exceeds ownership. These are commercial objects which speak to their premodern conditions of production and consumption, asserting their position within an alternative economic and political structure.

In *The Social Life of Things*, Arjun Appadurai drew critical attention to the cultural status of commodities, showing how across time, the value of economic objects has been determined by political and imaginative frameworks.[58] Nearly forty years on from the publication of that path-breaking volume, cultural critics continue to find new insights from analysing the social lives of commodities past and present.[59] The desire for commodities has been exposed as a driving force of colonial expansion – at the same time as colonialism shaped modern commodity cultures.[60]

In the Middle Ages, the term 'commodite' was already in use to describe objects of economic value.[61] The capacity for economic exchange is fundamental to the objects in my study, from manufactured silks to harvested spices to extracted minerals – all belonged on the merchant's ship. But these were objects with cultural and sacred significance: relic-like, fit for rituals. In Annabel Wharton's economic and art historical study *Selling Jerusalem*, she surveys 'Western' modes of possessing the Holy Land from medieval to contemporary sources, considering the 'relic', the 'souvenir', and the 'replica' as distinct categories across time.[62] The 'relic', derived from the Latin *reliquae* [remains], is venerated as an authentic object or fragment derived from a holy site or body: relic discourse elevates the material to sacred, transcendent status.[63] Personal 'souvenirs' were typically bought or stolen, tokens of human travel instead of divine miracle.[64] The medieval 'relic' and the commercial 'souvenir' were often inseparable. That realisation was often highly disturbing to medieval consumers, who found their religious rites tainted with the atmosphere of the market – a market which was dominated by non-Christian traders.[65]

In his essay 'The Otherness in the Focus of Interest: Or, If Only the Other Could Speak', art historian Avinoam Shalem asks: 'Can one compare our encounters with the foreign object with human encounters?'[66] The 'foreign objects' which Shalem has in mind are the portable Islamic items (such as beakers and pilgrim flasks) recorded in the Church treasuries of the Latin West. Shalem considers these objects as revealing the role of migratory artefacts as 'carriers of information in an intercultural context'.[67] The commodities treated as Syriana were mostly luxury items – with the exception of alum – but their impact was not only felt by the elite who were able to own them. Many of the craftspeople working with imported materials were themselves immigrants to, or within, England, living and working in cosmopolitan areas of cities. These objects remember their journeys in merchant vessels, jars, woven baskets, and travellers' pockets.

In my study, influenced by Rakowitz's artworks, Shalem's approach to premodern mobilc objects, and critical developments in commodity studies, I consider the goods on Sturmy's ship as political, aesthetic, and communicative artefacts.[68] These are goods which arrived here – and continued to recall their origins. Like the Lamassu casting its shadow towards the steps of the National Gallery, these imported objects left traces wherever they landed. Following the lives of medieval Syriana on their arrival reveals a narrated Syrian presence in premodern spaces often seen as more straightforwardly 'English', such as household larders, workshops in which wools were dyed, and the altar of Westminster Abbey.

The objects on Sturmy's ship arrived in Libya – not in England. This movement records the fact that the commodities which became Syriana in medieval England existed in other collections and categories around the world. As Syriana, these objects variously grieve the impossibility of their return, discard grief in favour of the production of gaudy new selves, or oscillate between these states of grief and self-invention. The alternative lives of Syriana under other names drift across the horizon of this project – but this study takes place at my home port.

Medieval Collections of Arabic Books

In a footnote of his work *Poetics of Relation*, Glissant writes that: 'The thought of the Centre was monolingual. The poetics of Relation requires all the languages of the world. Not to know or to ponder them, but to know (feel) that it is essential for them to exist.'[69] Glissant's theory was based on his observation of cultural formation in the Caribbean archipelago. He contrasts these multilingual poetics with a monolingual, colonial perspective. These contrasting forms of language – multilingual and monolingual – are the products of contrasting ways of being in the world. Glissant's theory has had a widespread influence in artistic and academic spaces: Jane Hiddleston and Wen-Chin Ouyang have argued that Glissant's concept of multilingualism could provide an alternative to current academic disciplinary categories – instead of the 'English' department, 'multilingual literatures'.[70]

Glissant wondered if the poetics of Relation might have existed in medieval Europe, before the rise of the colonial Voyages. Discussing creolisation as a synthetic process, in which African and European languages are combined without becoming fixed, he is curious as to whether his observations might apply to other 'languages in formation – here, for example, we would have to study the European Middle Ages'.[71] I take up Glissant's off-hand invitation for the study of the poetics of medieval relation. These poetics are not the same as those described by Glissant, which were formed in the conditions created by the transatlantic slave trade and the plantation. The medieval poetics of Relation reflect the unfixity of premodern languages and the unfixity of premodern global relationships.

In contact zones and through translations, borrowed words entered the English language. The arrival and translation of Arabic books in England intertwine with and frame the stories which follow.[72] The Graeco-Arabic translation movements in Syria, Palestine, and Baghdad from the eighth to tenth centuries CE preserved and extended the works of Aristotle and Galen, forming an influential Arabic corpus of scientific learning which transformed understandings of the body and the stars.[73] The twelfth- and thirteenth-century Arabo-Latin translation movements in the crusader Levant, Italy, and Spain disseminated this science throughout medieval Europe, with Arabic sources consistently foregrounded.[74] As Charles Burnett comments, crusader Antioch 'was a conduit through which Arabic works arrived in Europe'.[75] Mamlūk systems of patronage funded learning institutions and scriptoriums across the Empire: the book was a significant commodity.[76]

The late medieval period saw a surge of translations of Arabo-Latin texts into vernacular European languages. Critical work has recognised this phenomenon: in 1977, Dorothee Metlitzki showed that Middle English texts were situated amidst libraries of Hebrew and Arabic.[77] Archives and excavation sites have preserved medieval English collections of textiles, ceramics, and coins inscribed with Arabic script, which, like books, were seen and treasured.[78] But as Shazia Jagot argues: 'English literary studies has yet fully to embrace the possibilities that emerge from situating Arabic (along with Hebrew) as language(s) of multilingual medieval Britain.'[79] Fourteenth- and fifteenth-century English texts popularised Arabic translations to a new, non-Latinate audience. There is often an aesthetics of display in medieval translations of Arabic works, a foregrounding of origins.[80] Throughout the colonial era, Classical Greek and Roman texts were presented as providing a lineage for European civilisation, excising Arabic from the narrative of Classical reception. In contrast, premodern European translators of these Graeco-Arabic and Arabo-Latin texts continued to locate authority in their Arabic sources. Through these processes of textual transmission, Europe was decentred as a site of cultural production. Medieval Latin acted like the Mediterranean Sea – it was a midpoint, a cross-over space which absorbed and transmitted meaning in multiple directions.[81]

Geoffrey Chaucer is best known as a poet, but he also wrote scientific prose: the *Treatise on the Astrolabe*.[82] The astrolabe was a portable astronomical calculating device developed in the Islamic world which became seen as essential for navigation both on land and at sea, and for taking measurements using the stars. Chaucer's treatise addresses his ten-year-old son, Lewis, giving instructions for how to use the instrument. Two-thirds of Chaucer's text is based on a Latin edition of the works of Māshā' Allāh, an eighth-century Persian Jewish astrologer, who wrote in Arabic. He explains that he has translated the work

> in *Englissh*, since you can't read much *Latyn*, my little son. But don't worry, these *trewe* conclusions will be just as adequate to you in English, as the *noble clerkes Grekes* find them in Greek, and the *Arabiens* in *Arabik*, and the *Jewes* in *Ebrew*, and the *Latyn folk* in Latin, which Latin folk translated them first out of other *dyverse* languages.[83]

Identifying Greek, Arabic, Hebrew, and Latin as languages of transnational dialogue, Chaucer focuses attention on the intellectual outputs of the Graeco-Arabic translation movements. The present tense allows the reader of Chaucer's work to experience a kinship, a shared experience of thinking transnational conclusions in a local language. English reaches out towards Arabic, Hebrew, and the other 'diverse languages' which, although not necessarily known, are felt to be essential to exist.

In reaching beyond Latin towards the unread sources, medieval translators created texts which I call 'Arabo-English', the hyphen preserving the desire of the English text to touch the origin, the moment of crossing. The prefix 'trans-' means 'across', a process of becoming. In the Middle Ages the term 'trans-lation' and its equivalents in various languages – the act of 'carrying over' – was used to describe both the movement of meaning between languages and the movement of sacred relics between shrines. When moving the fragments of a saint's body, the pieces of earth from a holy site, the origins of these objects remained essential to their veneration in their new location. Likewise, borrowed words, which once arrived are held tightly, rely on their origins for their full meaning. These translations do not become static having been 'carried over'. The crossing continues, they continue to pull their new environment back towards the routes from which they have arrived, and which they continue to remember. Late medieval English translations of Arabic books are cultural and political vessels, carrying fragile and ambiguous histories into the present – their survival creating another crossing, the transhistorical.

Chaucer's Syria, Part II

In Chaucer's tale, news and letters travel rapidly across the seas from Rome to Syria, and the Syrian merchants in Rome are a familiar sight, but Chaucer's heroine Custance shudders at the prospect of going – 'she *wepte*' for being 'sent to *strange* nation'. 'Allas', the Man of Law says, pitying her (II. 267–8). 'Allas', Custance sighs – she calls her destination 'the *Barbre nacioun*', the barbarous nation (II. 281–2). Although the lawyer's description of Syria has been an aspirational scene, characterised not by the 'barbarous' but by scenes of elite counselling, he does not criticise his heroine's language – but only her father's lack of forethought. He should have spoken to his astrologers before arranging her transport.

Sympathising with Custance's dread at going to Syria, Chaucer's lawyer cries: 'O Mars, o *atazir*!' (II. 309). Deriving from the Arabic *al-ta'thīr*, 'atazir' means 'influence'. The term *ta'thīr* was used to describe astral influence in Arabic astrological and magical texts, circulating in the works of Abū Ma'shar (787–886), a renowned astrologer of the 'Abbasid court of Baghdad. The lawyer continues to lament Custance's journey, crying that if the Emperor had consulted a '*philosophre*', he would have been told that it was not an auspicious moment for her to travel. Since rich 'folk of high condition' typically know their birth time, this information should have been used before planning travel (II. 310–14). This advice is taken from a Latin version of the astronomer Ibn Bishr's *Kitāb al-Ikhtiyārāt* ['The Book of Elections', or in its Latin version, 'De Eleccionibus']. Sahl ibn Bishr al-Israili (82–850) was an astrologer and mathematician based in Baghdad – a contemporary of Abū Ma'shar. His name, 'al-Israili', speaks to his Jewish heritage. In medieval Europe, he was known as 'Zael Benbriz'. Ibn Bishr's works were available in Latin from 1138, the date of their translation by Herman of Carinthia.[84] His works survive in at least fifty-seven Latin manuscripts.[85] In the margin of the Hengwrt manuscript – one of the earliest and most authoritative copies of Chaucer's *Tales* – the scribe has copied out a Latin translation of Ibn Bishr's work beside the Man of Law's speech:

> Everyone agrees that astrological calculations are weak except in the case of the rich, for they possess the time of their birth, that is the root of their fortunes, which strengthens all unstable planets, as for journeys, etc.[86]

Including the Hengwrt manuscript, this passage of Ibn Bishr's text is preserved by Chaucer's scribes in the margins of twenty-seven manuscripts of the *Tales*.[87] In at least one instance, the scribe has moved Ibn Bishr's Latin text from the margin into the main text itself to appear before the Man of Law's adaptation, as in a late fifteenth-century copy made in Greenwich.[88] These scribes saw Ibn Bishr's text as an essential part of Chaucer's poetry – actively recopying it into the margins. These medieval readers recognised Ibn Bishr's works more easily than modern editors of Chaucer's poetry have typically done. The English scribal fragment has lost its authority – has lost its Arab-Jewish author, the 'philosopher'. Re-centering Ibn Bishr as a presence in the text, Chaucer's lawyer's speech becomes audible as an Arabo-English tale.

Reading Chaucer's Syria Now

Once in Syria, Custance survives the Sultaness's attack – but is taken and put into 'a ship al *steereless*' – a raft without a rudder (II. 439). The attackers tauntingly 'bid her learn to sail | Out of Syria again back to Italy' (II. 440–1). '*O my Custance*' (II. 446), gasps the Man of Law. She prays, set adrift. The lawyer describes how for 'years and days *fleet this creature*' – she floated through 'the See of Grece unto the Strate | Of Marrok', through the Mediterranean to the Strait of Gibraltar (II. 463–5). Custance is alone in the '*wilde* waves' (II. 468). Knowing how terrifying the scene will be to his audience, the lawyer reminds us of reassuring biblical precedents – remember, he says, that God saved the Hebrew people from '*drenchynge*', drowning (II. 489). Leaving the unconvertible Syrians behind her, Custance is afraid, but ultimately secure as she crosses the sea of faith.

Today the scene resonates with a different, ongoing reality: the experiences of those who have to sail across the same marine routes in fishing boats and dinghies, and who are not saved.[89] Asylum seekers cast adrift in rudderless boats are closed in by a legal system offering less sympathy than Chaucer's lawyer. On 18 April 2015, a fishing boat carrying an estimated 1,100 people collided with a freight boat attempting rescue, and only 28 survived. In May 2023, a boat without a working engine, which was carrying 500 asylum seekers, sank in the Mediterranean, 400 miles from Malta and Sicily. On 14 June 2023, a fishing boat carrying an estimated 750 people from Syria, Egypt, Pakistan, Afghanistan, and Palestine sank, forty-seven nautical miles off the coast of Pylos, Greece, having left Libya for Italy. Since 2014, the Missing Migrants Project has counted more than

32,345 missing migrants in the Mediterranean, the vast majority assumed to have died by drowning.[90]

In Chaucer's tale, Custance is washed from Syria through the Mediterranean until: 'she driveth forth into our ocean | Throughout *oure wilde see*' (II. 505–6). She has reached the North Sea, approaching the British Isles, the journey recalling the plotting points of medieval sea charts.[91] At last 'in Northumberland the wave her cast, | And in the sand her ship *stiked* so fast | That thence would it not, for a whole *tyde*' (II. 505–10). The boat digs itself into the shore. The tide cannot drag it back out into open waters. In Middle English, 'tyde' also means time – an hour, a day, a night, a season, or 'the interval between high tides' The fantasy of the rudderless ship is also a fantasy of miraculously facilitated arrival. Imagining the journey between Syria and England, Chaucer sketches a picture of two connected coasts.

When Custance arrives in England, she speaks a 'manner of *Latyn corrupt*' (II. 519), in which broken speech she is able to communicate. She might always have spoken like that, or her speech might be post-traumatic. The lawyer tells us that Custance has been '*mazed in the see*' – confused, dashed in the waves – so that she has lost her mind (II. 526–7). A sequence of dramatic events follows – Custance is framed for murder, marries King Alla of Norhumberland, gives birth, and is betrayed by her new mother-in-law, Donegild. Based on counterfeited documents, Custance is put 'in the same ship' as she was found – 'her, and her young son' – and ordered to be cast 'from the land' (II. 799–801). The small boat is pushed back out.

'O my Custance' (II. 803), grieves the Man of Law. Arriving on a rudderless ship, Custance finds herself on that same deadly raft, this time with a baby. 'Peace, little son', she soothes him (II. 836). She places her handkerchief over his eyes and rocks him to sleep as she prays. The idealised figure of the innocent Custance with her child echoes Christian iconography of the Virgin nursing Christ. Her ship passes back through the 'narrow mouth' of Gibralter until it arrives back in Rome, where the story began (II. 946–7). When Custance is found in Italy, she is so traumatised that she cannot speak at all – 'she *nyl seye*' (II. 972). Unable to act to prevent these past events, the lawyer narrates, repeating 'allas', 'O my'.

Since 2015, the Refugee Tales project has taken Chaucer's tales as a model for using storytelling as a mode of solidarity: walking and talking through the countryside to the coast, as part of a campaign to end indefinite detention in the UK. The project provides a space for asylum seekers, refugees, and those who have experienced immigration detention to speak – or to tell their narratives, anonymised, to a writer. In Dragan Todorovic's contribution 'The Migrant's Tale', translated extracts of Chaucer's 'Man of Law's Tale' are interleaved with a contemporary narrative of forced migration from Syria to Italy, and back to Syria, before 'Aziz' arrives in England. In Todorovic's version, the organised violence of the Sultaness's troops is juxtaposed with the violence enacted by Assad's regime, during the Syrian Civil War (2011–).[92] The medieval text provides a historic lineage for present-day experiences, asserting the transhistorical realities of human movement. Translating from the reaction of Chaucer's lawyer enables there to be language when otherwise no words can be found.

Chaucer's text reflects the present back to itself through a medieval mirror: showing an image of traumatic forced migration over recognisable and deadly seas. These texts continue to provide material for new literary imaginations of society and identity.[93] Here Chaucer's Syria provides a starting point for a new narrative of medieval English culture: based on recollected texts, images, and objects which were produced in the '*wyde-where*', made from the materials and stories which had been sent across the Mediterranean, I have not collected these stories for their contemporary resonance alone, but for the practice of restoring to view the remains of the past – not discarding what has been kept in archives.

What to Expect

In Chaucer's dream vision *The House of Fame*, the narrator is brought to a spinning house, shaped like a cage. Through the gaps in the walls arrive stories: brought by 'shipmen and *pilgrimes*, | With *scrippes* brimful of *lesinges*, | Intermeddled with *tydynges*'.[94] These are satchels of scraps. The true 'tidings' – reports – are mixed up with '*lesinges*' – lies, which are inseparable in the bags and become more so as the building spins. The word '*lesinge*' has another meaning: 'gleaning'. The sailors and pilgrims bring bagfuls of what they have 'gleaned' on their journeys: a mixture of facts and fictions. In Agnes Varda's film *The Gleaners and I* (2000), she observes acts of 'gleaning' – recording those who sift through the end of the harvest, or urban rubbish bins. These scenes of precarity become an image for her own practice as a documentary maker – making narratives out of 'gleanings' – collecting the debris. I have tried to present medieval culture in its intermingled state, without trying to sort my sources into neat piles of fact and fiction, fakes and originals.

I have aimed for a style of criticism which (like labels on curated artefacts) introduces, guides, and provides contexts but also allows texts and images to speak. To me this aim has meant translating and re-narrating more, not less, than in a traditional critical mode, in order to make Middle English sources more easily audible outside of the medieval academy, as well as – I hope – defamiliarising aspects of texts to scholars used to reading them. Having said that, it does not feel accurate to the present state of critical discourse to say that this approach to texts is 'untraditional'. Following (in particular) Rita Felski's argument that the critic's attachment to their source material should be integrated into the process of analysis, and Saidiya Harman's formulation of 'critical fabulation' as a way of approaching the gaps in historical records, there is a growing movement of criticism which seeks to integrate the imagination into the process of writing.[95] In a sense these approaches are especially appropriate for the Middle Ages: as Carolyn Dinshaw has argued, the discipline of medieval studies rests on – and continues to be enriched by – the work of 'amateur' scholars, from non-professionalised editors of texts to the organisers of re-enactments.[96] Taking inspiration from creative-critical methodologies, I have left myself present at brief moments within this text, not through my own biography, but through allowing my own visualisation of medieval scenes to remain within the frame: letting imagination guide my analysis without discarding the knowledge of these sources which my research has given me.

Along the way, we will read medieval pilgrim texts, travel narratives, romances, devotional, political, and moralistic poetry, dream visions, saints' lives, lapidaries, recipe books, the inventories of travellers, private wills, church treasuries, household books, parliamentary bills and legislation, herbals, dyers', and surgical manuals – and will look at manuscript illuminations, excavated silks, tapestries, enamelled glass, and museum displays.

Part I, 'The Dispensary', focuses on the consumables on Sturmy's ship: sweet wines and spices, reflecting on their medicinal, spiritual, and commercial value. Chapter One, 'Sweet Wine / The English Taste for the Blood of the Holy Land', analyses Eucharistic images which presented sweet wine as the Christian blood of the Holy Land, providing an ethnonationalist rationale for the essentialised Christianity of the lost crusader territories. Chapter Two, 'Spices / English Digestion and Indigestion', explores medieval English recipe books, poetry, and drama in light of the legacies of the crusades.

Part II, 'The Treasury', begins in Westminster Abbey, where imported silks and jewels were highly visible, and considers the difference between medieval practices of display and contemporary museum practice. Chapter Three, 'Silks and Velvets / The Fabrics of English Identity', unravels the meanings of Arabic and Pseudo-Arabic textiles in medieval England, as devotional and resistant texts. Chapter Four, 'Jewels / English Possession and the Unpossessable', addresses jewels as excavated geological witnesses of the Christian nature of the Holy Land, reflecting on their discomforting association with – and disassociation from – Jewish communities.

Part III, 'The Workshop', unpacks the cultural significance of the mineral alum, which was imported in bulk, as an essential mordant for the cloth industry. Chapter Five, 'Alum / The Demand for Sodomite Salt in England', revives the origin narrative of the essential mineral as the product of the Dead Sea – which itself was seen as the ashes of the destroyed cities of Sodom and Gomorrah. These narratives continued to inform the uses of alum in alchemical, surgical, and book-making practices. In the 'Coda' to Part III, 'The English Market as the Temple of Jerusalem', I reflect on the relationship between late medieval religious and economic practices, brought together through the theme of alchemy.

In the Conclusion, 'Christopher Columbus in Chios', I return to the relationship between Sturmy's voyage and the other ships which crossed the seas in the late fifteenth century. And finally – the moment you will have been waiting for – in the Epilogue, 'The Verdict of the Trials of the Genoese', I reveal the outcome of Heyton's case, reflecting on what these trials say about medieval English immigration laws, and their legacies today.

These fragments defamiliarise and reconstitute premodern English culture as a site of instability, fuelled by the desire for what came from Syria.

PART I

The Dispensary

As Robert lay bleeding out on the sand in Malta, John prayed the doctors would bring wines, sweet and strong to heal his partner's broken body. If the doctors had come in time to operate on the wounds with scalpels, then the surgeon might apply a sponge of myrrh and Malmsey. While his men lay dying around him, John longed for Robert's stolen cargo. Disappearing over the horizon, his boats contained a floating dispensary, with pharmaceutical products crucial for survival at sea and on land.

These were the consumables on Sturmy's ship: '*swete wynes* as *Tyer* and *Malvesies*' and '*dyvers spices*, that is to say pepper, ginger, cinnamon, sugar, green ginger'.[1] These were spiritual, aromatic, and healing plants – irresistible and essential. I start with the desire for these commodities which was created by the body – existing on the tongue and in the blood.

This is the body, medieval: it contains four humours, 'that one is hot. that other is cold. the third is dry. the fourth is moist'.[2] These elements had to be kept in balance – these humours were seen as the constitutive elements not only of the body but of the natural world. Everything edible has humoural properties. These notions of imbalance and rebalance explain why people get sick, and how they are cured. The body is not self-regulating: it has to be kept in check through dietary medicines. Too much cold and damp felt under the skin creates a need, a want for heat and dryness: for spice. These understandings of the body shaped the contents of Sturmy's dispensary. This was an ambivalent realisation: the wines and spices which were needed were not always available – too pricey, too far away. So merchants had to come with their cargoes and monks with their charity, dispensing essential peppercorns.

Along with spices, medicinal knowledge was understood to have travelled to England from abroad. One early fifteenth-century English manuscript presents itself as a translation of the '*bok* that *ypocras* sent to the *kyng*'.[3] The manuscript is miniature, at 10 × 13 cm including its binding, evoking the pocket of a travelling doctor. The name '*ypocras*' refers to the

Greek physician Hippocrates (c. 460 BCE–c. 370 BCE). The works of Hippocrates, along with those of the physician Galen (129 CE–215 CE), were developed through Arabic texts, which were then translated into Latin and brought to England in those Arabo-Latin versions.[4] This manuscript remembers these complex journeys, in the lightness of a book designed to be shipped like a letter. These travelling translations were the sources of humoural doctrine, underlying medical treatment and culinary practice.

When Galenic/Hippocratic medicine was translated and extended in Arabic, the Greek sources were altered to include products from nearby marketplaces. The physician Ibn Rushd ('Averroes', 1129–98 CE) dedicated a chapter of his *al-Kulliyyāt* [Generalities] to cataloguing the new pharmacological cures which he knew to be in current use, not mentioned in Galen's works: cloves, cubeb and betel pepper, bitter ginger and cardamom.[5] In Greek texts, sugar is rarely mentioned – but in Arabic pharmacology, written near the Levantine cane plantations, sugar became one of the most significant cures.[6] Translated into Latin, these Arabic medicinal works created transnational desire for the prescribed goods: the spices which had been locally available to Ibn Rushd and his contemporaries, but which were not originally available in medieval English fields.

The term 'dispensary' was used to describe an apothecary's cabinet, and contains within it the Middle English term 'spense': a storeroom in which food and drinks were kept.[7] In England, spices and wines settled in cellars, spicers' shops, and domestic shelves. Stocked with medically attested products, these various spaces became miniature apothecaries, their contents understood by cooks, vintners, and household stewards, as well as surgeons. In Arabic, Latin, and European vernaculars, cookbooks and medical texts were blended genres. In the earliest surviving cookbook in Arabic, the tenth-century *Kitāb al-Ṭabīkh* [book of cooking], Ibn Sayyān describes his work as a 'collection of whatever benefits the body'.[8] One late medieval English collection of recipes concludes: 'Here ends the [discussion] of cooking which is the best medicine.'[9] The maintenance and preparation of these prescriptions was the task of the steward, the cook, and the kitchen worker, who put theory into practice with powder-laced sauces.

Through necessity, commercial travellers were repositories of medical knowledge. In the Persian polymath Ibn Sīnā's *al-Qānūn fi al-ṭibb* [encyclopaedia of medicine], he advises that a traveller must 'take care of the matters concerning his body so that he might be safe from many diseases'.[10] Imagining the cases of wines and bags of sugar on Sturmy's ships as a 'dispensary', I do not see a closed-off storage unit, but a collection of boxes and jars to be opened in multiple spaces: at the operating table, in the church, in the kitchen, in the bedroom, on the deck. In all these places, sweet wines and spices were dispensed and put to work.

A Scene in the Dispensary

One recipe in the fifteenth-century Arabo–English 'bok of ypocras' appears under the heading: 'For to make a *drynke* of *antyoche*.' The author advises: 'Take a handful of *bugle* another of strawberry . . . another of *meneconsoud* another of *petyconsoud* of *conferye* . . . another of *sanycle* . . . another of crops of the red nettles another of *pympernele* . . . and three handfuls of *erbe robert*.'[11] The prescription of ferns, wildflowers, and hedgerow foliage evokes a local landscape. The term 'consoude' simply means a 'healing' herb – here in medium ('mene') and small ('petit') varieties. These are Anglo-Norman and Old English medicinal terms for plants, recalling the longevity of herbal medicine in the British Isles. The recipe goes on: 'wash the *erb* clean and stamp them and put them in a *newe* earthen pot and add there-to a gallon of white *wyn*'.[12] The quantity of a gallon clearly shows that the wine used was an inexpensive, homemade drink. But the recipe is still labelled 'of Antioch' – an aspirational rubric.

The locally sourced medicine was brewed according to ideas brought from Arabic sources, reimagining itself as belonging to an imported tradition. Sweetened with honey, the 'lycour' is left 'by the space of this psalm: Sing *miserei mei deus*'. The scene is that of herbs brewed to the sound of Christian recitative – 'Syng!' – bringing the laboratory together with the chapel in the imagination. Finally: 'put thy *lycour* in a vessel of pewter or of lead or of *glas* and when thee like to drink there-of give him a *sponeful*'.[13] Syrian glassmaking was a globally renowned industry, and there are records that Levantine glass vessels were imported to England.[14] This recipe was served in imported glassware or English-manufactured lead, luxurious or accessible containers for the foraged leaves.

The recategorisation of this herbal remedy as 'of Antioch' combines associations of the crusades and pilgrimage with mercantile and intellectual prestige. Sturmy's cargo was buoyed by the desire for the authentic Syrian product, a desire which, when fulfilment was impossible, led to the swift acceptance of available substitutes, sold as 'Syrian'. The wines and spices on Sturmy's ship were not local to England, like the herbs used for this 'drink of Antioch' – but neither were they straightforwardly 'Syrian'. Spices in Syrian marketplaces often originated in India and China, while many sweet wines were produced in Europe. In being named as an 'Antioch' drink, the domestic earthen pot filled with European herbs, honey, and cheap white wine expresses the dream of becoming a Syrian glass vessel containing a solution of Holy Land flora. Weeds and flowers from the English garden were distilled into Syriana, in a spiritual remarketing strategy which sold a blend of the real and the relabelled.

The stories and images which follow are samples of the imported goods which this herbal 'Antioch drink' aspired to contain: the spices and sweet wines which came by ship.

CHAPTER 1

Sweet Wine / The English Taste for the Blood of the Holy Land

The catalogue of Robert Sturmy's lost goods begins with: '*swete wynes* as *Tyer* and *Malvesies* in buttes and barrels to the number of 960 buttes, to the value in *Englond* of ... £3840'.[1] Recorded at the head of the list of merchandise, the cost of these wines is equivalent to around £2.5 million in today's currency.[2] In Sturmy's view, the home market for 'Tyer and Malvesies' was booming. The labelling of wines as the produce of 'Tyre' or 'Antioch' – the former Syrian crusading cities, now Sūr in modern-day Lebanon and Antakya in Turkey – recalled the lost Christian settlements, even though these products were known to have travelled from Mediterranean marketplaces.

In this chapter I retrace the transportation, consumption, and misremembering of sweet wines. Introducing my first object-based example of post-Acre melancholia, I show how Eucharistic images represented sweet wines as the Christian blood of the Holy Land, providing an ethnonationalist rationale for the essential Christianity of the lost crusader territories. These crusading associations coexisted with medicinal and mercantile understandings of sweet wines, from medieval pilgrim texts and travel narratives (John Mandeville, William Wey), Chaucer's 'Wife of Bath's Tale', romances (Mallory's *Morte Darthur, The Squire of Low Degree*), and medical texts.

To me, these contradictory narratives are blended, as will be seen finally in the industrial-devotional image of the mystical winepress, with which this chapter will close.[3] The category of sweet wine was celebrated and policed.

Francisco and Panino's Tavern

In 1353, a London tavern run by Francisco of Genoa and Panino Guillelmi, the servant of Francisco de Spynola of Genoa, was forcibly closed down by the Mayor and Aldermen of London for illicit practices. The crime: the men had stocked 'two adjoining cellars ... and have stowed away wines of Crete and other sweet wines in one of the said cellars, and red and white wines in the other cellar, for making sale of in the same tavern'.[4] It was illegal to sell sweet and non-sweet wines together, under pain of imprisonment. Laws and taxes separated these drinks from the 'ordinary' wines of Gascony or Bordeaux.[5] The case was serious enough that the accused sought aid directly from Edward III, who was sympathetic to their cause.

On 24 February 1353, Edward III wrote a royal injunction 'in favour of two Genoese, keeping tavern in the City' to the mayor and sheriffs of London: 'wishing to act graciously as towards the same Francisco and Panino ... to the end that other alien merchants may not thereby be minded to decline to come to the said city with their wines and merchandises'.[6] The term 'alien' derived from the Latin 'alienigena', meaning one 'born elsewhere', as distinct from a person 'indigenus', 'born there'. Edward III's letter to the Mayor of London resonates with anxiety: it would be a terrible outcome for 'aliens' to stop travelling to England with their wines. This incident from nearly a century before Sturmy's voyage shines a spotlight on the highly regulated late medieval division of sweet and non-sweet wines. The closure of Francisco and Panino's tavern and its royally backed reopening are events which are only explicable in the context of a culture deeply preoccupied with the symbolism and practical availability of sweet wines.

Through association with the Eucharist, sweet wines held spiritual significance.[7] In devotional representations, Christ's blood was described as sweet, meaning that the fortified wines of the Holy Land reminded consumers of the Passion, through both their taste and location of origin. Malmsey, Romney, and Osei were produced in the Mediterranean using the same techniques.[8] These wines were routinely purchased by pilgrims on their way to Jerusalem, and were absorbed into the same cultural category as those produced in Syria. Unlike 'ordinary' wines, sweet wines were viewed as relics, as salvific blood. Sweet wines were relics of the Passion – but they were also commodities and surgical cures derived from translated Arabic medicine.

The Wine Industry after Acre

Sweet wines were first transported to England from vineyards in Crusader Syria.[9] As the archaeologist Rabei Khamisy writes: '[i]t seems likely that large areas of the plain of Acre were covered by vineyards', with villages established for the express purpose of wine production.[10] In 2021, Khamisy directed an excavation project in his hometown, the hillside village of Miʿilyā, which uncovered a Crusader winepress so large that it is thought to have functioned as a wine factory, with owners of local vineyards bringing their grapes to the press.[11] With twenty-five Frankish winepresses already excavated and unknown numbers undiscovered, it is clear that winemaking in the Kingdom of Jerusalem was a major organised industry.[12] The technologies of crusader winemaking combined the indoor fermentation practices of European peasants with the local Levantine technique of drying grapes in the warm sun.[13] These Frankish winemaking practices left agricultural and architectural remnants across Syria, and left a reservoir of recollected crusader wines in late medieval imaginations.

After 1291, sweet wines continued to travel from the Levant and the Mediterranean to England, mainly traded by Italian merchants. Southampton was the staple English port for sweet wines, principally visited by Genoese merchants.[14] It was not until December 1504 that a Southampton-owned ship, the *Charity*, brought back sweet wines from Morocco.[15] The late medieval sweet-wine trade was not a trade dominated by the English, but a trade in which the English acted as avid consumers. The anonymous author of the fifteenth-century political poem *The Libelle of Englyshe Polycye*, which argues for nationalist controls over marine trading routes, comments bitterly that 'The great *Galees* of Venice and Florence | Be well laden ... With *sweete* wines'.[16] It was common for Italians resident in England to act as agents for consignments: in November 1442, Paolo Morelli collected sixty-six butts of malmsey wine from a Venetian carrack, which he sold on to English merchants for shipment around the country.[17] Occasionally, Italian traders fell foul of English regulations: on 14 February 1463, twenty butts of sweet wine were seized from the Venetian merchants Filippo Cini and Andrea Morosini, who were alleged to have avoided the customs tax.[18] These resident and visiting Italian merchants brought their first-hand knowledge of Levantine markets to England.

Sweet wines were transported via separate trading connections to non-sweet wines. For example, the Hundred Years' War between England and France caused the Gascon wine trade to fluctuate, but did not impact the arrival of sweet wines. In the years after the battle of Aquitaine, between 1453 and 1458, 568 tons of wine arrived in Southampton, over half of which was sweet wine transported on Italian carracks.[19] Given that expensive sweet wine was usually only a fraction of the wine trade, comprising 2.5 per cent of total wine sales in the late fifteenth century, this rebalancing of the volume of sweet and non-sweet wine imports witnesses the sharp decline of the French wine trade at this pivotal moment in the conflict, in comparison to the stability of Italian sweet wine imports.[20]

In England, private ownership of sweet wine was a sign of high wealth. In 1411–12, the Staffordshire aristocrat Lady Talbot bought 144 gallons of sweet wines, including Romney, Malmsey, and Tyre.[21] The household records of the East Anglian gentry woman Alice de Bryene (d. 1435), compiled by her steward, witness the more restrained consumption of sweet wine in a wealthy gentry household. While 'ordinary' wine was drunk daily, only one annual record is made in 1419 to the purchase of '2 small barrels, whereof one of "rumneye" and the other of "Malmesyn"' at London.[22]

Outside the aristocracy and the gentry, sweet wines were drunk in religious houses. In his will, Edward IV left one ton of 'ordinary wine and one ton of sweet wine' to the convent of Henton.[23] The records of Durham Cathedral Priory indicate that an average of 0.4 tons of sweet wine was bought per year between 1464 and 1540, with a regular annual purchase of one butt of malmsey by the 1490s.[24] The Durham monks were chiefly supplied by Newcastle merchants, such as John Sample, William Carr, and Edward Baxter, who also imported Levantine goods such as silks and minerals.[25] The consumption of sweet wines in religious contexts was dependent on the contact between traders and monks, and the financial capacity of the Church to access luxury goods.

Holy War and Holy Grapes

The monks' taste for sweet wines had a theological basis: transformed into Jesus' blood during the Mass ceremony, wine became the ultimate symbol of communal Christian identity. During the medieval Mass, only the Host was distributed to the public; the consecrated wine was kept for the priests. As Caroline Walker Bynum comments, 'withdrawal of the cup only increased the people's sense of its power': the cultural significance of the wine persisted as a widespread phenomenon.[26] Devotion to the Eucharist was frequently expressed as a form of relic worship, drawing attention to the Jerusalem origins of the transubstantiated blood.

Recalling Christ's Passion in taste, sweet wines travelled along the same routes as blood relics. Stained earth and browned remnants of the holy blood were transported in vials from pilgrim sites. In 1247, Henry III processed with a relic of Christ's blood towards Westminster Abbey, in a manner reminiscent of Corpus Christi ceremonies, as depicted by the St Albans cartographer and monk Matthew Paris [Figure 1.1].[27] In the

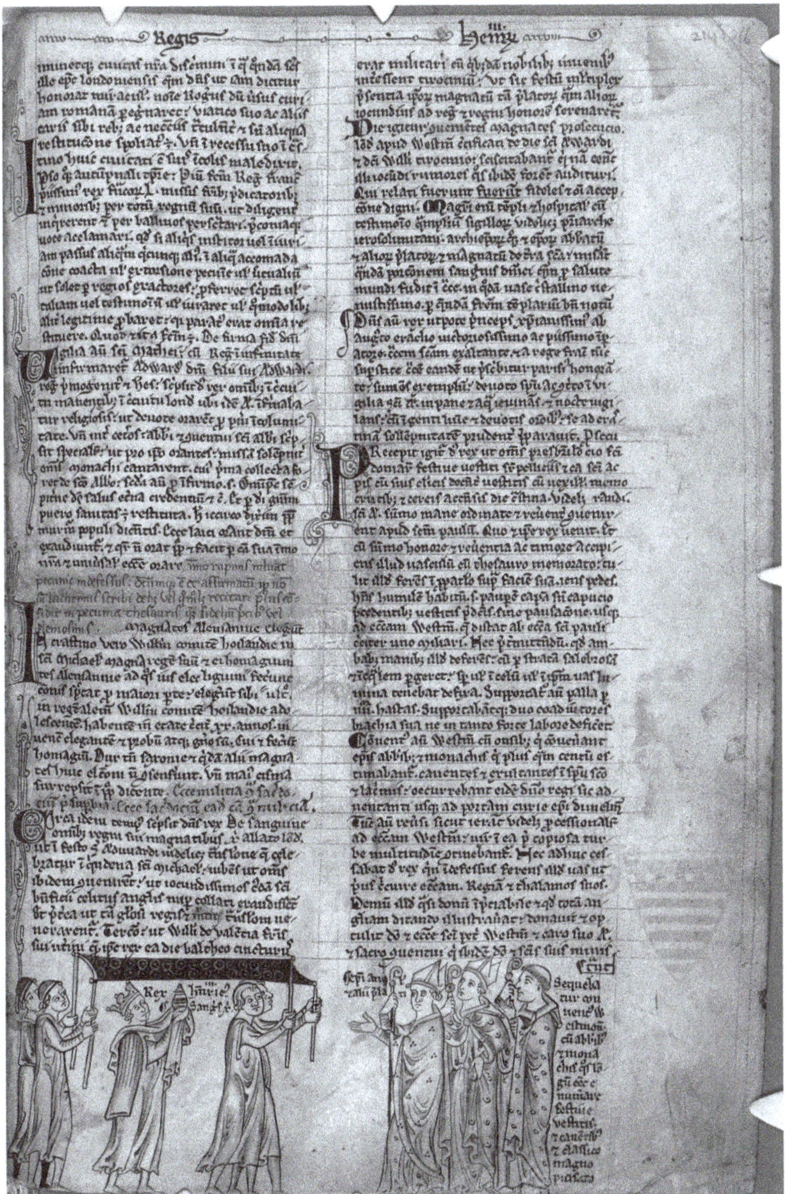

Figure 1.1 Matthew Paris, the Westminster blood relic. Source: Corpus Christi College, Cambridge. MS 16, fol. 215 r. Printed with permission of the Parker Library.

Abbey, the relic was stored not in a pyx or crystal vial as was customary, but in 'a *cuppe* of gold with *stonys* with the *blode* of our lord'.[28] Henry III's Westminster blood cult was not a success: partly due to scepticism about the authenticity of the relic. After all, Henry III had not been to Jerusalem. Why should the laity put their trust in his blood?

For the theologian Thomas Aquinas, devotion to the physical relics of Christ's blood was not permissible – since Christ's physical body ascended to heaven in the Assumption, how could traces of his blood remain on earth? – but devotion to the Eucharist *as* a blood relic was acceptable.[29] Becoming a form of relic in its transformation, the wine was experienced as a more reliable trace of the Holy Land than physical blood.[30] The ceremony of the Eucharist was often accompanied by prayers known as 'collects', such as *pro terra ierosolimitana* [for the land of Jerusalem], which combined the Mass with an explicit call for the recapture of the settlements. In addition, the Mass was used to justify holy war as a sacrificial deed.[31] The military expedition was seen as salvific, likened to the consumption of the Host. The perceived connection between the Holy Land and the Mass ceremony also motivated unarmed pilgrimage.[32] In the fifteenth-century Middle English translation of the *Liber Celestis* of the mystic Bridget of Sweden (1303–73), Bridget receives instruction from Christ to travel to Jerusalem in these terms: 'when you come into my temple that is hallowed with my *blode*, you are also cleansed of all your sin'.[33] Across the region, and especially at the site of the Holy Sepulchre, Christ's blood was felt as a spiritually curative, ongoing presence.

The fourteenth-century *Travels* of John Mandeville presents itself as the work of a returned pilgrim, a knight who left St Albans for Jerusalem and has witnessed the Holy Land and the lands beyond. The identity of the author is unknown. The narrative persona is typically read as a fiction. The self-named knight begins with an exhortation for the reader to reflect on how: 'the *holi lond* . . . is blessed and hallowed of the precious blood of our lord Jesus Christ . . . Right well ought men to love and worship and praise such an *holy lond* that brought forth such *fruyt*.'[34] Represented as the 'fruyt' of the Holy Land, the birth of Christ is likened to the generation of grapes in a local vineyard. The language recalls the Mass ceremony – and vice versa, the wine used in the Mass ceremony recalls its Jerusalem origins. Likened to the consumption of the Eucharist, visiting Jerusalem allows the pilgrim to experience the presence of Christ's sweet blood.

Grown from the ground on which Christ's blood had been spilt, these sweet drinks were brought out of time. Medieval pilgrims were motivated to travel to the Holy Land through an awareness of the historic and transubstantiated presence of Christ's blood-as-wine, and once there, regarded the landscape in biblical and sacramental terms. Moving along the same routes as physical relics, sweet wines were desired as if they were traces of Christ's blood.[35] Infused with these narratives, sweet wines became a self-evidently Christian substance, with ethno-nationalist significance: a fragrant fluid drained from Holy Land earth, as naturally distinguished from the non-Christian blood as sweet wine is distinct from sour grapes.

Expressing Identity

For medieval pilgrims, the wines pressed in contemporary Jerusalem were still viewed as traces of the Passion. When he returned from his 1458 and 1462 pilgrimages to Jerusalem, the former bursar of Eton William Wey settled down in Wiltshire to write *The Matter of Jerusalem*. The text was based both on his experience and on his readings of previous accounts, including Mandeville.[36] Wey guides his reader through the contemporary landscape via the biblical sites of wine consumption and production. He gives some general advice: '*at Jherusalem hyt ys goyd wyne*'.[37] In the context of sacramental pilgrimage, the 'goodness' of Jerusalem wine is layered: the fluid is 'good' in both a marketplace and a ritual sense. Describing the location of the Last Supper, Wey writes, in snappy verse:

> There gave he his body and *blode*
> To his Apostles that were right *gode*
> Under the form of *wyne* and *bred*.[38]

The deictic 'there' encourages the reader to remain contemplatively focused on the landscape whilst considering the origins of the Eucharistic wine. The 'fruit' of the Holy Land, the curative human presence of Christ on earth, shaped views of the grapes with which contemporary wine was made. Wey also recommends that the pilgrim visit 'a town called Cana, where Christ converted water into wine'.[39] Wines drunk in contemporary Cana or seen as imported from the region were construed as a vestige of the historic miracle. The present-day sites of biblical wine production were destination locations, appealing to pilgrims' devotional and sensory desire to taste the holy grape.

At the same time, medieval pilgrims witnessed the contemporary realities of the sweet wine trade, reinforcing the knowledge gained from merchants in England. Wey records the origins of wines in the Mediterranean: '*Malvesey* grows in the kingdom of Crete. Romney grows on the island Modin

(Methoni) in Greece.'[40] For travellers, wine was often safer to drink than water: Ibn Sīnā's *al-Qānūn fī al-ṭibb* contains a section dedicated to the 'Protection of Travelers against the Injurious Effects of Various Waters'.[41] Those who travelled to the Holy Land were advised to drink plenty of wine for physical as well as spiritual health. Wey included amongst his essential Greek phrases for the English traveller: '*Wher ys the taverne*?', 'Woman, have ye *goyd wyne*?', 'Man, have ye *goyd wyne*?' and '*Bryng* hither *wyne*'.[42] He gave step-by-step directions for wine purchase and storage along the journey, advising the pilgrim to purchase a barrel of red wine at Venice, to sample the wine in Cyprus, and to bring 'gordys' of wine from Port Jaffa.[43] He even provided a plan for a hamper to take from Jerusalem to the river Jordan: 'when you shall ride to the *flum* [river] Jordan, take with *yow* out of Jerusalem bread, *wyne*, water, hard cheese, and hard *eggys*'.[44] This wine was likely to spoil on the journey if it was not stored properly – mid fourteenth-century recipes detail a range of dubious- sounding methods for treating spoiled wine, such as adding eggs, salt, saffron, or the sulphurous mineral alum.[45] Stored alongside hard cheese and boiled eggs, the wines drunk in the Holy Land were an everyday necessity, and a practical concern. Wey cautioned the pilgrim that on returning from the desert where '*drynke* no water, but rest *yow* a little, and then . . . *drynke clene wyne* . . . after that *grete* heat water engenders a great *fluxe*'.[46] Wine could rebalance the humours within the body when water might cause illness. Given that water was often the cause of disease, this advice can be seen both within the context of medieval humoural frameworks and in line with more recent understandings of the dangers of drinking unclean water.

The book of the mystic Margery Kempe (c. 1373 – d. after 1438) gives a dramatic sense of the significance of wine to pilgrims. Kempe 'had eaten no *flesch* [meat] nor drunk no *wyn* for four years before she went out of *Ynglond*', but was convinced by her holy father to drink wine as an exception on her pilgrimage.[47] Kempe found herself unpopular – her mystical inspiration came in the form of uncontrollable, noisy weeping, which saw her thrown out of churches and accused of heresy. Her self-characterisation lingers on these moments of ostracision – being misunderstood, she feels saintly. The non-provision of wine becomes an instance of her exclusion from the group with whom she travelled, recorded in Kempe's aggrieved comment that they bought '*vessellys* for their *wyn* . . . but *nothyng* for her'.[48] The denial of drinking vessels was a mark of deliberate hostility, the deprivation of a basic resource. Having been reluctant to consume wine at all in England, even the contrary Margery Kempe wanted to drink wine in the Holy Land.

The Desire for Wine

In Chaucer's *Canterbury Tales*, Alison, the Wife of Bath, is introduced as a seasoned traveller – she has been to Jerusalem three times and knows much about '*wandryng* by the way' (I. 463–7).[49] Her three trips to Jerusalem – like her five husbands – are a sign of her exuberance, her excess. Reflecting on her youth, Alison tells us she used to dance to the sound of a harp, and sing – *ywis*! – like a nightingale, when she had '*dronke a draughte of sweete wyn!*' (III. 457–9). Referring to a parable of the '*foule*' Metellius – the swine! – who killed his wife with a staff because she drank wine, Alison boldly claims that even if she had been his '*wyf* | He should not have *daunted me fro drynke!*' (III. 460–3). The Wife's determined adherence to wine drinking is stated against the explicit backdrop of proverbial, violent male resistance. Sweet wines make her feel free. Geoffrey Chaucer was the son of a wine merchant. When his father died, his mother remarried another vintner.[50] The Wife's attachment to the qualities of wine draws on the dockside trade in which the poet had been raised.

These scenes of wine drinking and dancing are not given an explicit location – they could take place in England – but the narrative cuts between this memory and direct memories of the Holy Land. Juxtaposed with physical travel, the consumption of sweet wine is associated with the liberty of movement. During her Jerusalem pilgrimages the Wife becomes a mobile consumer, having been cast, as a married woman, into the role of property.[51] Having disclosed her memories of drinking, dancing, and flirting during her fourth marriage, she comments that 'he died when I came back from Jerusalem' (III. 495): the reference to pilgrimage frames the scene of wine-consumption.

Along with travel and wine, the Wife feels freest when she experiences sexual desire. She discloses that 'after *wyn* on Venus must I *thynke*' (III. 464). Sweet wines make her sing – libido-enhancing and disinhibiting. The reference to Venus here recalls medicinal frameworks: as the Wife has a Venerian complexion, the balance of her body will be acted on in a certain way. Alison's blood is stirred – instead of the unity of sweet wine transmuted into Jesus' blood, here the reader receives sweet wine as a sexual stimulant within the Wife's receptive body. Rejecting the reverence of wine as a relic-like vessel of purity, the Wife delights in Jerusalem and its produce as sites of worldly joy, her experience of which gives much-needed relief from the men of medieval England. The thought of these wines and her travels prompts Alison to muse nostalgically: 'I have had my world as in my *tyme*' (I. 473). Alison's world is geographically expansive, sensual and relational.

Her next lover was abusive and violent: Alison looks back on her fourth marriage as a time of singing, wandering, and drinking, with sweet wines recalling the taste of her well-spent youth. The sensory pleasures of sweet wines were not only enjoyed with the Eucharist in mind – their tastes did not have one single association, even among groups of Christian pilgrims.

Judeo-Muslim Wine Cultures

In order to see Holy Land wine as a Christian fluid, medieval travellers had to extract the drink from its proximity to resident non-Christian communities. In the *Travels*, the Mandeville author lays great emphasis on the prohibition against wine drinking in Islam. He writes:

> all that dwelleth in Bethlehem be *cristene* men. And there be fair *vynes* about the city and great plenty of *wyn*, for their books of their law that *Macomet* bitook them (which they call *Alkaron*, and some call it *Massap*, and some call it *Harme*) forbids them to *drynke wyn*, for in that book *Macomet* curseth all those who drinketh *wyn* and all that sell it.[52]

The Qur'ān had been available in Latin translation since 1141, the date of its translation by the Englishman Robert of Ketton.[53] Ketton's translation was intended as a conversion tool, disseminating knowledge of Islam in order to refute it. In keeping with this practice of translation, the Mandeville author draws on canonical Muslim traditions as a means of asserting the Christianity of wine. This understanding of the Qur'ān is brought into the text in order to Christianise both the holy city of Bethlehem and the wine that is cultivated there. The wine sold in markets becomes evidence of the continued presence of Christian viticulture. Communities of Syrian Christians long preceded the Frankish settlements and were active in Mamlūk society long after the fall of Acre.[54] The Mandeville author's description of active Bethlehem wine merchants was not a fantasy, but a recognition of the diversity of Mamlūk Syria. But in this context, the essentialised Christianity of Bethlehem wine also stands for the rightful Latin Western possession of the Holy Land.

The prohibition is repeated later in the text: Muhammed 'cursed *wyn* and all that it *drinketh*. And therefore *Sarasyns* which be *devoute* drink no *wyn*.'[55] In medieval Christian texts, the Prophet Muhammed is often represented as a 'contra-image' to Christ – in its most extreme form, this is seen in iconography of Muhammed as the Antichrist.[56] The idea that wine is cursed in Islam appears as the inverse of the Christian sacralisation of wine. At the same time, the understanding that wine was forbidden was founded in transmitted knowledge of the Qur'ān and *ḥadīth* collections.[57] The Qur'ānic prohibition against intoxicants was expanded in *ḥadīth* compilations to encompass condemnation of drinking, pouring, selling, buying, producing, or transporting wine: rules noted in Mandeville's *Travels*. The statement '*al-khamru miftāḥu kulli sharrin*' [alcohol is the source of all evil] was frequently affixed to the start of *Kutub al-Ashriba* [*Books of Drinks*], specialised chapters within *ḥadīth* collections.[58] Mandeville's text can be seen to 'reorient', to swivel between perspectives, revealing the imaginative pull of alternative traditions.[59] While there is an impulse to Christianise, there is also a curiosity about different viewpoints, an ambivalence and a hesitancy in remaining fixed in one voice.

In both instances, Mandeville's record of the wine prohibition is framed by an uncanonical anecdote which is used to explain the motivation for the Prophet's condemnation of wine:

> *Macomet* loved well a good man, a hermit, that dwelled in the *wildernesse* a mile from mount *Synay* in the way as men shall go from *Arabye* to *Caldee* . . . a day's journey from the sea where *merchauntis* of *Venys* cometh many times for to buy *merchaundises*. And *Macomet* went so often to this hermit to hear him preach that all his men were angry . . . So it befell upon a night that *Macomet* had so drunken of good *wyn* that he was *drunke* and fell asleep. And while he *slepte*, his men took out a sword out of his own sheath and with that sword they slew this hermit.[60]

Historical scenes and contemporary trade collide, as Muhammed's route is mapped through the paths taken by medieval Venetian merchants. The episode of Muhammed's supposed drunkenness is not taken from *ḥadīth* records – but it is a departure too from the more typical modes of misrepresentation of the Prophet in medieval Christianity.[61] Muhammed as he appears in this incident is neither God nor idol nor Antichrist, but a flawed human – Mandeville describes him as a '*grete astronomere*' well versed in authoritative Arabic science.[62] The wine on which Muhammed is said to have become drunk is the same wine as the Mandeville author himself claims to find on his journey to the Holy Land.

Mandeville finishes his account of Muslim attitudes towards wine with the acknowledgement that: 'some *Sarasyns* drinketh *wyn* gladly but not openly but in private . . . But their drinketh *goode* beverage *swete* and nourishing, which is y-made of *calamele*.'[63] The secretive nature of 'Saracen' wine drinking is in contrast both to the 'devout' who abstain and to the public and communal ceremony of the Christian Mass. Contemporary Muslims are half revealed and half concealed here under the 'Saracen' label. The Christian sacred symbol becomes illicit, deviant. But these private acts of drinking are not straightforwardly condemned either, accompanied with a description of the sweet, nourishing, desirable alternative to wine which is also drunk among the 'Saracens', made of caramel, the sugar-cane.

When buying wines in the Holy Land, medieval pilgrims came into contact with the contemporary realities of the sale and production of wines under Mamlūk rule: that is, with the multi-confessional nature of Mamlūk society. Levantine wines were often traded and produced within established Jewish communities – a fact which is typically absent from English pilgrims' accounts. However, the letters of the Italian-Jewish merchant Meshullam of Volterra (before 1443 – after 1507) testify to these scenes. Meshullam was a Tuscan trader of wine, jewels, pearls, oil, and cloth. In 1481, Meshullam made a pilgrimage to Jerusalem. In the Levant, he joined a family dinner party, recording in Hebrew flecked with Italian loan words that: 'they bring raisin wine [Italian: *zibbino*, from Arabic *zabīb*, 'raisin'] which is a thousand times stronger than the *malvasin* . . . If you were to refrain from drinking, you would greatly insult the host.'[64] Meshullam himself was apparently unwilling to partake, feigning illness to avoid drinking – but the vivid scene remains a focus of his narrative.

Another late medieval record of Jewish wine drinking in the Levant is preserved in the family correspondence of Rabbi Obadiah (c. 1450–1515), who emigrated from Bertinoro to Jerusalem. Obadiah attended Shabbat in Alexandria, noting the observation of the Kiddush [wine blessing]. He commented that wine was drunk with yellow plums, candied fruit, fresh ginger, dates, and coriander seeds: 'sometimes raisin wine, which is very good, and sometimes *malvasin di Candia*, or local wine; and I drank with [the host] and was exhilarated'.[65] The holiness of Levantine Jewry impressed Obadiah: 'there is no sinner or transgressor in these parts who would drink the wine that was touched by an Ishmaelite [a Muslim], much less by an uncircumcised idol worshipper [a Christian]'.[66] This praise of kosher Jews testifies to the cultivation and production of wine within the Jewish community. The participation of these European Jewish travellers in local drinking customs – whether somewhat reluctantly, like Meshullam, or eagerly, like Obadiah – provides essential insight into the spiritual significance of sweet wine to residents of, as well as visitors to, the Levant. Witnessed scenes of the consumption, production, and sale of sweet wine by Syrian-Jewish communities contradicted narratives of the essentialised Christianity of the territory and sweet wines of the Holy Land.

The interpretation of Holy Land wine as a Christian fluid relied on the erasure of resident, less observant Muslims and kosher Jews, whose homes and vineyards remained free of the blood of God, stocked with untransformed wine. The knowledge, gained through travel and trade, that many of these individuals were responsible for producing and transporting the Eucharistic wine risked the dissolution of the theological framework. Post-Acre representations which emphasised the Christianity of sweet wine offered the melancholic taste of a Christian Syria, out of reach except in being savoured in the imagination.

The Chalice at the End of the Quest

The Holy Grail is the transcendent object which King Arthur's knights seek for the end of their quest: the archetypal image of Christian desire. Thomas Malory's prose version of *Le Morte Darthur* translated the already influential and popular Arthurian legends into the English imagination. Malory states that the Grail refers to a relic of Christ's blood preserved by Joseph of Arimathea and brought from Jerusalem to Britain.[67] The backstory was represented in illuminations of the Grail narrative, such as one early fourteenth-century manuscript of the *Estoire del Saint Graal* which shows Joseph of Arimathea collecting Christ's blood in a dish.[68] The presentation is reminiscent of Henry III's Westminster chalice: a Jerusalem blood relic stored in a Eucharistic vessel.

In Malory's version, one night, the Grail appears to the gathered knights at dinner: '*Than loked they and saw a man com oute of the holy vessell that had all the synges* [signs] *of the Passion of Jesu Cryste bledynge all openly.*' The doctrine of transubstantiation is given bodily manifestation: the man of sorrows rises from the chalice. Galahad 'kneeled down and there he received his Saviour'. After him each knight kneels to receive the saviour in their mouths, and 'they thought it so *sweete* that it was *mervaylous* to tell'.[69] These kneeling men beg to taste the body of Christ and do receive it, delicious on the tongue. In this scene, sweetness stands both for the spiritual elevation of the moment and the pleasure of the experience. The community is formed around the embodied Eucharist, a band of Christian men unified through their group desire, experienced together. This vision of an all-male ritual formed around the body of Christ is erotic in its explicit sensory desire. These men will have to prove their worthiness of sweet pleasure through violence. Throughout Malory's *Morte Darthur*, there is a strong impetus towards Christian conquest, symbolised in this scene of Eucharistic consumption.[70]

The Taste for Crusade

Like the *Morte Darthur*, the anonymous fifteenth-century romance *The Squire of Low Degree* explicitly celebrates crusade as an ideal – and explicitly records the elite desire for sweet wines. As is characteristic of this popular verse tradition, the narrative is loosely plotted and relies on the suspension of disbelief. The Princess of Hungary falls in love with a Squire. The King believes he is unworthy – and so the Squire sets off to Jerusalem, vowing to 'prove my *strengthe* with my right hand | On God's enemies in *uncouth land*'.[71] Like the loosely plotted storyline, crusading ideology is characteristic of the genre of 'recovery literature' – late medieval English romances which continued to enact fantasies of Christian domination.[72] While the Squire is proving his worth, the Princess is falsely led to believe that her low-born lover is dead.

Seeing that the Princess is pining away, her father tries to comfort her with the material wealth of the Hungarian court, starting with his wine cellar:

> Ye shall have *rumney* and *malmesine*,
> Both *ypocrasse* and *vernage* wine,
> *Montrose* and wine of *Greke*,
> Both *algrade* and *respice eke*,
> *Antioche* and *bastarde*,
> *Piment* also and *garnade*;
> Wine of *Greke* and *muscadell*
> Both *claré*, *piment* and *rochell*.[73]

The catalogue reads like a fantasy wine merchant's inventory, listing all the most expensive, imported products. These wines come from Antioch, Greece, and Grenada ('garnade'). With both Antioch and Grenada evading Christian conquest in this period, the list is predicated on trade with Muslim-ruled empires. The paradox is evident: the squire sets off to battle 'God's enemies' singlehandedly in order to gain entry to a Christian Hungarian court in which Muslim-traded goods are the most prized commodities. The cognitive dissonance is irresolvable: both within this tale, and in late medieval culture more widely, desires for crusade and trade were sustained simultaneously. The ability of the Christian elite to possess these wines is presented as a victory, the ownership of commodities acting as a surrogate for the futile dream of conquest.

Alongside the sweet wines which the King offers to the Princess, he promises her 'spices that be good and *fyne* | Gentle *pottes* with ginger green, | With *dates* and *dainties*'.[74] Recalling historic merchants' lists, these dates and pots of green ginger are both luxurious and realistic, the material produce of the marketplace inserted into the romance. The Hungarian court is fictive and loosely situated in the medieval world, both in time and political circumstance – but these commodities are real. The romance foregrounds the produce of the erstwhile settlements, in exoticised modes of representation, overlaying late medieval trading networks with a post-Acre melancholic consciousness. These fantasies were not the result of a lack of awareness of contemporary trade, but a means of reframing known realities.

Reaching the Holy Sepulchre in Jerusalem, the Squire lays down his sword. In this narrative, the 'recovery' of the Holy Land is beyond fantasy. As much as crusade continues to be an aim, the ambition ends in scattered conflicts across the Mediterranean. The Squire's battles do not take place in Jerusalem, but on the way: in 'Gascoyne, Spayne, and Lumbardy': contact zones, trading sites.[75] At home the Princess grieves, still believing him to be dead. Reality and fantasy coexist. The Princess falsely grieves her living lover. Christendom yearns for the lost territories. Both individual and community are in a suspended state of mourning, awaiting the impossible return of the lost object.

Curative Wines

Aware that the curative uses of sweet wines were based on Arabic science, medieval English medicine troubled the view of that product as a straightforwardly Christian fluid. The Middle English *Cyrurgie*, a translation of the surgical works of the French doctor Guy de Chauliac (c. 1300–68), positions itself amongst 'the *bookes* translated *out of Arabye* tongue'.[76] In this work, Ibn Sīnā – or '*Avicen*, the noble prince' – is cited as the source of medicinal uses of sweet wines.[77] Chauliac's Latin work was circulated in miscellanies alongside the fourth book of Ibn Sīnā's *al-Qānūn fī al-ṭibb* [*Encyclopaedia of Medicine*].[78] These manuscript traditions kept translation and source in close association – when the Latin text was then translated into English, the original Arabic source was repeatedly cited in order to preserve its authority. In the Middle English *Cyrurgie*, the author writes: 'If the ulcer forsooth be *fretyne* . . . *Avycen* taketh of three kinds of *pome gernatz*, of *bittre*, of *swete* and of *soure*' – but if there are no pomegranates available, the doctor should 'turn again to the pelettes of *aldaron* and of *calidico* dissolved with *swete wyne*'.[79] The 'pellets of aldaron' were medicinal corrosive pills of unidentified substance.[80] The 'fretting' ulcer needs swift treatment. Another recipe 'after *Avicen*' recommends 'Take of the rind of pomegranates' and mix them with gall, myrrh and '*swete wyne*'.[81] These Arabo-English medicinal works both reflected and motivated the commercial circulation of sweet wines in England. The discomforted, ulcerous patient demands sweet wines not as a luxury for the dining table but as a vital cure for relief from pain – dabbed on the outside of the sore body.

In medieval surgical practice, imported wines were applied both externally and internally. In one Middle English version of the *Philomena*, originally composed in Latin by the royal surgeon John Bradmore (d. 1412), the anonymous translator explains the rules of bloodletting:

> The 7th rule is convenient and wholesome to give the patient that *bleddys* at diverse times some *swete wyne* to *drynke* as *malmsey bastard rumney osei* with a *toste* therein and if it be a poor body take good ale for such things shall for the time comfort nature.[82]

Bradmore's original Latin text does not include this list of wines.[83] This vernacular translation appears in a late medieval medical miscellany which also contains an 'Englished' edition of the works of the Iraqi physician Yūḥannā ibn Māsawayh (777 CE – d. 857 CE). This was a practical book designed for a readership with access to imported products, and a desire for translated knowledge. These wines are known to be prohibitively expensive for most patients – as acknowledged in the advised substitute of 'good ale' for a 'poor body', unable to afford malmsey. But the ale does not carry the symbolism or the scientific authority of sweet wine.

Medieval medical texts often brought translated Arabic frameworks together with devotional practice. In the *Cyrurgie*, one cure for paralysis prescribes a mixture of herbs and spices: '*confecte* them with *oximel squylletik* and with *swete wyn*, and be he *gargarized* day by day'.[84] If the patient gargles with sweet wine daily, their speech will marvellously return: the medicinal cure evokes the action of relics. In John Trevisa's fourteenth-century *On the Properties of Things*, sweet wine is defined as a cleansing cure: '*swete wyn* that is full red helps to cleanse evils of the breast and of the lungs, and . . . clenseth and wipeth away *unclennesse* and *gleymous* [viscous] humour'.[85] The description of sweet wine as 'cleansing evils' recalls the sacramental cleansing action of the Eucharist. Elsewhere the *Cyrurgie* author writes: 'Some *thinges* forsooth . . . engender good blood and subtle, as . . . *swete wyne.*'[86] The connection between sweet wine and blood – established in the theological doctrine of transubstantiation – was scientifically reinforced in the image of good blood being produced by the consumption of sweet wine.

The Franciscan monk and alchemist John of Rupescissa (1310–62) recommended sweet wine as a means of producing the quintessence, a medicinal remedy and source of the alchemical Elixir. In one late medieval English translation of Rupescissa's *De consideratione*, the author advises: 'Thou shall take *wyne* not over clear ne watery, neither black *wyne*, *erthely* and *thicke*, but *noble wyne* and glad savoury and *swete smyllyng*, the best that may be had, and distil it by a canon *ofte tymes* till thou have made good *brennyng watre* at the highest degree.'[87] Like surgical instruments and practice, the apparatus and method of distillation were derived from Arabic sources.[88] Rupescissa claimed that his quintessence, an early form of distilled ethanol, was more potent than other alcohol-based medicines, being incorruptible and free from earthly elements.[89] For Rupescissa, the distillation of sweet wine produced the fifth element, the substance of the celestial spheres.[90] Leah DeVun has commented that a likely source for Rupescissa's understanding of the healing properties of the quintessence exists in the Latin *Tractatus de vinis* [Treatise on Wines], attributed to the Catalan physician Arnaldus de Villanova (c. 1240–1311).[91] Arnaldus' medical works were explicitly based on Graeco-Arabic sources, including Ibn Sīnā's *al-Qa'nūn fi al-tibb*, an extract of which Arnaldus himself translated into Latin.[92] Based on Graeco-Arabic traditions, the *Tractatus De Vinis* listed fifty types of medicinal wines and was widely circulated in England.[93] Specified as the basis of the ethereal quintessence, sweet wine held a high status in the interlinked alchemical and medicinal traditions. These medical and alchemical texts were expressed in the language of religious transcendence – and were reabsorbed into medieval English religious texts, providing a scientific authority for the idea that Eucharistic wine was a spiritual and bodily cure.

Christ the Physician

Following their introduction in surgical contexts, medicinal views of wine are found throughout religious descriptions of the wines of the Holy Land. With the Eucharist being represented as a medical resource, there is an overlap between understandings of spiritual and bodily healing. The Middle English translation of Bridget of Sweden's revelations exemplifies this motif: 'Christ likens himself to a *potecari*, the which makes wholesome *drinkes* . . . Right so it is of *gosteli drinke*, that is, the grace of the *holi goste*.'[94] Elsewhere Bridget hears Christ's words in a vision, telling her: 'I do as a *kinge* that sends wine to his servants, and bids them *drinke* of it, for it is wholesome and will heal sickness.'[95] These are both images based on reality. Christ mixes his drinks, the grace of the holy spirit, like an apothecary mixes prescriptions, and he generously sends out his wine, like a good king – as Edward IV left his sweet wines to the Henton nuns.

In the anonymous devotional text *The Privity of the Passion*, the author describes 'our great *wikkidnes* that might not be washed away but with the precious *licoure* of thy *precyouse blode*'.[96] The description of Christ's blood as 'licour' draws on the language of medieval medicine, and on medieval understandings of viticulture. Trevisa describes how 'the *vyne* is a good tree and a *medicynable* . . . and thereof cometh *licour* that is better and passeth the juice of all trees'.[97] These images of Christ as physician, and of Christ's blood-as-wine as medicinal cure rely on the language and associations on scientific representations of wine.

In the Middle Ages, devotion and medicine were overlapping cultures, as is seen in texts and in material artefacts such as the late fifteenth-century Coventry Ring. The Coventry Ring depicts Christ's wounds, originally enamelled in gory red, and Christ in the tomb alongside the Latin inscription 'the Cross and the passion of Christ are my medicines', and the pseudo-Hebrew charm word '*ananyzapta*'.[98] This charm ring, designed for personal possession and intimate touch, indicates medieval affective piety in action, combining medical lore and religious faith in one object. Similarly, the medicinal uses of sweet wines integrate devotional and scientific discourses. Christian images of curative wine were founded on cross-cultural scientific lore and based on the taste of an interfaith-traded product. These drinks were paradoxical, their narratives blended.

Christ of the Mystic Press

The image of the mystic winepress combines the main narratives of sweet wine: trade, industry, crusade, medicine, devotion. Crushing out healing wine from traded grapes, the mystic press remained informed by an awareness of the scientific and mercantile milieu of contemporary Mamlūk society. At the same time, the mystic press was integrated into the discourse of the crusading Mass, framing the Holy Land as the source of Christian wine grown from consecrated soil. The *Christ of the Mystic Winepress Press* tapestry, c. 1500 [Figure 1.2], offers a detailed representation of the literalised sacramental imagery. Christ is shown in the press, dressed

Figure 1.2 *Christ of the Mystic Wine Press*, c. 1500, South Netherlandish, tapestry weave, wool, silk, and metallic threads (73.5 × 77.5 cm). Source: Metropolitan Museum of Art, New York. Accession Number: 1994.484. Gift of Mena Rokhsar, 1994. Image permission granted under Creative Commons Zero (CC0) Open Access License.

in a red robe, the colour recalling his Passion, but calm, unwounded, and looking directly into the eyes of the viewer. The image is based on the biblical iconography of the crushed man of sorrows, in Isaiah 63. 3. Here the Cross is refigured as an enormous and highly functional winepress – such as Khamisy excavated in Miʿilyā – with Christ in the position of the pressed grape. In addition to Isaiah, the scene draws on John's description in Revelation 14. 19–20 of the Apocalyptic winepress of God's wrath: the angel gathered 'the vineyard of the earth and cast it into the great press of the wrath of God', from which blood flowed. The sweetness of Christ's blood-as-wine is shown in a context of mechanical production, crushed from a press shown with geographical specificity, located in the historic land of the Passion and the contemporary land of vineyards. The mystic press is shown producing the imported wines of the Holy Land: not the 'ordinary' wines of France but an elite drink from Jerusalem.

Here the scene is free of visible trauma. Behind Christ's ringleted head a small representational cloth hangs, in place of a halo – as in *mise-en-abyme* for the tapestry itself. An illegible text is situated to the right of the image, hanging from the press, with the rubricated initial 'M' evoking manuscript traditions. Another text, a red-bound book, stands on the ledge behind Christ. A representational chalice and red rose are painted on a panel at the top of the press. The press is complete with ropes and grooved pillars, giving a tangible sense of its mechanical function. The frame of the winepress assumes the role of the aesthetic frame of the image: occupying three out of four sides of the square cloth, replacing the need for an ornamental border such as is visible in the lowest corners of the tapestry. Through this frame, the Holy Land appears: trees and architectural forms rise behind Christ in beautiful still-bright hues of green and stone-grey. The frame of the winepress mediates the viewer's contemplative encounter with Jerusalem.

This tapestry belongs to the 'Mystic Grapes Group' of four associated works from the Netherlands, small-scale, wrought with incredible attention to detail, and luxuriously created in the most precious Eastern-imported silk threads. Elizabeth Cleland has suggested that these tapestries were designed to hang as altarpieces.[99] The 1547 inventory of Henry VIII alludes to a 'square pece of Arras of Christe and one giving him grapes & our Ladie standing by', which Cleland identifies as a lost example of the same tradition.[100] Tapestries from the Mystics Grapes group were, then, present in late medieval England, whether imported from Dutch workshops or – as in the case of Henry's tapestry – remade by the King's personal Flemish workman. The altarpiece location of the tapestries is crucial, linking these objects directly to the practice of the Mass, as well as to private devotion in their intimate size.

In addition to this tapestry, the scene of Christ in the Press was common in illuminated manuscripts of the Apocalypse.[101] The image was replicated in different visual and material forms – including chalices in the shape of Christ's body, with functioning spouts in the places of his wounds.[102] The humanity of Christ is essential to the devotional function of these objects and images. But in the tapestry winepress, the scale of liquid evoked is not an individual's oozing wounds, but the scale of industrial production.

The Christ Child Pressing the Wine of the Eucharist, c. 1500 [Figure 1.3], an associated tapestry, shows a similar attention to the landscape in which the mystic grape is situated.[103] Here the infant Christ, dressed again in a robe and with marvellously dextrous hands for his age, squeezes a bunch of

Figure 1.3 *The Christ Child Pressing the Wine of the Eucharist*, c. 1500, South Netherlandish, linen warp; wool, silk, and gilt weft yarns (50.5 x 46.4 cm). Source: Metropolitan Museum of Art, New York. Accession Number: 14.40.709a. Bequest of Benjamin Altman, 1913. Image permission granted under Creative Commons Zero (CC0) Open Access License.

grapes into a Eucharistic chalice. In the background tall Mediterranean trees and buildings are visible. The bunch of grapes recalls an image from the fourth book of Moses, in which Joshua and Caleb, the 'Spies of Canaan', return from their explorations with a gargantuan grape cluster, evidence to the gathered Israelites of the divinely sanctioned nature of the land towards which they travel (Numbers 13. 23–4). The grape cluster was commonly interpreted as a prefiguration of Christ. The journey of Joshua and Caleb through the Holy Land with their treasured grapes was also represented with geographic clarity. One Parisian Book of Hours (c. 1500) includes a representation of the two spies – wearing turban-like hats, a variant on the common Jewish signifier of the pointed hat – in which blue hills and a hazy horizon stretch beyond the foregrounded grapes [Figure 1.4].[104] Visual cultures emphasised the location of Eucharistic grapes in their Holy Land origins.

The wooden, material apparatus of the winepress brings to mind the physical processes of production and exchange which underpinned trade

Figure 1.4 The spies of Canaan. Source: Pierpont Morgan Library, New York. MS H.5 fol. 40 v., detail. Printed with permission of Pierpont Morgan Library.

between England and Syria, integrating these trading networks into an imagination of holy geography and space. The Mandeville author describes the location of the Passion in the language of the mystic grape, alluding to 'trees of which a cross was made that bore *good fruyt, Jhesu Crist*'.[105] The woodenness of the Cross is here given organic agency, rendering the Cross capable of engendering the redemptive fruit which that same Cross would subsequently crush. The growth of Jesus from the animate Cross both literally and figuratively roots the image in its land of origin, Christ's historic blood mingling with contemporary wine. As a figure for the wooden Cross, the winepress was brought into the milieu of True Cross relics which, along with vials of blood-stained earth and cloth, were venerated throughout medieval Europe. The winepress was revered as a relic without being stripped of its mechanical qualities.

The Tavern of Heaven

In the widely circulated collection of saints' lives, the *Gilte Legende*, the wine of the mystic grape appears, connected with another worldly context, the tavern:

> The cross may well be likened to a *presse* in which he was so sore pressed that his precious *blode* went out largely of all the parts of *hym*. And also the *devell* is called a press, the which *wrappeth* so *mankinde* with the *cordes of synne* and straineth them so sore . . . But this noble fighter *defouled* so the *presse* that he broke all the *bondes of synne* and *stied* [ascended] into *hevene*, and after that he opened the *taverne of hevene* and poured out the wine of the *holy goste*.[106]

The cords of the winepress are both metaphysical and technical, the tightening action emphasising the material reality of the object even while they are unambiguously glossed within the text as the 'bonds of sin'. There is a mechanical repetition of 'presse . . . pressed . . . presse . . . presse'. The scene is graphic, hyperbolic, and mechanical: Christ is envisaged being flattened, drained to a raisin skin. The motif is given a further worldly association. After the Ascension, Christ is imagined as a vintner of a heavenly inn, holy wine running not so much from his wounds, as from his taps. The extension of the mystical winepress motif to the 'tavern of heaven' is coextensive with a tradition which had at its core the integration of the material apparatus of winemaking into a means of accessing the divine. The space evoked is not a chapel, but a secular urban environment. Rather than showing the wine pouring into the Eucharistic chalice reserved for priests, the author of the *Gilte Legende* offers us scenes of communal wine drinking, of popular consumption: the wine of the Holy Ghost is rendered convivial, a fantasy of the elite fluid made accessible.

The winepress remained rooted in Jerusalem as it was seen in the English imagination, both in its reverential conception as blood relic and in its evocation of the landscape and mechanics of the wine trade. The repeated circulation of the winepress image did not weaken a sense of the importance of its Holy Land origins but rather multiplied those origins through replication, each illumination, tapestry, statue, marginal detail, or verbal description acting like a fragment of the True Cross. The moment of the Passion was recalled to mind in its historical and geographic contexts, blended with the contemporary networks which brought sweet wines to England. When Francisco and Panino poured out sweet wines in their London tavern, they mingled these fantasies with the idea of ordinary wine, kept illegally in one cellar – the tavern of heaven had to be kept apart.

Postscript: Malmsey as Murder Weapon

Following the death of George Plantagenet, Earl of Clarence, in 1478, a new use for sweet wine entered the popular imagination. A rumour spread about the manner of Clarence's death, accompanying the increasingly defamatory histories of Richard III written by John Rous (d. 1492) and Polidore Vergil (b. 1470). Shakespeare retold the story in his *Tragedy of Richard III*, in the dialogue of Richard's anointed assassins in the Tower, as they prepare to kill Clarence:

FIRST MURDERER: Take him on the costard with the hilts of thy sword, and then throw him into the malmsey-butt in the next room.
SECOND MURDERER: O, excellent device; and make a sop of him.[107]

Here the audience witnesses the descent of malmsey from the signifier of Christ's blood to an ominous fluid implicated in crime: from symbol of divine sacrifice to material of human slaughter. The full horror and significance of the deed is understood only by retaining a memory of the transcendent associations of sweet wine in which Clarence is drowned, historically locating Shakespeare's play in its medieval context. In making the Earl a 'sop', the murderers align their act – and so the King – with the moment at which Satan enters into Judas, with Christ's proffer of dipped bread to the traitorous disciple (John 13. 26). The barrel in which the malmsey is stored preserves echoes of the barrel in which Christ treads grapes in medieval illuminations of the Apocalypse. The subverted spiritual vocabulary allows Richard III to be cast as Antichrist in synoptic, vivid fashion.

The Eucharist was the archetypal medieval sign of the sacred, a sign capable of miraculous transformation into the object signified. Sweet wine should have stabilised its own meaning within this framework, continually recalling Christ's blood in unilateral and unambiguous figural fashion. But instead sweet wine continued to transform and be transformed, remaining malleable, open to subversion and unexpected expansion, in spite of regulations which attempted to control and delimit its use. Clarence's death in the malmsey-butt is no simple instance of the degeneration of the holy but typifies the absorbent nature of the medieval sacred sign, capable of accepting secular or entirely unholy new meanings. Sweet wines were practical, spiritual, healing, erotic, ethnonationalist, interfaith-traded, and relic-like all at once: existing in intoxicating irresolution.

CHAPTER 2

Spices / English Digestion and Indigestion

Robert Sturmy's ship was filled with '*dyvers* spices, that is to *sey* pepper, ginger, cinnamon, sugar, green ginger, raisins of Corinth, rhubarb, turpentine, cotton and gunpowder ... to the value in *Englond* of £2600'.[1] Sturmy was familiar with the spice trade both from his travels and from home: a record of the city made after his death describes 'a place upon the back of Bristol called Spicers hall, wherein sometime dwelled a full notable Worshipful Merchant of the said Town called Robert Sturmy whom God late hath taken to his mercy'.[2] Named after the group of merchants who traded there, Spicers Hall would have once been an aromatic site of exchange – Sturmy's house was built on the foundations laid by their profits.

In medieval England, spices were already 'right here' in marketplaces and at fairs. Despite their high price, spices were common enough to be used as rent payments in both rural and urban areas, from the late twelfth century to the late fifteenth. For instance, in 1279, William Burgan paid 1 lb of pepper and cumin for his landholding in Cowley, Oxfordshire; in 1487, tenants held their lands in Little Milton through an annual payment of 1 lb cumin.[3] In the late medieval period, the Levant was a centre of sugar production.[4] In addition, cinnamon, cloves, ginger, and pepper were exported from the Levant to Europe.[5] These spices had first been imported from Indonesia, India, and China, origins which were integrated into medieval imaginations. Spices were said to have been brought as a gift from God to Adam and Eve in Paradise to comfort them. In medieval images of Eden, spices are often shown growing in the garden; when Eden was drawn on maps, it was usually located in the East.[6] The arrival of spices in premodern Europe eventually brought European colonialists in search of their origins.[7] The legacies of European colonialism and the transatlantic slave trade are the lingering aftertastes of these premodern desires. But Robert Sturmy was not travelling towards the spice groves – and the scenes which follow do not envisage their conquest. In this chapter, recalling their origins in the marketplaces of the eastern Mediterranean, these spices are melancholic and multilingual, contextualised in the histories of the crusading settlements and the continued transmission of translated science. Bought on the way back from the Holy Land, spices were agential and symbolic: eaten by the animals on the English crest.

Henry of Derby's Leopard

Sailing back from Jaffa after visiting Jerusalem in December 1392, Henry of Derby, the future King Henry IV of England, docked in Famagusta, in Cyprus. When Acre fell, Cyprus had become home to many who left the last crusader settlement – travelling from the Kingdom of Jerusalem to the Kingdom of Cyprus, a short distance across the sea.[8] Since then, the island had been under sequential occupations, which shaped the architecture and cultural environment. Traces of past conflicts littered the island. In Famagusta, Venetian settlers built the Palazzo del Provveditore, as the royal palace and the governor's residence. Following the Genoese conquest in 1373, the harbour town was the main point of entry for trade between Cyprus and Mamlūk Syria. Henry was treated to the hospitality of the European ruler of Cyprus, James I. He was put up in the castle. And he was given a leopard, which he fed spices. The animal is found in the treasurer's records taken by the steward Richard Kyngeston (d. 1418), who accompanied his employer on his journeys, keeping an itemised portrait of elite travel. In Cyprus, payment was made: 'for diverse spices bought by the keeper of the leopard in that place, for the said leopard, 4 ducats 7 asp'.[9] Whatever spices the English court thought the leopard wanted to eat, it seems to have liked them, or at least agreed to eat them, because later on, additional payments are made 'for diverse spices and oils bought . . . for the leopard' in Italy, and on return to England.[10] Starting the discussion of Sturmy's spices here, I want to reposition the leopard as a known consumer in the medieval English court. In Cyprus, Henry restocked his stores with sugar, as well as with saffron, ginger, pepper, figs, and syrup.[11] The trading connection between Syria and Cyprus was so close that Cypriot products were often relabelled as 'Syrian' and vice versa – Eliyahu Ashtor has shown that the product sold in England as 'Cyprus sugar' would usually have been grown in Levantine plantations.[12] The leopard might not have been Sturmy's typical target market, but it was still a high-status consumer, whose tastes have survived in these documents.[13]

Henry's leopard had its own cabin on the ship: the treasurer lists that wood was bought for that purpose.[14] There were other animals on board:

a parrot, and some falcons, but no large mammals. Henry hired a special keeper to look after it. The leopard first enters the records in a mention of two horses bought for 'the custodian of the leopard'.[15] The other records are of foods which were bought for the leopard. Mostly, the leopard ate sheep.

When I picture Henry's leopard, I see it resting on its haunches, turning its head to profile over one shoulder. It is skinny, like a greyhound – but with a thick neck, and large paws, claws retracted. Its large, clear, cat eyes look out from a broad face. It has small pointed ears. Its back is dappled with large dark spots across its sandy coat. Someone has fastened a collar around its neck, heavy metal dotted with glassy jewels. It stares back with a slight smile – no barred teeth. I picture an animal like those seen in medieval tapestries – because the real leopard is lost, except for these traces in the inventories.[16] The real 'leopard' might have been what is still called a leopard (*Panthera pardus*), or might have been a cheetah (*Acinonyx jubatus*), or a lion (*Panthera leo*); medieval European understandings of the difference were not always clear. Starting with the woven leopard, I visualise the animal through the perspectives which brought it to England – as part of the world which it inhabited.

During the First Crusade, Richard I wore an emblem with three golden leopards on his arm – now usually called the three lions, as in the song by David Baddiel and Frank Skinner. The leopard was associated with English royalty, both in imagination and in reality. In 1235, Henry III was gifted leopards which then lived in the menagerie in the Tower of London. It can be assumed that Henry of Derby's leopard was destined for the Tower on its arrival. There is a sense of monarchic command being articulated through the possession and transport of a leopard.

As a predator, the leopard could not have been sustained by fragrant oils. But there would have been a practical rationale for these purchases, based on the same medical humoural theories which shaped human desires for spice. Like humans, animals were thought to have four humours – and tamed animals were thought to have a different humoural balance from those in the wild.[17] The spices could have been fed to the leopard in order to alter its humours, so that it ceased to be wild, became manageable in the cabin. Or, since spices were typically used to aid human travellers' health, it might have been that the leopard was sick – and these oils were part of an attempt at cure.

The leopard's consumption of spice feels symbolic. In the Aberdeen Bestiary, the leopard is represented as degenerate, and thirsting for blood.[18] Turning the folio, the panther is represented as gentle, a symbol of Christ which – we are told – gives out a sweet odour when it roars. The 'leopard' and the 'cheetah' are blurred in medieval taxonomies, later becoming distinct modern categories – but the 'leopard' and the 'panther', which are distinguished in medieval encyclopaedia, are now considered as variant names for the same species. The perfumed breath of the panther draws all to it, except the devilish dragon, which flees into caves. In one late twelfth-century bestiary, the breath of the panther is described as follows: 'from his mouth comes a very sweet scent just as if it were of all the spices'.[19] Fed with 'diverse spices', Henry's leopard's breath might have become sweet – might at least have been sweeter than if it ate sheep carcases alone.

The Leopard's Mountains

In Robert Alter's resonant translation of the Song of Songs, the lover speaks as if murmuring: 'With me from Lebanon, bride, | with me from Lebanon come | . . . from the lions' dens, | from the leopard's mountains'.[20] These mountains are not a region which can be possessed but an expression of that which is beyond possession. The leopard comes into the text from that uncontrollable wildness.

The Song of Songs is a late biblical collection of love poetry, a series of dialogues between two lovers. Set in the landscape from Lebanon to Ein Gedi, the texts were written in Hebrew, likely in the fourth century BCE.[21] The imagery of the Song of Songs was both influential and problematic for medieval Christians – the poetry is pervaded with the deep sense of the need for bodily pleasure. Monastic commentators allegorised the representation of carnal love as the spiritual union of the soul and God, among other interpretations – but that did not exactly resolve the dilemma. Inviting monks to imagine themselves as the bride, with Christ as the bridegroom, the erotic remained the subject of extended, mystical contemplation.[22] 'Let him kiss me', the song begins, 'for your loving is better than wine' (1. 1). The physical senses – taste, scent, and touch – are both elevated and realistic.

In the Song of Songs, the desire for spices is an expression of an embodied desire: for a lover's body. Describing the bride, the groom sighs over her scent, her sweet tongue dripping with honey and milk and her robes perfumed like Lebanon. She is a 'locked garden', an orchard where pomegranates grow, with henna and spikenard, saffron, sugar cane and cinnamon, trees of frankincense and aloe (4. 11–14). The text records a spiritual geography: the enclosed garden is believed by many to have been located in present-day 'Artas, an occupied Palestinian village near Bethlehem. In the poem, it is springtime: the garden is at its freshest, most verdant. These spices are desirable because of their origins in these lands – although that conjunction is not made here with explicit territorial intent. These desires seek fulfilment through a proximate bodily experience. When medieval European readers received these lines – typically in Latin translations of the Hebrew – they found the Holy Land brought proximate through the imagined scent and taste of skin. Written in the vocative mode – the lovers addressing each other in turn – the longing expressed is not the melancholic desire for a lost object, but the active longing for a desire which can still be realised. The sensory delight of spices brings that possible experience into the hands, into the mouth of the reader, and into the nose. As scent, the sensory object is drawn into an affinity with the immaterial. Incense: intangible delight.

In the Song of Songs, the bodies of both masculine and feminine lovers are described in the same fragrant language. The bridegroom's cheeks are like beds of spices (5. 13) – his beard grown from the same garden as his bride's body. The sensory ecstasy of spice gives rise to an enduring spiritual language, an olfactory aesthetic which preserves the transhistorical experience of touching and being touched by another's body, aroused by their scent. As Jonny says to his teenage lover in the 1987 film *Dirty Dancing*, 'You've gotta understand what it's like, Baby . . . these women . . . they smell so good . . . .' Each longed-for lover remains their own agent: not coming because they are desired, but because they desire to come.

The collection closes with the bride's cry for her groom to flee like a deer, like a gazelle 'on the spice mountains' (8. 14). Running passionately across the fragrant hills – which might also be read as her breasts – the lovers join the animals who already inhabit that untameable landscape. The deer and gazelles are fleeing – from what? Perhaps from the leopards, who prowl through the spice groves.

When Henry of Derby's leopard was fed spices, that was a scene of the containment of the uncontainable: a regal, biblical animal kept calm through the provision of the produce of its own biblical habitat, dried and powdered for transport.

The Pilgrimage to the Spice Markets

The geographical location of Paradise in the 'East' traditionally found in medieval maps meant that the sense that spices had travelled along trading routes from (for example) India to England via Syria reinforced, instead of contradicting, their spiritual significance.[23] The spices sold in earthly Jerusalem were laced with the associations of that city's heavenly counterpart. Versed in the text of the Song of Songs, visitors arrived expecting to find the spice mountains of Lebanon and the groves of Ein Gedi.

At Ṭawāḥīn al-Sukkar near Jericho, sugar mills have been documented from 1116.[24] Ayyubid and subsequent Mamlūk rulers developed a major irrigation system in order to support the sugar crops. In order to prevent overheating, Palestinian industrialists began to use minerals to clarify the syrup, using the mineral alum, as well as wood ashes and lime.[25] When the crusaders occupied these pre-existing sites of sugar production, they took over supervision of the process, which was complex and large-scale: water flowed through a chute to operate the gearing mechanism of the mill, while the industrial waste of charcoal and by-products, inedible crystals and excess liquid had to be kept at a remove, in the dump. These archaeological details demystify premodern sugar as the product of an organised industry. The crusaders encountered sugar mills and wine factories, remembering these as practical sites from which goods were brought back to England.[26] The crops processed at Ṭawāḥīn al-Sukkar outlasted the Christian Kingdom of Jerusalem: the mills were still in use in 1484.

In Mandeville's *Travels*, the author records that near Hebron, on the way to Jerusalem:

> in that vale is the field where men draweth out of the earth a thing that men call *chambille*, and they eateth that thing instead of spices. And they beareth it to *sille* [market]. And no matter how deep or so wide a man may dig, at the year's end it is full again up to the sides through the grace of God.[27]

The report of '*chambille*' is an allusion to a medicinal spice mix known in Arabic as *kinbil*.[28] The description here makes the medicinal use of *kinbil* clear through the contextualisation of its consumption 'in stede of spices'. The commercial value of the mix is made evident in the reference to its sale at 'sille': the market.[29] At the same time as these practical elements are foregrounded, the scene is overlaid with wonder: the earth replenishes itself endlessly through God's grace. The landscape is biblical, the vale described in relation to a cave in which Adam and Eve lived after their expulsion from Paradise, spices situated within references to Seth and Abraham's passage through the land. If merchants could not trade in the garden of Eden, they could still trade in the traces of Eden as they appeared on Earth. The marketplaces of Jerusalem are imagined as sites in which the produce of miraculous intervention is readily available for sale.

Like wines, spices were necessary purchases for pilgrims – as medicinal safeguards whose healing properties were tangible witnesses of God's grace.

Henry of Derby bought 'one box of rose sugar' at Rhodes and 'sugared water' at Ramla, along with wine. On his way to Jerusalem, Henry went to Venice, where spices were bought from Anton Potecario [the apothecary]: 'saffron, mace, cloves, sugar candy, caffetin sugar, almonds and rice'. The surname of the salesperson Potecario shows that these were medicinal items. He also bought Greek wine in bulk, a jar of Romney, a vase of Malmsey, and amphorae.[30] The group travelled onwards to the Holy Land in a hired Venetian galley, surrounded by these goods. The pilgrim William Wey also advised that Holy Land pilgrims should buy spices in Venice: 'laxatives, restoratives, ginger, rice, figs, raisins great and small, which shall do you great ease by the way, pepper, saffron, gloves and *poudre douce*'.[31] These practical goods gained their value from their association with the Holy Land, put to use in order to reach the lands of their imagined or recorded origin. As Susan Harvey has described, understandings of the medical properties of spices directly influenced Christian traditions of representation and use, with shared practices of hygienic customs and ritual anointing developing into a broader overlapping medical and spiritual imaginary.[32]

An incident in the *Book* of the fifteenth-century mystic Margery Kempe further illustrates the overlap between the practical and spiritual function of spices. Finally arriving within sight of her destination of Jerusalem, Kempe was overwhelmed with the sweetness that she perceived God had wrought in her soul. Some German priests accompanying her saw her on the verge of falling off her donkey, and 'put spices in hir mouth to comfort hir, thinking she had been sick'.[33] Spiritual and material sweetness collide in Kempe's body, the symptoms of her religious ecstasy soothed with medicinal spice.[34] The reaction of the priests might be seen as a misinterpretation of the situation, a failure to recognise Kempe's joyous vision. But as Caroline Walker Bynum has commented, medieval Christianity was 'a piety characterised by intense awareness of the power of the material'.[35] The prescription of the market produce of the Holy Land at the gates of Jerusalem is in keeping with medieval attitudes. Margery Kempe's spices – bought nearby – were naturally suitable for curing both bodily and spiritual faintness.

Margery Kempe's mystical inspiration often came to her in the form of unstoppable tears. Wailing and moaning, she found herself an unpopular, disturbing presence in churches around England. Her noisy devotion seemed to some to be evidence of demonic possession. Praying for comfort, Margery was told by Christ that 'thy tears are angels' drink, and it is very *pyment* to hem'.[36] Piment is a spiced wine – a medicinal drink, a luxurious treat. The image of the angels drinking Margery's tears as spiced wine in heaven closes the gap between physical healing and spiritual solace.

The biblical, medicinal, and practical associations of spices for pilgrims carried through into their wider imaginative representations. In Chaucer's translation of the popular French text the *Romance of the Rose*, a dreamer enters the garden of the God of Love. There he finds:

> There was also *wexyng* many a spice
> As *clowe-gelofre* [clove] and *lycorice*
> *Gyngevre* [ginger] and grain of Paradise
> *Canell* [cinamon] and *setewale* [zedoary] of price,
> And many a spice *delitable*
> To eat when men rise from table.[37]

The scene continues the sense that the representation of spices as spiritual did not lessen an understanding of their practical traded realities. The location of these spices in an enclosed garden recalls the imagery of the Song of Songs, and other biblical fragrant gardens – like Eden. The phrase '*greyn de parys*' (grain of Paradise), describing the spice *Aframomum meleguet*a, places the reader further inside that imagination. These biblical allusions do not erase the actual knowledge of the spice trade. These products are grouped together in the garden, as they were in Henry's inventories or Alice's household book. Trade routes are acknowledged in the reference to the 'prys' of zedoary ('setewale'), which was exported from Syria.[38] Even in dreams, the commercial potential of the garden is not forgotten. The list of spices is succeeded immediately by the physical image of their consumption after dinner. The introduction of the table into the Edenic garden blends experience with imagination, playing with the varied associations of spices rather than attempting to draw distinct lines between them. The spiritual fantasy is constantly tugged back towards the economy and digestive medicines, and vice versa: these practical spices remained wonderful substances. Like the garden in the Song of Songs, this enclosed space is both romantic and saleable, a place articulated through its mobile products. The Christian awareness of the power of the material was consolidated by a canny understanding of the marketability of that power. Miraculous spices contributed to the spiritual and economic status of the Holy Land – both of which were sources of medieval English desire.

Bitterness at the Margins

Italian merchants trading in Levantine goods became the target of medieval English distaste, based on an envious desire for the proceeds of the trade. *The Libelle of Englyshe Polycye* is an anonymous fifteenth-century polemical work which lists the main products imported to England, via the groups who imported them.[39] The critic Paul Freedman comments that while the *Libelle* generally 'celebrates trade', Italian goods are singled out for deliberate hostility.[40] The author mocks:

> The great *Galees* of Venice and Florence
> Be well laden with things of complacence,
> All spicery and of *grossers* ware:
> ...
> Apes, and Japes, and marmosets tailed.[41]

On these Venetian and Florentine ships, spices are brought back with animals: not leopards this time, but monkeys. The captive primates are 'things of complacence' – disposable luxuries, unnecessary purchases. The Grocers were the guild associated with the spice trade. The Southampton Port Book records the arrival of imported projects on English shores, including the arrival of Levantine and Italian-traded goods, and indicates the significant role of Venetian merchants and other immigrant traders in the spice trade.[42] The majority of imported spices are listed in the 'Alien Book': records which were kept separately to those of English merchants' vessels.[43] The *Libelle*-author's polemic was directed at proximate subjects. In resistance to the flow of goods, the *Libelle*-author continues defiant:

> In our England are such commodities
> Without help of any other land
> ...
> That all humors might be voided sure,
> Which that we gather with our English cure.[44]

Like the 'Antioch' drink discussed in the 'Dispensary', the claim here is that English herbs and plants can be used for humoural medicine. However, unlike the 'Antioch' drink, the *Libelle*-author suggests that this product of Arabic science and foraged herbs would be 'English'. The *Libelle*-author repeats: 'a man may void infirmity | Without drugs fetched from beyond the sea'. All these spices are 'licking ware'.[45]

In Trevisa's encyclopaedia, 'medicinal spicery' is a specific scientific category. He states that cinnamon 'heals the bites of creeping worms' and 'dissolves' abscesses, is anti-inflammatory and antiseptic, and is recommended to encourage menstrual flow. Pepper 'maketh *fnesynge*' – sneezing! – but also 'purgeth and clenseth the brain', corrodes 'dead flesh, and consumeth and wasteth the *webbe* in the eye [cataracts]'.[46] Instead of being the impotent objects of luxurious consumption, these spices were thought to act upon the body in specific, urgent ways.

In rejecting spices, the *Libelle*-author was pushing back against the mainstream medical and spiritual discourses of his time. The demand to close trading borders alongside repeated assertions of national identity resonates with later political discourses – these are the early traces of a developing ideology. The *Libelle*-author was pushing against a strong imaginative current in which spices were the subject of desire and wonder. The *Libelle*-author makes one exception. All of these imported goods are fripperies, apart from: 'but *sugre*'.[47] That remains desirable and necessary: local herbs could not make up for the curative properties of sugarcane.

Sugar as Medicine

The medieval desire for spices relied on the idea of their imported origins, which were viewed as the source of their agency. In John Trevisa's fourteenth-century encyclopaedic text *On the Properties of Things*, he writes that sugar is 'y-made and cometh of certain canes and reeds that groweth in lakes and ponds fast by the river Nilus'.[48] The sugarcane grown along the banks of the Nile situates sugar in its imperial contexts of production: Egypt was the political centre of the Mamlūk Empire, with Syria as a secondary administrative base. Trevisa describes the industrial process of sugar production. When the cane is boiled:

> The best thereof sinketh down into the bottom, and what is fatty and foamy abideth and floateth above, and is less sweet and full of holes, and cracketh not between the teeth when it is chewed, but vanisheth suddenly and melteth.[49]

The powdered sugar described as floating in the cauldron and vanishing in the mouth was the cheapest form of sugar in the late medieval period, and was the main form of sugar exported from Syria in the late fourteenth century.[50] Trevisa was translating from the twelfth-century Latin text of Bartholomaeus Anglicus, who himself had drawn on Latin editions of the *De materia medica* of Dioscorides of Anazarbus, written c. 50 CE. Written in Greek, Dioscorides' treatise was translated into Syriac and Arabic, via which versions it reached the Latin West.[51] While Trevisa translated from these pre-existing sources, his text was situated in his contemporary historical contexts: the transport of powdered sugar from the Mamlūk Empire to late medieval England.

When that Nile-watered sugar arrived in medieval English mouths, it remained marvellous. Trevisa's description of the sugar vanishing and melting on the tongue is Eucharistic, recalling the melting of the wafer in the communion service.

In humoural frameworks, the lands in which plants were grown were viewed as integral to the formation of their properties. In his chapter '*De Radice*' [on the root], Trevisa writes:

> the root is y-gendered of humour of the earth by working of heat . . . Also of place and disposition of the ground the root taketh disposition and complexion, for he that groweth in sweet ground . . . be better than other.[52]

In this passage, an essential link is forged between the ground and the plant. The 'disposition' of the root is determined by the properties of the soil, the intensity with which the sun has shone on the ground, the sweetness or moistness of the water in which the plant has grown. The sugar grown near the Nile brought the qualities of that river with it when it travelled.

Drawing on Greek and Arabic medicinal lore, sugar was viewed as healing. Trevisa writes that sugar is 'most profitable in medicines, in powders and in syrups'.[53] In the Syrian cookbook *Scents and Flavors*, sugared sweets are recommended as 'a digestible dish for invalids'.[54] The Syrian physician Ibn al-Nafis wrote a treatise entitled *Akhām al-Sukkar* [*The Principles of Sugar*].[55] More benefits could be drawn from sugar when it was combined with rose petals. Trevisa writes:

> Of rose well y-pounded and well incorporated with *zugre* is made *succura rosacea* or '*zugre roset*' which hath virtue to comfort and to bind and helpeth against distemperance of heat and feverish ague and maketh to sleep.[56]

Switching between English and Latin, Trevisa's text gains scientific authority through code-switching. Sugar was a high-status substance with curative properties which made it a necessary item, not only a luxury.[57] *Succura rosacea* was advanced medicine, needed for health both at home and abroad.

Before his travels in 1390, Henry of Derby bought spices in bulk, in London, in preparation. Hankyn Spicer – whose name records that he was a professional spice-buyer – purchased 'Cyprus sugar', sugar caffetin, ginger, pepper, cinnamon, cloves, and dates at Calais. Adam Wikerell also purchased Cyprus sugar for Henry at St Botolph's.[58] It seems strange that a medieval traveller would take imported spices with them – but since these were essential medical products, Henry could not wait to get to the Holy Land to buy his sacks of 'ginger, ginger in confit, cloves in confit, royal *gobbets*, flat sugar, red and white, sugar candy, paste royal, ginger *madrean*, *penydes*, *drage royal*, pepper, bought by himself at London on 4 July'.[59] Henry's clerk recorded sugar in all its forms: sweets, digestive sweetmeats (*drage royal*), red sugar, white sugar, sugar candy, barley sugar, and '*paste royal*', a mixture of sugars and spices. The effect of luxury is developed through accumulative listing. Wealth is asserted not only through quantity but through the repeated adjective 'real' [royal]. Luxury is expressed in borrowed language. Sugar *candy* evokes Arabic *qandī* [candied], Persian *qand* [sugar] and Sanskrit *khanda* [piece].[60] 'Penydes' is a corruption of the Arabic *fanid* [refined sugar].[61] These inventories are multilingual, written in a combination of Middle English, Latin, French, Arabic, Sanskrit, and Persian.[62] The marketplace terms for spices were absorbed by medieval English tongues, along with the tastes of the goods which they labelled. These words and tastes were proximate realities. The trading fairs and stalls in London were pulled towards the sea – and so was the English language, as a language in formation.[63] Middle English was hyper-absorbent, acquisitive, and hybrid, a mixture of translated and miscopied words from other languages. As Henry moved towards Jerusalem, and spices moved towards England, the English language moved back and forwards, revolving at the meeting point of these journeys. With biblical and medicinal frameworks in mind, medieval consumers were kept aware of the geographical origins of their curative sweets – these preserved words kept their origins on medieval tongues.

The Horizons of Desire

In the fifteenth century, Genoese and Venetian traders began to cultivate sugar in Crete and Cyprus using enslaved labour.[64] This shift in practice has been described as the traders' response to the rise in the price of sugar production, following the Black Death in the fourteenth century: waves of plague had resulted in population decline, which had impacted the workforce for this labour-intensive product.[65] The surviving sugar workers could demand better pay. Instead of continuing to meet their demands, those in charge of sugar production brought in enslaved people, whose exploitation cut costs for their enterprise. In the sixteenth century, sugar became the first crop to be cultivated using the plantation system of slave labour in the Americas, based on the methods already developed in the Mediterranean.[66] In the face of competition from the colonial plantations in the Americas, Levantine sugar production went into rapid decline, having first been part of the system which created the mechanisms of those new plantations.

The hostility to Italian traders in the *Libelle* was paired not with a critique of their labour practices, but with an explicit desire to emulate patterns of settlement and extraction. The *Libelle*-author extends the previous disregard for Venetian traders who, we are told, 'bear the gold out of this land . . . as the *Waspe* sucks honey from the bee, | So diminishes our *commoditee*'.[67] The poet's frustration at the failure of English traders in comparison to foreign merchants leads to a direct call for exchange to be abandoned in favour of open violence. The author encourages 'good men called *werriours* | . . . To purge the sea . . . | And *winne* them goods'.[68] In combination with this tactic, the poet speculates that England's gold shortages could be solved through extraction in occupied territories in Ireland, where 'of silver and gold there is the ore, | Among the *wilde* Irish though they be *poore*'.[69] Writing in 1433, the *Libelle*-poet advocates the systematic mining of raw materials from colonised lands at a profit to the occupying nation, a system which was to become hegemonic within the British Empire.[70] The idea that the spice groves could become part of an English system of extraction and control was not on the *Libelle*-author's horizon – the elements had begun to be set in place, but their full consequences were not yet realised.

Spices on Stage

Along with Italians, a typical scapegoat for medieval English fears about international trade was the figure of the Jewish merchant. The action of the *Croxton Play of the Sacrament* takes place in 1461, in the imagined city of Heraclea, in the non-imaginary region of Aragon, Spain. The play was performed in East Anglia, although may have toured around England. The prologue outlines the action which is to come: a Christian merchant will meet 'a Jewe' who comes from 'the city of *Surrey* [Syria] (this full true!)'.[71] When the Christian enters, he boasts: 'Sir Aristorius is my name . . . Full wide in thys world springeth my fame.'[72] The phrase 'thys world' is repeated – emphasising the global horizons of the merchant's ambitions. Aristorius is known in Genoa, Syria, Antioch, Cologne, Denmark, Holland, Faro, Jerusalem, Jericho, Rome, Milan, Naples, Lombardy, and Turkey.[73] He sends his clerk, Peter Powle, to see if any merchants' ships have docked from Syria, Saba, or Salerno. In the clerk's words, he goes 'to search at the *waterys syde*' for a 'pleasant bargain' at the 'haven' – the port.[74] Heraclea is on the coast – the sea is unnamed, although mapping the imaginative geography onto reality, the water corresponds to the Balearic Sea, flowing into the Mediterranean. Although the prologue suggested that the action would take place in a forest, the opening scene is definitely urban, located in the mercantile region around the docks.

The Syrian-Jewish merchant enters, played by a Christian in Jewish costume. I see him briefly through the eyes of a medieval East Anglian audience: a spectacle from a biblical nightmare, a caricatured, hook-nosed monstrosity, spitting and smelling sour. When Jonathas enters, he prays: '*almyghty Machomet* . . . whose laws tenderly I have to fulfil . . . I thank thee highly, that hast sent me gold, silver, and precious stones, and abundance of spices'.[75] These definitively Syrian-Jewish merchants remind me of Chaucer's traders, who are unspecified in faith – raising the question of whether Chaucer's characters might have been received as Jewish by a medieval audience. Presented as signs of un-Christian excess, these precious jewels and spices caused a problem for the medieval audience. Their problem was: spices really do taste delicious.

Jonathas' prayer to Mohammed as the Jewish God creates a figure of fear and difference, summoned by medieval suspicion. Medieval European Christians regularly confused Jews and Muslims. However, the elision of Jewish and Muslim faiths in the context of premodern Mediterranean trade is not straightforwardly a sign of ignorance. Seen through a distorted lens, Jonathas' speech remains a gesture towards the multi-faith realities of Mamlūk Syria, and the locally embedded nature of Jewish communities and especially of Jewish trading communities.[76] For centuries before and contemporary with the composition of the *Croxton Play*, Jewish merchants did operate within Islamic law, in intimate dialogue with Muslim communities.

Geraldine Heng has commented on the number of anti-Islamic polemics written in medieval contact zones.[77] The Syrian-Jewish merchants in this play can be seen in the same light: as figures drawn from observation of cross-cultural contact, seen from up close by a hostile viewer. The unbearable proximity of these Syrian Jews is part of what makes them monstrous from the perspective of the English drama. These are not fantasy, virtual Jews, but encountered people whose lives brushed up against those of Christians in the Mediterranean.[78]

Reflecting their locally embedded lives, the lingua franca of Jews across the premodern Mediterranean was Judeo-Arabic: Arabic written in Hebrew letters. For example, take one Judeo-Arabic letter sent in the twelfth century from Fez to Almeria by a young Spanish merchant trading in textiles, perfumes, and dyes. The merchant was writing to his father to complain about having to pay customs taxes, which apparently made him 'sick for three days out of anger and sorrow'.[79] At the header, in Hebrew characters בשמ רחמ, appears the Arabic phrase: بِسْمِ رَّحْمَٰنِ '*bism raḥmānī*' – in the name of the merciful – an abbreviated version of the Muslim invocation – '*bismillāhi al-raḥmāni al-raḥīm*' – in the name of God, the most gracious, the most merciful. This twelfth-century letter, from the Cairo Geniza, shows that Muslim prayers were in fact borrowed by medieval Jewish traders. Although Jonathas' prayer appears to be a caricature, the entanglement of cultures means that the representation is a more complex blend of stereotype and reality.

Instead of seeing only the Jonathas who stands on stage, a Christian-in-Jew's-clothing, I start to imagine a historic, unknown merchant, whose life would be mappable onto these details of the text. Filling in the character from my readings of his world, I see an elegant man with curling hair, olive skin, and soft hands, covered in rings. His cotton shirt is a fine fabric, and he smells of musk and leather. In his speech, I start to hear beneath the Middle English text an echo of a Yiddish accent: an anachronism of my own imagination.

Having prayed to Mohammed, Jonathas dangles his wares before the East Anglian audience: 'fat figs to please *yow*', sugar 'as *yow* may see'.[80] He lists the spices which he has in his ships: ginger, liquorice, pepper, saffron, dates, cloves, green ginger, mastic gum, cinnamon, long pepper, Indian liquorice, oranges, apples, pomegranates.[81] These spices recall those which were recorded in Henry of Derby's inventories: the listing is luxurious but accurate. At the same time, these spices remain marvellous: spices offered alongside pomegranates, like the trees which grew in the garden of the Song of Songs.

There are records which show that Jonathas' spices were bought and consumed in fifteenth-century East Anglian households. The household book of the gentry woman Alice de Bryene, taken by her steward, carefully records the goods purchased, in daily, monthly, and annual accounts. The opening flyleaf of the accounts book for 1412–13 records that figs were bought at Stoke-by-Nayland in December, dates, sugar, and pepper were bought at Stourbridge market, near Cambridge, more pepper was bought in London, more sugar was bought at Bury St Edmunds in February, 13 shillings worth of saffron was bought at Stourbridge, as well as ginger, cinnamon, and cloves.[82] Alice invested in the spices which were exported from Syria in large quantities: in 1413, Venetian cogs purchased pepper in Damascus to the value of 729.5 ducats.[83] Alice's household book is a small-scale witness to the wider networks which brought spices from Syria to Suffolk. In Alice's household book, these spices are filed next to local goods – recorded alongside a list of purchases of '*cheese*'.[84] The impression given is that imported spices were as necessary to the household as dairy – although spices were more expensive, bought on dedicated trips to fairs, marketplaces, and urban centres. The 1412–13 accounts are not an anomaly – in Alice's other surviving book, from 1419, the steward again records two trips taken for the 'purchase of spices' at London and Stourbridge, to buy pepper, ginger, cinnamon, cloves, white sugar, saffron, and dates.[85]

These spices would have been used to make treats such as this fourteenth-century recipe for apple blossom fritters:

> Take crumbs of white bread & and the flowers of the sweet apple tree and yolks of eggs and . . . temper it up with white wine and make it to seethe. & when it is thick add thereto good spices of ginger, galingale, cinnamon and cloves, and serve it forth.[86]

The spices combine with the sweetness of the apple blossom: no sugar is needed.[87] These apple fritters were both delicacy and cure: 'good spices' with medicinal properties. Local apple blossom and eggs are combined with imported products, prepared with the knowledge derived from translated medicine, which was circulated through kitchens across England. These are not goods which were strange – but which were regularly bought and mixed together.

Imagining Alice's steward or her cook in the audience for the *Croxton Play*, Jonathas' list starts to look less fantastical. The traders operating in regional marketplaces would have come into contact with international traders, who would have sold them these goods. Along with the spices themselves, anecdotes of life in the Levant and Mediterranean filtered through to English consumers. Dripping with moralised wealth, Jonathas is both a scapegoated stereotype of the religious-racial enemy, and a representation of the Syrian-Jewish merchants who worked in Mediterranean marketplaces. His inventory of spices is a plausible product of the trading networks from Syria to England.

Gilroy writes that today the 'postcolonial migrant' has become an 'anachronistic figure bound to the lost imperial past'.[88] I see Jonathas as a figure bound to the lost past of the crusader settlements: the threatening, ethno-religiously different inhabitant of a formerly Christian-occupied land. Beneath the caricature, the character of Jonathas preserves traces of a real community.

Selling the Divine

The main events of the *Croxton Play* are set in motion by Jonathas' treatment of the Eucharist as a commodity. He plots to use his extraordinary wealth as 'the greatest merchant in all *Surre*' to buy and kill the Christian 'God, that is full mighty, in a cake!' as he puts it.[89] In this drama, the bread of the Eucharist is carefully distinguished from commercial objects – it is clear that Jonathas' purchase of the wafer is blasphemy. Jonathas' actions appear against a backdrop of intense Christian anxiety around their own relationship to the marketplace, an awareness that commercial value and devotional value were often impossibly interwoven. Playing into the stereotype of Jews as essentially materialist, Jonathas misinterprets the Eucharist as an inanimate 'cake'.[90] His view of consumption is the wrong kind of eating. Jonathas and Aristorius haggle over the price of the wafer, until Jonathas hands over the sum of £100. His sale of spices is set against the backdrop of his misguided mercantilism.

As in the *Libelle*, the rejection of Jonathas and his spices comes with the rejection of medical frameworks. Having bought the Host, the Jews torture the wafer, in a restaging of the Passion. When they stab the wafer, it bleeds. Astonished, Jonathas picks up 'that cake', and it sticks to his hand. Not deterred, they pin the wafer to a post – and Jonathas' hand comes away from his arm. He needs medical assistance: the doctor, Master Brundyche, is sent for – and is found sitting 'with some *tapstere* [barman] in the *spence*'.[91] Here the 'spence' is a tavern. The governor of the dispensary, the medical cabinet, should not – it is implied – be found in this environment, drunken and at ease. In Trevisa's text 'on medicine', he advises that 'a wise doctor taketh heed of things . . . and cureth the matter that is hard and corrupt within with medicines of digestion, as with oxymel'.[92] When Master Brundyche describes treating a patient with oxymel – a drink of vinegar and spices derived from Arabic sources – the strong implication is that the patient has died. The sense is that earthly medicine will do no good: calling a doctor is another of the Jews' errors. For spiritual and bodily healing, Christian understanding is the only cure. It is clear that these Syrian Jews do not understand this difference between the material and the spiritual. Jonathas commands his associate Jason to wrap the wafer in a cloth 'and throw it in the cauldron'.[93] The scene is of the domestic made terrible: the oven, surrounded by Jews, becomes an emblem of evil. The fire beneath a 'cake' is devilish when the 'cake' is Christ. The raw body in the bread must not be cooked. The distinction between religious communities is articulated in terms of consumption: the Christian wafer – opposed to Jewish spices.

Staging its resistance to the mis-preparation of the Host, the oven explodes. From its bleeding depths appears an image: Jonathas' servant Masphat cries out at the 'great wonder!'.[94] Jesus speaks to the Jews, pleading for the torment to end. The Jews begin to speak in Latin quotations from the Psalms, processing towards the Church. Aristorius is punished for his sinful act in selling the Eucharist to Jonathas: he is forbidden from continuing as a merchant. The now converted no-longer-Jewish merchants continue 'Forward on *owr vyage*'.[95] The converts become pilgrims, but their precious cargo is still on the ships on which they sail away – not explicitly forbidden, still available to be sold. English audiences could still long privately for Jonathas' spices – some of which would have been available to buy in nearby markets following the performance. Jonathas' luxurious lists cause the imaginative richness of spices to persist against the strongest suspicions towards the Syrian Jews who sold them.

The histories of the 'lost Judeo-Muslim hyphen' pervade the *Croxton Play* like a denied aroma.[96] The sweet scent of Jonathas' spices is absorbed in spite of the spectacle on stage, in spite of the text which told the audience that they ought not to desire what their mouths were watering to taste.

Consumption and Display

When Henry of Derby's leopard joined the English group, it became part of a parade: a procession of troops and servants followed the court, and had to be fed. Across medieval Europe, banquets were sites at which ideology was displayed and consumed. In one fifteenth-century manuscript illumination, the French King Charles V is shown dining with spice vessels modelled in the shape of ships, while a tableau of the siege of Jerusalem takes place beneath his table [Figure 2.1]. Before the pilgrimage, Henry ordered the purchase of 120 pewter plates, and fifty-six pewter saucers, plus a sack 'to put spices in'.[97] The sack and these stacks of metal plates sketch a scene of large-scale consumption, into which the leopard arrives, licking spices. There are records that animals could play a part in the spectacle of courtly dining: one account of Duke Philip of Burgundy's 1454 Feast of the Pheasant describes how a statue of a young woman 'jetted hippocras [sweetened spiced wine] from her breasts the entire duration of the supper' with an 'entirely alive lion' chained to a pillar nearby.[98] The leopard could have been intended for this kind of dramatic performance, wine spraying from inanimate breasts over its iron-clad paws: a breathing symbol within the stagecraft of tableware.

Along his journey, Henry encountered a man at Rhodes – original name unknown – who was converted to Christianity and baptised under the name of Henry. The converted man was displayed as a token of the fulfilled pilgrimage. Echoing the miracle of the Syrian-Jewish merchants, this is conversion as spectacle. The newly baptised Henry joined the itinerant court back to England. As Marion Turner comments, 'When a great noble

Figure 2.1 Charles V dining. Source: Bibliothèque Nationale de France, Paris. MS Fr. 2813, fol. 473 v. Image permission granted under Creative Commons Zero (CC0) Open Access License.

such as Henry travelled, he did so in a profoundly imperial manner.'[99] A faux-imperial Henry might not conquer the Holy Land, but he still preserved the fantasy of English conquest, to be realised at a distant future date. And for individuals, for 'Henry Saracen', the medieval English court could do damage. There were still consequences and causalities to the performance of royal power even in the form of a charade. Details of the man's presence are found in the purchases which are made: 'a hackney horse for Henry the convert', a pilgrim gown 'for Henry *baptizato*', material 'to make a toga for Henry the Turk', shoes for 'Henry the Saracen'.[100] He rode a horse, wearing a gown, a toga, and new shoes. Reclothed and renamed, the transformation still left him marked as a 'Turk', a 'Saracen'. These shifting terms show that the man's identity was illegible to the English court into which he had been taken – his origins were seen differently at different times. The collapse of these terms records a failure of communication, and the instability of these externally defined categories.

Performances of the 'Saracen' are also known to have taken place at medieval banquets: the 1454 Feast of the Pheasant included a performance by a 'Saracen giant', dressed in green silks and wearing a turban, leading a silk-clad elephant into the room, on which sat Holy Church, represented by a lady wearing white satin.[101] At Philip's feast, the tableaux of the 'Saracen' was followed by a call for aid to Christendom in the aftermath of the recent Fall of Constantinople to the Ottoman Empire. 'Henry Saracen' walks through and past these imagined scenes, an uneasy guest in an unhospitable fantasy.

The After-Taste of the Crusades

The movement of spices from Syria to England began during the period of the crusader settlements. In reflection of the continued desire for the tastes of the settlements, the surviving fourteenth-century English collections of recipes preserve a dish: *Blank de Syria*. There are variant names for this recipe: 'Blanc Desire', 'Blank de Surry', 'Blank de Syry', 'Blank Dessorre', 'Blank Desire', 'Blandesyre', or 'Blandesire'.[102] These different spellings all mark the recipe as originating in 'Syria'. In some, the prefix collapsing into the place name brings out another meaning – the food of desire. Still in use centuries after the fall of Acre, the existence of this dish hints at a continued fantasy of eating as reproducing the vanished experience of being in the crusader Kingdom. An example recipe is as follows:

> For to make *blank de surry*, take flesh of cocks or of hens . . . & take *mylk* of almonds . . . and put thereto sugar a good part, and a part of white grease, and boil it; & when it is done in dishes strew upon *blanke poudere*, and put together *blank de sury* & *maumene* in a dish & serve it forth.[103]

This stew of boiled meat, almond milk, sugar, and fat was a rare treat, a delicacy. The sprinkling of '*blanke*' powder was a spice mix. The dish suggested as a suitable pairing, *maumene*, derives from a dish known in Arabic as *ma'mūniyyah*, which was introduced to European consumers during the period of the crusading settlements.[104] The fourteenth-century Syrian cookbook *Scents and Flavours* contains a number of variations on *ma'mūniyyah*, in which the essentials are rice, fat, sugar, and pistachios.[105] The thirteenth-century physician Ibn al-Quff, who lived in Damascus, recommended sugared rice for good health.[106] In England, *maumene* was made from minced meat, spices, sugar, almond milk, and wine. The wine was a European addition.[107] Served together and dusted with spices, these dishes were the product of Christian crusaders' adaptation of local cuisine. Recreating a scene of Syria, the recipe books evoked both the present realities of trade and the recollected histories of the crusades. These were the remembered tastes of the settlements: imported goods contained within fantasies of Christian control. The continued preparation of these recipes in elite kitchens across medieval England shows how these ideologies were preserved in sensory experience.

Another dish which accompanies 'blanc de syre' and 'mawmene' is 'Sawce Sarzyne' – 'Saracen Sauce'. This is how you make it:

> Take rosehips and make them clean. Take almonds blanched . . . Boil it up with good red wine, and put therin sugar enough with *powder fort* . . . colour it with *alkenet* and mess it forth; and flourish it.[108]

This is cuisine as exoticism, a caricature of the foods of the erstwhile – although no longer literal – enemy. This is a menu designed to appeal to the Christian subject. The imported dye alkenet combined with the red wine to make the whitened almonds blood red. Freedman writes that 'Saracen' dishes were often 'merely red'; red was associated with Islam in medieval art.[109] The religious-racial category of the 'Saracen' is used as an advertisement: inviting English enjoyment of the Other's cuisine. Phillips has described late medieval eating as a state of 'broad-mindedness'.[110] The role of spices in medieval English culture does direct attention to the complexity of English–Muslim relations in the later Middle Ages. But at the same time, some of the English were dining in the past: licking their boiled flesh and dreaming of the days of Frankish domination.

The edible displays at the English court were faint echoes of the culinary spectacles of Islamic feast days in the Fatimid and Mamlūk Empires. The Persian travel writer Nasir i-Khosrau visited Egypt in 1040 CE, and observed one Ramadan feast at which he claimed to have seen a tree made of sugar, among other displays amounting to 73,000 kilos of sugar.[111] As a style developed during the Crusader settlements, these English feasts scattered with spices and sugars aspired to the condition of imperial banquets in territories out of reach.

Despising Courtly Consumers

In England, regular private feasts were aristocratic events. Peasants would have eaten spices more rarely, on special public feast days, while those in poverty or enclosed in leper colonies occasionally received small quantities of medicinal spices through the charitable donations of monks.[112] The popular romance *The Feast of Tottenham* is a burlesque comedy which was likely performed in urban contexts to a broad social milieu. The poem considers the consumption habits of the court. The aristocracy are imagined to eat:

> millstones in *mawmany*
> ....
> And bell clappers in *blawndisare*
> With a noble curry
> ...
> And *blobsterdis* in white *sorre,*
> ...
> With *spicery* strong.[113]

Here the dishes of *maumeny* and *blank de Syria* are made indigestible through the addition of mill stones, bell clappers, and 'blobserdis' – horse shit. 'Sorre' is a dish of chopped eels, sometimes dyed red, like 'Saracen sauce'. These are unattainable luxuries made disgusting – the elevated recipes colliding with the debased English court. The repulsive scene created from the collision of these products does not rely on xenophobic horror at imported goods – like in the *Libelle.* Instead, the poet mocks the pretention of the spice-eating classes. These melancholic recipes are undercut as status symbols – through the refusal to elevate those who, through their material wealth, were able to eat them more often.

The fifteenth-century anonymous poem *London Lickpenny* describes the frustrated wanderings of an impoverished man from Kent around the city. A spice vendor:

bade me come near and buy some spice
Pepper and saffron, they urged me to bid
Cloves, *grayns* and *flowre* of rice
For *lacke* of money I might not succeed.[114]

The penniless visitor to the spice market experiences desire from a distance. The presence of spices is tantalising, placing healing substances at arm's length. The non-encounter with spices was the dominant medieval experience: present in the street but rarely in the mouth. Like the lay devotees who observed monks tasting the sweet wine of the Eucharist while being denied from drinking the blood, those who witnessed spice consumption numbered far greater than those who were able to purchase them. In *London Lickpenny*, the narrator is unable to survive in the inaccessible city. These spices stayed transcendent through their status as healing, spiritual artefacts, and as luxury commodities. The desire for spices was encouraged through biblical and literary sources, in expensive markets and on other people's tables. The *Feast* meanwhile provides an antidote to jealousy, with its caustic comedy directed not at Syrian traders, but at noble English consumers.

Spices Come Down to Earth in England

Chaucer drew on these popular literary traditions, recirculating the motifs and jokes developed in comic forms. Chaucer had family connections to the spice trade: the first husband of Chaucer's grandmother was a pepperer, John Heron, and although Mary Chaucer twice remarried after Heron's death, she continued to live in her first marital residence, in the spicers' district around Sopers' Lane.[115] Chaucer grew up visiting his grandmother in the streets of the spice trade in London. The movement of spices was part of the culture from which Chaucer emerged.

'The Miller's Tale' is the second narrative in Chaucer's collection *The Canterbury Tales*. In deference to his social status, the Host calls upon the Monk to speak – but the Miller, drunk, pushes ahead to tell his tale. The heroine of the Miller's story is Alison. An eighteen-year-old newlywed, Alison's rich carpenter husband is significantly older than her; we are not told by how much, but enough to make him evidently meaningless to her as an object of desire. They live in Oxford, near the lodging house of a university student, Nicholas.

Nicholas is poor, his clothes threadbare – but he has strewn his bedroom with sweet herbs, and is 'himself as sweet as is the root | of liquorice or any *cetewale* [zedoary]' (I. 3206–7). Described in the romantic terms of the spice-trade, he is surrounded by his books, astrological texts from Arabic sources, and instruments. He even has an astrolabe – like Chaucer's son, little Lewis (I. 3209). All of these make him a suitable candidate for Alison's desire, who herself has a mouth as 'sweet as ale and mead' (I. 3261). The imagery of the Song of Songs is playfully rendered for a local audience: her mouth tastes not of milk and honey, but sweetened beer. And unlike the Song of Songs, the union of these spiced lovers is definitely extra-marital. Although Alison's husband longs for her as his 'spouse' (I. 3610), conjugal desire is mocked and sidelined. The erotic here cannot be allegorised as a spiritual metaphor, taking place inside the worldly genre of the fabliau, the popular comic tale.

Aiming to impress Alison, Nicholas comes and catches her 'by the *queynte* [cunt]' (I. 3276). A bad start: she springs away from him, but is won back by his gentle words. He calls her 'lemman', sweetheart (I. 3280). They make a plan to have sex while her husband is away. Nicholas knows that he has a rival – Absolon, a clerk with curling gold hair and fancy clothes. Attempting to place himself in the running for Alison's affections, Absolon 'sent her *pyment*, mead and spiced ale' (I. 3378). These material offerings are no match for Nicholas' fragrant sweetness. Absolon's offerings of spices fail not because of their impotence, but because of the one offering them. For all his 'love-longing' (I. 3679), Alison's desire remains her own.

Successfully managing to be alone together, Nicholas and Alison are interrupted by Absolon's amorous address to Alison from below her window. He calls up: 'my sweet cinnamon' (I. 3699). Unimpressed, Alison devises a trick to play on her would-be lover. If she kisses him, will he leave her alone? Yes! He agrees. She unlatches the window and tells him to hurry up. Absolon wipes his lips carefully and leans up – the night is pitch-black, and so he does not see that before his face is not Alison's mouth – but 'her hole' (I. 3732). Expecting to taste cinnamon, instead Absolon 'kissed her naked arse | full savourly' (I. 3734–5). How strange! He always thought 'a woman hath no beard' – but he 'felt a thing all rough and long y-haired' (I. 3237–8). 'Tehee!' she says, totally unashamed.

Alas! The Englishwoman's body intrudes onto the scene, undercutting Absolon's romantic discourse of spices. Alison should taste like imported cinnamon: erotic and transcendent, healing and wonderful. To me Chaucer is playing with these biblical and medicinal frameworks in this moment – which are invoked in order to be rejected, creating bathos. Absolon's reaction to the event is that: 'he was healed of his malady' (I. 3757). In other words, expecting to consume cinnamon, Absolon finds a cure of a very different nature: he is cured of his desire for women. The expectation of encounter with fragrant spice is subverted by the encounter with the English body. The cinnamon, zedoary, and spiced beverages with which the tale is scented are mingled with the less elevated awareness of the baseness of English actions.

'The Miller's Tale' is not a narrative about transnational encounter, but a narrative which takes place in a culture already informed by those encounters. Absolon's confrontation with Alison's body, instead of with the metaphoric cinnamon of her sweet, spiced mouth, cannot be reduced to a single interpretation. The referent of the spiced garden of the Song of Songs has been lost. The romantic associations of spices are fractured. The subversive comedy remains enriched by the imaginaries of the lost symbolisms. The wonder of medicinal, spiritual spice haunts Absolon as he '*frotteth* now his lips' with straw (I. 3747). In Chaucer's verse, spices are integrated and disintegrated in comic re-orientations that play with the traditions of these products as elevated wonders. These products were rooted in their local context, as well as in their histories of movement. Cinnamon was at home in medieval English markets, minds, and bodies – even if it was not found by Absolon when he came to kiss Alison's arse.

Lingering Contradictions

Where Orientalism is the agent of digestion, the 'West' feeds and grows from the 'East' whilst remaining apparently unchanged in substance. Edward Said summoned the nineteenth-century poet Paul Valéry to express these ideas: writing on 'Oriental influence', Valéry stated that 'the real question in such matter is to *digest*', proceeding to clarify that the aim was to effect 'the transformation of everything into our own substance'.[116] The metaphor of digestion here suggests an impermeable 'Western' body, whilst 'Eastern' culture remained the passive object of consumption. In Valéry's formulation, the transfer of knowledge from 'East' to 'West' resulted only in the Westernisation of the ideas transferred. But there is a distinction between premodern digestion of imported spices and modern Orientalising processes of digestion.[117]

In medieval digestion, imported spices are not transformed into the unchangeable substance of the 'English' body. Instead of the digested object being viewed as passive, spices travelling through the body were viewed as agential: an agency which was both medicinal and spiritual, akin to the Eucharistic experience of God's body dissolving in the mouth.[118] Whereas Orientalist digestion relies on the idea that 'Eastern' culture is the passive object of digestion by the 'Western' consumer, medieval discourses of humoural balance instead relied on the idea that the unruly English body required temperance from rational combinations of imported spices. Instead of being obliterated, spices remained transnational, communicative artefacts, bringing knowledge first across the seas and then down the throat.

The food-based art of Michael Rakowitz offers a means of understanding the premodern movement of consumables. In his project *RETURN* (2004–ongoing), Rakowitz reopened his grandfather's date import business, Davisons & Co., in New York.[119] For those who – like Rakowitz's grandparents – had left Iraq for America as exiles, entering the shop acted as a form of 'return'. For the dates, the 'return' was a continuation of movement, a 'return' to the long-established paths of export, a 'return' to travelling the world as they had done for thousands of years. As the theorist Ella Shohat, with whom Rakowitz has worked closely, comments: 'Contrary to the exotica industry associated with Middle Eastern restaurants and cookbooks, Rakowitz's food projects comment on the transnational flow of images and sounds, of smells and tactile impressions.'[120]

Arriving in medieval Europe, spices were witnesses of trade and conflict, continued histories of human movement and violence. In his project *Enemy Kitchen* (2003–ongoing), Michael Rakowitz (with the help of his mother) compiles Baghdadi recipes and teaches them to different groups, including schoolchildren, discussing Iraq through the framework of cooking.[121] Those who are taught Iraqi recipes (such as American schoolchildren) are transformed into guests; the 'enemies' become their hosts. The collective consumption of Iraqi food is a simultaneous digestion of politics and cuisine. The paradoxical image of the *Enemy Kitchen* can be taken as a framework for many of the medieval scenes of spice-eating encountered: Jonathas selling his suspicious, coveted wares; the *Libelle*-author scowling against Levantine imports while knowing that his readers longed for such luxuries. In medieval England, spices were sacramental cures and sinful luxuries, the immaterial product of Christian traditions and the commercial product of interfaith trade. There is an impulse to resolve paradoxes. But these spices remain resistant and contradictory.

The presence of spices 'right here' posed a challenge to Christians steeped in crusading nostalgia, anti-Jewish hatred, and fear of Islam. Those who stayed rooted in the present had to find a way to process Syrian spices as the witnesses of a trading and intellectual relationship: crusading narratives provided a palatable fantasy. The English often seemed left with a bad case of indigestion, spitting out their medicine. But spices remained present in kitchens and markets across England, reminders of a complex world which could be digested, but which could not be consumed.

Postscript: The Undigestible

Brought back from Cyprus, Henry of Derby's leopard did come home to England. As the gift of the King of Cyprus, the leopard played its role in maintaining the elite diplomatic networks which spanned centres of trade and travel across the Mediterranean. But the leopard was not only a symbol. It was hungry and difficult to care for. The sheep and spiced oils in the inventories from Henry's journeys are traces of attempts to cater to the leopard's desires. Whether in its cabin or as part of a parade, the leopard was an unavoidable embodiment of fierce alterity, resistant and active: like the spices which it was fed.

In August 1393, four boats were hired at Dover to carry Henry's baggage ashore, with a dedicated transport for the leopard. On 2 September 1393, Henry took his leopard with him to Rochester.[122] And then it slips out of the records. The converted man, 'Henry', disappeared too. On arrival in England, he was taken to Peterborough with Henry of Derby's luggage: and that beginning marks the end of the records. Henry and the leopard vanished in England, leaving these spare traces: the purchase of shoes, wood to make a cabin, a slick of sweetened oil in a steward's accounting book.

PART II

The Treasury

As the light began to leave Robert's eyes, John wished he could place pearls in his hand, close his partner's fingers over the stones. If he could, he would have wrapped cloth of gold around Robert's chest and pressed his hands into the damp fabric. Robert's blood was not holy but it was precious to him – he would have tasted it like a saint's, tangled bright threads of silk through his hair and prayed for forgiveness. Offering up their treasures to God, John might have received mercy.

The second part of my book focuses on silks and jewels, recorded as travelling together in '300 great chests and coffers' on Sturmy's ships. Although Sturmy's treasury was redirected to Libya, examples of these precious objects were found in churches and residencies of the nobility around England. An especially visible collection was held at Westminster Abbey – which remains a high-profile site of ceremonial display. As Susan Jenkins writes, today the 'Abbey has been acknowledged as *the* public space in which the erection of monuments to heroes encouraged visitors, both native and foreign, to reflect on British national ideals and gaze on figures of national importance'.[1] But some of these objects in the medieval Abbey are records of the alternative state of premodern global relations and exhibition practices. In the Middle Ages, Westminster Abbey was not yet a museum, and not yet a national monument. The Abbey was a reliquary, a tomb, a building site.

In the eleventh century, this small Benedictine monastery by the Thames was rebuilt and greatly enlarged by King Edward. When Edward was canonised as a saint in the twelfth century, the presence of his body transformed the Abbey into a shrine. For centuries afterwards, monarchs were interred close to his sacred remains, in the (futile) hope of gaining saintly status themselves.[2] From Henry I onwards, Westminster became the site reserved for coronation ceremonies, and a series of forgeries followed, fake royal charters produced by the Abbots at Westminster, creating new privileges for the monks.[3] In 1245, Henry III ordered another reconstruction of the building, and it is much of this that stands today. Mosaics, sculptures, and paintings were added. The Gothic style was French influenced – one of the architects was Henry of Reyns, and it has been suggested that the cathedral of Reims was a model. But Gothic architecture itself did not originate in Northern France. As Nagel and Wood write: 'The earliest Gothic architecture itself emerged in the mid-twelfth century during the period of the Latin occupation of Jerusalem and in an intensive dialogue with Holy Land architecture; indeed, the Crusader additions to the church of the Holy Sepulchre are among the earliest examples of Gothic architecture.'[4] To me, this background is more relevant than whether or not the Abbey was modelled on a cathedral in Northern France: in origins the style of both French and English buildings were part of a widespread project of European replication of the Crusader settlements in the Holy Land.

Henry III's works for the 'New Abbey Church', as it was called, cost around £41,000, over £29 million in today's currency.[5] Unfortunately for Henry, across the Channel, Louis IX was building Sainte-Chapelle – a harsh contrast. Dedicated in 1248 to house the Crown of Thorns relic, which Louis IX had acquired on Crusade in the Holy Land, Sainte-Chapelle is built like a glass reliquary, its arched ceilings splitting into transparent panels which let the light through in pale pinks and greens onto the mosaic floor.

In 1247, Henry III processed with a relic of Christ's blood towards Westminster Abbey [Figure 1.1]. The blood relic was stored in a jewelled beaker in the Abbey. But Henry III's blood cult failed to catch the English imagination – pilgrims continued to travel out of Westminster to see the relics of Thomas Becket at Canterbury, while in Paris, pilgrims flocked to see Louis' Holy Thorn. In 1268, Henry III laid down the Cosmati Mosaic, a Roman pavement in the sanctuary – a Papal art form, and a clear token of his Imperial ambitions. But there was no empire to match Henry's fantasy. In fact, as these stones were being set in mortar, the Kingdom of Jerusalem was collapsing overseas. Henry III died in 1272, buried in the Abbey without a campaign to make him into a saint. When Louis IX died in 1297, he was canonised by Pope Boniface VIII as a crusading icon, with Sainte-Chapelle as an enduring witness to his perceived sanctity. Westminster Abbey stood as an embarrassing, expensive emblem of Henry III's failures. He had not succeeded in starting a blood cult, or in becoming a saint, or in heading an empire. Successive kings looked at the project with relative disinterest. In the fifteenth century, Henry VI donated to the foundation of King's College Cambridge and Eton school instead of financing the completion of the Abbey.

The treasures stored in the Pyx chamber of the Abbey proved irresistible. In 1303, a man called Richard Pudlicote (allegedly) broke into the storeroom and stole £2,200 worth of jewellery and ceremonial objects – a crime for which he was convicted to death, after the loot started appearing in pawn shops around London. Pudlicote may have been scapegoated – perhaps to protect the Westminster monks and abbots, who would have been in a much better position to crack the locks from within the Abbey, but whose convictions would have thrown the Crown into disrepute, through proximity.

The image of a cathedral under scaffolding is a familiar contemporary sight. The presence of steel bars over stones, on first sight, looks like a juxtaposition of modern and medieval elements. But these construction sites, in a sense, more accurately evoke the reality of medieval architecture than do the restored buildings, without their metal shrouds. From the thirteenth to the fifteenth century, Westminster Abbey was under more-or-less constant redevelopment, with scaffolding (made from wood, not steel) being put up again as soon as it was dismantled. 'Scaffolder-Monks' were trained to work on the site, but many of the labourers who physically built the Abbey – quarrymen, plasterers, mortar-makers, stone-cutters, masons, workers who transported, laid, and bound the stones – were itinerant workers paid by the day or by piece. Some names of the master masons are known: Henry of Reyns, John of Gloucester, Robert of Beverley. Some craftsmen carved their maker's marks on the walls – other painters of frescoes, sculptors, and stained glassmakers left their work anonymous.

These centuries of unfinished labour made the Abbey into a site of monumental debris, drawing attention to its incompletion. The chapel continued to function as a contemplative and ceremonial site – but these rituals took place from within an unfixed building. There are traces of modernity in the medieval Abbey: elements of an aesthetics of display which would later become museum practices, nationalist ideologies which would later become the rationale for colonial expansionism. But like the Abbey walls themselves, these elements are unstable in their premodern state. In the Middle Ages, Westminster Abbey not only had no global status – there was no British Empire to be the centre of – it struggled to be accepted within England. The undocumented workers who constructed the Nave and the Pyx were not at the time building a symbol of the nation – at the end of the day they moved on to another church.

That is not to say that Westminster Abbey was ever exactly just another church. Proximate to the royal palace and the administrative capital, the Abbey was pivotal to the monarchic project, and to an elite monastic network, both of which imagined English national power, before that international power became a reality. By the end of the fifteenth century, Westminster Abbey had shifted in meaning – it was now known as 'the head of England, the kingdom's coronet' – to use the phrase of the monk John Flete.[6]

The Holy Land was crucial to the identity of the medieval Abbey. In the 1380s, Abbot Nicholas Lytlyngton commissioned the Jerusalem Chamber: a room which he used as his personal dining room. Consuming sweet wines and spices in the Jerusalem Chamber of the Abbey, Lytlyngton could sit back and relax in blissful luxury, not at the sacred centre of the world, but within a very expensive, incomplete English replica.[7] The room was hung with tapestries, adjoining a church which was strewn with imported silks and jewels.

The Westminster Abbey Silks

In 1388, the monks Richard Cirencester, William Sudbery, John Beynte, and Ralf Tonworth compiled an inventory of the contents of the Westminster Abbey Vestry. The Abbey can be visualised using these documents. The tombs were draped with silks – for example, the tomb of Edward III (1312–77) was draped 'with the arms of England and France in red and blue velvet with leopards and fleurs-de-lys'.[8] Walking through the medieval Abbey to perform rituals, the priests were dressed in fantastical garments. They wore white floor-length silk vestments, called albs. Some of these white robes were embroidered with fighting grotesques – 'babewynis' – and others were decorated with 'griffons and other beasts with women's faces'.[9] The aesthetics of these fabrics echo the stone grotesques and the illuminated books in the Abbey chests – somehow more subversive and surprising when found on priests' bodies.[10] The women-headed beasts overlooked the ceremonies.

Other priests wore white velvet robes 'with stripes of gold and silk', one of which had a design of 'moon and stars of gold intermingled'.[11] The pattern of moon and stars recalls the style of Islamic design work. Another floor-length robe was made 'of cloth of gold of Cyprus', embroidered with gold falcons and flowers.[12] Another cloth of gold made in Lucca had 'stripes of various colours and [was] inscribed with diverse letters'.[13] The 'diverse letters' could be Greek, Hebrew, Arabic, or another non-Latinate script. These cloths create a sense of marvel, their calligraphy marking them out as the product of travel.

The priests wore gloves embroidered with gems and pearls. The mitres, headpieces worn by abbots and bishops, were studded 'with precious stones and pearls', and their crucifixes were studded with jewels.[14] For the Mass ceremony, these lavishly dressed men covered the elements with silk veils, called *sudaria*. As they were carried to the altar, the wafers were draped in 'striped silk' and 'from white silk with stripes of gold and with silks of varied colours for the principal festivals'.[15] Reaching the altar, the sacred site of ceremony was hung with six red silk curtains 'of Sarsinet *cotidianum*' hung around the altar.[16] The Latin word *cotidianum* can be translated as 'for daily use', or as 'everyday' – these red 'Saracen silks' in the Abbey aspired to evoke the Kingdom of Jerusalem, with its imagined endless wealth of silks, an everyday abundance. A small portable altar – the 'super altar' – was made entirely out of jasper stone.[17] A crucifix was made 'of chalcedony stone, with two red stones of Israel in the middle'.[18] The label '*de israel*' might refer to the style of engraving instead of the origins of the stone. The language still draws the Holy Land into the English chapel – the crucifix is imaginatively made into a biblical relic. Glittering, the Abbey was a site of ceremony, memory and fantasy.

The Melancholic Abbey

The medieval Abbey was a site of melancholia, expressing a post-Acre condition which both predates and resonates with later postcolonial habits of display. There are now 600 tombs and more than 300 memorial stones and windows in the Abbey – among which are, displayed in the Diamond Jubilee Galleries, Admiral Nelson's funeral effigy and, in the entrance to the Abbey, a paving stone for Winston Churchill. These statues and signs keep the unmourned past in view, grieving these imperial figures as a means of forgetting the realities of Empire.

The display of Holy Land artefacts in the Abbey has been seen as among the early origins of colonial-era museum practices.[19] These were objects in the medieval Abbey which had travelled from Christian settlements, presented in the royal chapel as tokens of power. After the collapse of the Christian Kingdom of Jerusalem, these artefacts assumed an altered resonance. They became melancholic souvenirs, recalling the erstwhile territories and refusing to mourn the loss of the Holy Land.

The medieval English crown did possess territories nearer to home, in Scotland, Ireland, Wales, and France. In 1295, Edward I had moved a number of chests of jewels from the Scottish royal treasury in Edinburgh to the King's wardrobe in Westminster: a physical and a symbolic gesture of control. But in spite of the desires which brought them to England, the objects which travelled from Syria to the medieval Abbey displayed the futility of Christian aims for reconquest. Presented within an unfinished, underfunded site of royal non-command, these artefacts evoked the cultural capital of the Mamlūk Empire. The Damask cloths – purchased, not stolen – were named after the global centre of Damascus. English monarchs could not dream of conquering that city: they stitched their lions to their hems instead. The possession and display of these silks and stones articulated not the reality of control, but its absence: the void of international power at the centre of the unfinished Abbey.

In the Middle Ages, the Abbey was not the heart of an empire. But the aesthetics of the medieval Abbey produce a negative affect: the consequence of the refusal to mourn the loss of Christian territories. In the premodern Abbey, the silks and jewels on display had travelled – or were worshipped *as if* they had travelled – from the symbolic global centre of the Holy Land. These silks and jewels processed through the Abbey in rituals which constructed Christian community based on a complex, and contradictory, combination of fantasy and reality.

On display within a shrine under construction, the objects in the medieval Abbey remained unfixed. The Abbey is haunted by the memories of this untold medieval past, contained in the treasury.

CHAPTER 3

Silks and Velvets / The Fabrics of English Identity

Robert Sturmy's ship was stacked with '300 great *chestes* and coffers and more stuffed with clothes of silk as *velvettes*, *damasks*, *satens*, *tarterons*, *chamelettes*, strips of gold and silke clothe of gold, *baudekyns*, purses ... *rawsilke* ... to the value in *Englond* of 5200 marc'.[1] Sturmy's silks locate us in an interwoven world of authentic and imitative Holy Land wares.

The wearing of silks was considered an element of a healthy lifestyle, as expressed in Ibn Butlan's *Taqwīm as-Sihha* [Handbook of Health], translated into Latin as the *Tacuinum Sanitatis*. These fabrics were considered beneficial for the skin, and for the humours in allowing perspiration and heat to escape the body.[2] One fourteenth-century French illuminated manuscript of the Latin *Tacuinum Sanitatis* features a detailed scene of silk making [Figure 3.1]. Worn as a sign of good judgement and deep pockets, these fabrics were not only used to make clothes.

In this chapter silks will appear as the materials of spatial and self-construction, excavated and bequeathed, dreamed up and legislated against – from romances to private wills, poetry, and parliamentary bills. Silks are often seen in motion: used for boats' sails or nailed to wagons as part of the set of moving theatrical productions. Medieval silks hung from walls and over the altar were cut into veils, ribbons, belts, covers and pillows for books, and sheets for beds. And above all, silks were needed to construct Jerusalem.

Building Jerusalem in England

Edington is a village in the Cotswolds where, not long after 1476, down the lanes, with the sun catching the flowers through the hills, medieval churchgoers would travel through the village to the Holy Sepulchre, to be near the earth on which Christ walked.

The Wiltshire Holy Sepulchre was a replica, built on the design of the former bursar of Eton William Wey, who wrote the *Matter of Jerusalem*.

Figure 3.1 Silk making, pictured in the *Tacuinum Sanitatis*. Source: Bibliothèque Nationale de France, Paris. Nov. Acquis Lat. 1673, fol. 95 r. Image permission granted under Creative Commons Zero (CC0) Open Access License.

Returning from his travels in 1458 and 1462, he brought with him a handful of stones – from Calvary, from the Holy Selpuchre, from the Hill of Tabor, from the site of the pillar on which Christ was whipped, and from the holy cave of Bethlehem. Slipping these stones into his pocket as he travelled, these objects were reminders and traces of sacred earth. In his will, he left his souvenirs to the monks at Edington – along with a detailed plan for a new building, in which they were to be displayed: 'These be the goods of master William Wey's gift to the chapel made to the likeness of the Sepulchre of Our Lord at Jerusalem.'[3] The chapel was to be joined onto the side of the chapterhouse. The chapel was likely destroyed during the Reformation, but a bricked-up door in the church choir shows that it was built.

It is easy to visualise Wey's chapel – he planned it in detail. On the altar lay a hair shirt, and a canvas, a few towels and silks, painted with scenes of the crucifixion and Mary breastfeeding 'our lord'. A '*mappa* of the *Holy Lond*, with Jerusalem in the *myddys*', hung above the altar – a world map, with Jerusalem as its sacred centre. Wey donated silk vestments for the priests to wear, in red and green, with fringes and stripes of gold. He left cloths of gold and black silks for use in the Mass ceremony, to cover the Eucharist. He left blue curtains to hang around the chapel, and wall hangings with scenes of Jerusalem. There were silver chalices, and a wooden reliquary box containing Wey's precious, sacred stones, and silk pillows, to place books on. He ordered the construction of a collection of wooden planks, cut to sacred measurements, like devotional rulers: marking the length of the Lord's Tomb, and the circumference of the Cross. Lastly he specified that the Church of the Nativity and the Church of Bethlehem should also be 'made with boards'. These were miniature models for display. Wey finished: 'My will is that these afore writ be not removed from the chapel of the Sepulchre, nor from the holy monastery of Edington.'[4]

The music for the English hymn *Jerusalem* was written by Hubert Parry for performance in 1916, commissioned for the First World War 'Fight for Right' propaganda initiative. It redeployed lyrics from William Blake's *Preface to Milton* for the imperial war effort. The song asks, 'And was Jerusalem builded here?' In 1917, Parry's anthem was echoing around Women's Institute halls as British troops were entering Palestine. Set to music, the rural landscape of Blake's lyrics becomes an emblem of both an idealised English nation and an idealised pre-industrial past – which combine to create an image of 'ancient' natural space as the site of authentic Englishness. As civilians dreamed of Jerusalem existing in an English field, on the battlefield it was England that was being built in Jerusalem: the British Mandate for Palestine, established as a colonial settlement. As I read Wey's will now, Parry's choral music echoes over the scene: *Bring me my arrows of desire*. But the anthem belongs to a later era of imperial history.

When Jerusalem was built in England along Wey's specifications, the chapel was a surrogate for settlement. These silks and stones were brought home without bows and arrows, paid for and pocketed by an unarmed pilgrim. The wooden models were sawed and placed carefully in the chapter house: in that recorded act of construction, there was no need for a sword. In so far as the replica was part of a propaganda initiative for military action, it expresses a desire for action which was inextricable from the awareness of its own futility. In a crucial difference from the narrative of premodern England as a site of rural authenticity, the space which was created in Wiltshire was defined by its artificiality. The Wiltshire Jerusalem was a symbolic reconstruction which did not attempt to be taken as the original. The silks which filled the chapel were on devotional display. Instead of an origin point for a stable 'England', Wey's chapel reveals a premodern space which was essentially inauthentic, fabricated.

In Wey's chapel, precious fabrics and relics were used to re-create Jerusalem as a place.[5] Relics are imaginatively non-substitutable, effective only if authentically brought from their stated site of origin, claiming to occupy one stable time and place.[6] As Susan Stewart writes, such souvenirs 'envelop the present within the past'.[7] The silks with which Wey filled the chapel were imaginatively returned to the lands from which they originated, at the same time as the Holy Land was itself symbolically reconstructed through these materials.[8] Returning pilgrims could dwell on the experiences had whilst in the holiest of destinations. For those who had never made the journey, the space could go some way towards conjuring the dreamed-of experience of being in Syria.[9] Wey's own experience of travel both authenticates the objects and unsettles the replica through the recollection of the realities which brought its elements to England. In the chapel silks are both the abstract representations of holy space and complex traded items. There is a contradiction here: an awareness of the traded, constructed reality of these items risks undermining the principle of non-substitutability on which their contemplative value relies. These are openly textual objects layered with intersecting, contradictory fictions, histories, and imaginations.

Labelling Fabrics

The medieval names of fabrics gesture to historic, fantasised, and corrupted locations of production. Before 1291, Acre acted as one of the main sources of silks to Europe.[10] 'Damask' derives from Damascus, which was a global centre of the silk trade. High-quality, luxury textiles made in Syria were imported to Europe – these were the most desirable fabrics. Ibn Battuta recorded that Damascus was home to 170 silk markets. Al-Maqrisi wrote that there were 4,000 silk looms in Tripoli.[11] Syrian silk production was a world-leading industry in both scale and quality. However, other Damasks were made in Europe, imitating Syrian techniques and designs. By the fourteenth century, the Italian imitation silk industry had risen to such a high standard that, as David Jacoby comments, it was often 'impossible to determine whether they were genuine Oriental silks'.[12]

There was never a single, continuous 'Silk Road'. There were always several routes and several centres, including but not limited to Damascus, Antioch, Baghdad, Venice, Genoa, Florence, Milan, Cyprus, and Andalusia.[13] Following silks on their journey from Syria to England does not erase the routes which could have been followed, from Quanzhou to Venice or Baghdad to Milan. Medieval silks were laced with the traces of these other journeys. The term 'baudekyn' is a modification for the Old Norman word for Baghdad – 'baldacco'; the term 'tabby' preserves the core of the Arabic *'Attābiy*, a quarter of the same city.[14] The word 'satin' echoes the Arabic *zaytūnī*: 'Zaitun' was the Arabic name for Quanzhou, in China.[15] Several terms are drawn from technical Arabic or Persian vocabulary. The term 'camoca' derives from the Arabic *kimkhā*, originally referring to multi-coloured silks; 'taffeta' echoes the Persian *tāfta*, twisted linen or silk. These echoes of Arabic sit alongside terminology derived from crusading-era religious-racial categories: 'sarsinet', 'Saracen silk' and 'tartarium', 'Tartar cloth'.[16]

In the medieval period, the routes of the silk trade were woven around the world, tangled from country to country through the sea. On Henry of Derby's 1392 journey to the Holy Land, his treasurer Kyngeston records 'three pieces of silk from Damascus bought by the master on the fifteenth of December at Venice'.[17] On the way back from Jerusalem, in 1393, Kyngeston records: 'English scarlet bought by Henry of the wardrobe for the master at Venice on 6 April.'[18] Buying Damascus silk on the way to Jerusalem and English scarlet on the way back to Dover, English and Syrian cloths collided in Venice, with fabrics travelling 'home' in both directions.

Arriving in England, silks were imported alongside other associated commodities: for instance, in 1513–14 the Newcastle merchant Edward Baxter sold silk, alum, raisins, and wine to Durham Cathedral priory.[19] *The Libelle of Englyshe Polycye* describes Genoese carracks 'arrayed withouten lacke | With cloth of gold, silke, and pepper blacke'.[20] Chaucer's comic knight Sir Thopas appears dressed in '*syklatoun*, | That cost many a *jane*' (VII. 734–5). The fabric known in Arabic as *siqlātūn* was a red and white brocade associated with Antioch.[21] The 'jane' was the Genoese currency: the combination of Arabic vocabulary and Genoese currency in this description of Thopas' precious gown traces a distinct path of import, from Antioch production (or its imitation) through Genoese traders, into the hands of luxuriant knights.

In Lucca, Italian weavers were recorded as the producers of 'soriani'.[22] Used to describe these weavers' work, the label of Syrian origin was a marketing tool, more than an accurate description. These imitative silks – in which I first saw the term Syriana – intermingled with the genuine produce of the Holy Land. In England, Syrian place names were affixed to fabrics as markers of prestige, such as a red fabric 'de Antioche' [of Antioch] recorded at Canterbury Cathedral – again, this label could signal an original or imitative cloth.[23] The ritual use of these fabrics relied on the suspension of disbelief in order to conjure the desired feeling of proximity to sacred earth, a devotional encounter which many medieval Christians experienced through contact with Syrian fabric and 'soriani' alike.[24] Being read as sacred, these textiles were used to evoke the lost crusading settlements and the present realities of Christian pilgrimage sites. In a world where imagination was not separate from reality, knowing that an image was constructed did not cause it to fall apart. In England, Syriana was used to remake holy sites and the heavens above them.

The Heavens Are a Silken Construction Site

As well as in chapels, silks were used for medieval stage sets. The York Cycle of pageant plays was a series of religious dramas, dated as early as 1376, and still in performance in the sixteenth century. The pageants were performed on wagons, which were wheeled around the streets on Corpus Christi day, stopping at pre-arranged locations. Each pageant staged a religious episode, performed by a relevant guild. The Pinners acted out the Crucifixion (a showcase for their nail-making skills) while the Mercers were responsible for bringing the Last Judgement, the climax of the cycle, which usually took place at night. Like Wey's Jerusalem Chapel, the York Mercers' Indenture provides a record of silks being used to construct imaginative space.

A list from 1433 records the huge volume of props, costumes, and scenery used for the Mercers' performance that year. There was an iron grate for God to sit on, designed to ascend from the wagon, on a pulley system of ropes. Two pairs of angels' wings were wrought from iron. There were nine red mechanical angels, which would run around the roof of the wagon – the heavens – when a cord was pulled. Two timber rainbows were arched over God, alongside four cloth clouds in red and blue, and gold cloth sunbeams. The spectacle, visibly made from iron, wood, linen, and pins, demanded that the viewer marvel at the labour which went into its construction – human labour which paid tribute to the divine making of the world. The Last Judgement begins with God reflecting on the time when first 'I this world had wrought'.[25] Then the world is systematically deconstructed, as it comes to an end. The backdrop of the whole scene: 'A great *coster* of red damask painted for the back side of the pageant.'[26] As the red mechanised angels ran around, and the iron grate was hoisted upwards, the precious cloth stayed still. The colour echoes the red ink used in illuminations of the Apocalypse – standing for the burning sky, and the flowing blood, but also for the Heavenly Jerusalem which awaits the saved.

Gazing on the red damask, glimmering in the dark on the streets of York, was to gaze on Paradise. But since the Mercers were a trading guild, the cloth was also on display as an example of their high-quality wares which were available for purchase. The damask was both material and symbolic – an advertisement for traded goods and a reminder of biblical prophecy. These woven signs were traces of divine revelation and human labour.

The Stolen Supernatural

These combined associations of divinity and labour remain part of medieval silks in their narrative and material forms. The action of the fourteenth-century romance *Emaré* pivots on a silk cloth which is shown being made in a human context, but which gathers magical associations in its appearance and actions.

Emaré is a version of the Constance narrative, the same base narrative which was later retold by Chaucer in his 'Man of Law's Tale': indeed, *Emaré* is considered as a source for Chaucer's tale.[27] *Emaré* takes place primarily in Wales and Rome, rather than Syria and Northumberland as in Chaucer's retelling. In this version of the narrative, a symbolic cloth is brought from 'Babylon' to an unnamed Christian Empire. The scenes of romances were part of the soundtrack of medieval silks: along with rituals, these narratives shaped how people saw the cloths in marketplaces and churches. *Emaré* begins with: 'Minstrels who walk far and wide | Here and there, on every side' – who used to sing 'Of a lady, fair and free, | Her name was called Emaré'.[28] The jaunty, slightly clunky rhythm of the verse brings the performative context of the original composition to mind. The main audience for this tale were merchants and their families, gathered in domestic spaces in urban locations.[29] The fair lady is born to Sir Artyus, the Emperor – of what region, it is unclear, but definitely somewhere in Christendom. When the Empress dies, in Emaré's infancy, Sir Artyus hires a nurse, Abro – an ambiguous name, which has been suggested as implying corrupted Arabic.[30] As well as good manners, Abro teaches Emaré to sew gold and silk. In teaching Emaré to produce silk-work, Abro provides her with her primary character trait – as will be seen later on.[31]

Meanwhile, in 'heathenness', the daughter of an Emir – of which country it is also unclear – is making a silk for her beloved, the son of the Sultan of

'Babylon'.[32] The 'Emerayle' [Emir's] daughter stitches medieval love stories across the cloth.[33] Tristan and Isolde is retold in topaz and rubies. She represents herself on the cloth as a unicorn: a symbol often used to represent Christ. The cloth is given to the Sultan's son – and that is the last we hear of the Emir's daughter's romance. The narrative cuts away, but takes the silk with it.

Back in the first, unnamed Christian country, the King of Sicily arrives at the Emperor's court, bearing this jewelled cloth as a 'rich present'. When the Emperor looks upon the cloth, he cannot 'see | for *glysteryng* of the rich stones; | *Redy* sight had he none'.[34] The brightness of its jewels strips him of 'ready sight': in the first instance, 'redy' here means quickly, easily, but contains within it the verb 'reden', 'to read'. The displaced cloth cannot be read, resists being seen, at the same time as demanding attention through its glittering, fascinating surface. The King of Sicily is proud of his gift, and of its origins: 'My father was a noble man; | From the Sultan he it won | With mastery and with might'.[35] The looted cloth recalls the items stolen by Frankish crusaders.[36]

Perhaps the stolen cloth has cursed the recipients, because what happens next is that Sir Artyus becomes 'enamoured' of his daughter.[37] She is so fair! Bearing in mind, this was a story designed to be read aloud, often by a father to his assembled kin – the discomfort of the scene is vivid. Sir Artyus calls his counsellors and sends to the Pope, seeking permission to marry her – which is granted. The moral dichotomy between Christendom and 'heathenness' falls apart when that language is matched with the actions witnessed in these distinct spaces. So-called 'heathenness' is characterised by silk-work, the cloth woven as part of a highly suitable romance between two elite offspring. In Christendom: looting and Pope-sanctioned incest. In Chaucer's version, this Christian incest plotline was discarded, replaced with the marriage of Custance and the Sultan of Syria. The binary representation in *Emaré* undermines its own construction.

Sir Artyus has the stolen silk cloth cut into a gown, for his daughter to wear: 'And when it was put upon her | She seemed *non erthely* woman'.[38] The unearthly quality of the gown is read as supernatural, a foreign magic in the weft. 'I will wedde thee', says the King, gazing on her.[39] 'Nay, sir', she replies, God forbid that 'we should play together in bed'.[40] 'God forbid – God forbid', she repeats, to herself, to the court – to her family. Humiliated and furious, Sir Artyus throws her into the sea without food, drink, anchor, or oar: with only the bright cloth on her back to protect her.

The cloth is a stolen artefact, but in this story it appears to be a willing guest: a non-Christian stranger ready to take part in the Christian narrative. Perhaps Emaré is a more suitable guardian of the cloth than her father: the silk haunts her sympathetically, clinging to her as she is cast out to sea. Abro has brought Emaré up, taught her to make silk. Even the name 'Emaré' brings her into association with the 'Emerayle' daughter who made the cloth which she now wears, the sonic echo collapsing the apparently fixed cultural distance. The gown is a foreign surface containing properties not inherent in the heroine herself, but through its agency, she seems to be guided to safe harbour. Where Chaucer's lawyer thanked God for Custance's safe journey, here the agency of the cloth is unspoken, and ambiguous.

Exhausted by the waves, Emaré is washed up on the Welsh coast, where a knight, Sir Kadore, is walking, as he usually does: 'everyday' he would go with a 'squire or two, | And play him by the sea'.[41] The knight and his squires typically enjoy themselves at the seaside uninterrupted – but today is not like other days: 'A boat he found by the brim, | And a *glysteryng thyng* therein'.[42] Still wearing the gown, Emaré becomes a 'thing': she looks like shipwrecked treasure, miraculous washed-up cargo. The indefinite article locates the audience in Sir Kadore's perspective, not 'the boat' whose journey has been followed already, but a surprise encounter. Looking through the knight's gaze at an unidentified arrival – a '*ferly*', a marvel – the reader enters into Sir Kadore's gradual realisation that there is a person on the raft. The abandoned figure causes him '*gret dele*', a great sorrow. The gold cloth has saved Emaré's life, drawing attention to her when she is on the brink of death. Sir Kadore takes her home and Emaré – who has, for unclear reasons, temporarily changed her name to Egaré – ingratiates herself by teaching the Welsh 'to sew and marke | All manner of silken work'.[43] Emaré's ability to teach the Welsh to sew enables her to regain agency, her silk-work a marker of her civility, assuring the Welsh of her respectability. Guided by her silks, Emaré's integration into Welsh society is so successful that she marries the King and has a son, Segramour.

Silk-work is at once a token of craft and marvel, human labour and the supernatural. To some in Wales, the persistent alterity of the cloth remains a source of fear. Introduced to the Welsh court, the cloth shines so brightly that again Emare 'seemed *non erthly* thing'.[44] The Queen of Wales cries that she 'is a fiend, | In this *wordy wede*!'[45] The use of 'wordy' is a variant, Northern spelling of 'worthy', referring to the value of the dress. But it is hard not to read more into the chosen term. The gown is 'wordy': a complex text made in jewels, and travelling between multiple contexts. Emaré's gown remains a surface resistant to interpretation, a detachable threshold in the text.

These imagined scenes of the romance bear a complex relationship to those which occurred outside the text: imagination and reality are interwoven, one thread pulled over the other. This was a text produced and read among a mercantile audience with an in-depth knowledge of the silk trade and its wares – wares such as were woven and brought into historic coastlines, not only imagined beaches.

Fabricated Origins

In 1977, an excavation at 2–7 Duke's Place, London, EC3, revealed a collection of preserved objects from the precincts of Holy Trinity Priory, in Aldgate. The collection included nine fragments of lampas weave: a form of expensive double-weave, produced in the eleventh or twelfth century.[46] The fabric was still in use as vestments until the fourteenth century, when it disintegrated from centuries of use and was thrown away into the cesspit, in which it was preserved. These scraps of precious debris have survived through chance, and are valuable witnesses to the trade, use and re-use of imported fabrics. The pattern on the cloth has been carefully reconstructed from these nine fragments. The vestment was originally decorated with eight-pointed stars, each with radiating acanthus leaves and Arabic inscriptions. The Aldgate priests wore these cloths until their inscriptions started to fade – and the clay beneath East London rubbed away at their surfaces. Between each point of the stars, the Kufic letters are now debased, ambiguously legible as either *Allāh* [God] or *baraka* [blessing]. In constant use for nearly 400 years and then buried for 700, now the recovered text can be rearranged and restored to view, but cannot be read.

Touching the fabric carefully on a piece of acetate in a room above the Museum of London, the thread shimmered under the lights. Wanting to turn it over to see the back – if I pick it up, will the fabric tear? I asked the archivist, who looked over me and shrugged encouragingly as I warily raised the fragment which had survived for a thousand years between my fingers: the threads held. Fragile exile: this unlikely remnant.

In Aldgate, generations of priests took up these same vestments, repairing and recycling the silks to keep the past in active performance. The repeated Arabic motif and the plant ornamentation belong to a school of incised twills, many of which were produced in Syria, c. 1000. The lettering on this cloth more closely resembles Spanish imitations, suggesting that it was produced in an Islamic workshop in Spain.[47] The Arabic text of the lampas weave reached its destination of Aldgate, as part of a significantly altered world.[48] Made in Europe, imitating Syrian techniques, used in England, the silk drifts between times and places. Like the gown in *Emaré*, the excavated silk travelled between contexts, introduced into a Christian setting in which it became attributed with marvellous power.

In 1972, another excavation at Baynard's House, London, EC4, turned up a fragment of light pink lampas silk from another late fourteenth-century deposit, decorated with a spray of three flowers and cursive, non-linguistic script [Figure 3.2].[49] These woven 'letters' are found in no real alphabet. This design was highlighted with lichen dyes, rather than being woven into the design: an overt counterfeit. Placing it next to the Arabic-inscribed scrap of vestment on the table at the Museum of London, the difference in quality was reflected in the intensity with which these two fragments caught the light. Where the Arabic-inscribed design gleamed, this pseudo-Arabic script was dulled: a clear counterfeit.

This scrap of a faux-Islamic textile was found near the harbour of medieval London. The excavation of the fabric near the London docks locates this item in close proximity to the trade networks which facilitated its existence. Pseudo-Arabic script was a popular design feature in Italian fabrics of the period: European artefacts which sought to embed themselves in the world of Islamic art.[50] These cloths – painted and excavated – show the imitation of Arabic script, or the use of Arabic-inscribed material for an audience to whom Arabic was illegible but attractive. Lisa Monnas has suggested that this rise of pseudo-Arabic inscriptions on textiles in the Latin West was linked to a Christian association between Arabic and the Holy Land. By the late medieval period, it had become commonplace for saints' robes to be embellished with Arabic-style inscriptions in European paintings.[51] At one level, the style was tied to a view of Arabic as a Christian

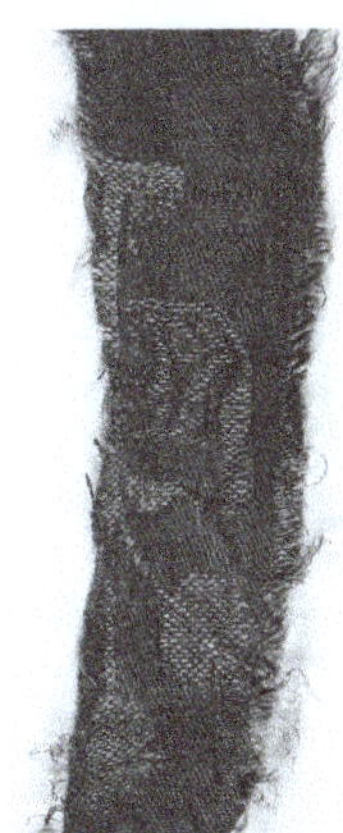

Figure 3.2 Pseudo-Kufic design, Museum of London. Source: Museum of London, London. TB91[55]<1645/15>. Printed with permission of the Museum of London.

language which was used to reinforce the crusader belief in the rightful Christian possession of Syria.

But for the majority of the time during which these silks were in use, the Christian possession of Syria – like the pseudo-language on the fabrics – was a visible fabrication. Like the jewelled stories on the cloth in *Emaré*, it is hard to read these embroidered Arabic-style scripts on Christian cloths. That is: both literally and conceptually, it is difficult to decide what they mean.[52] The crusades were a period both of heightened ethno-religious division and intense transference between cultures: these contractions filtered through into the aftermath.[53] Imitative designs rendered the lands from which silk-making techniques originated visible to their medieval viewer, albeit though a distorted lens.[54] While the Pseudo-Arabic texts on cloths were being constructed, manuscripts were being translated from Arabic into Latin into English: borrowed words, re-fashioned inexactly in English. As archival objects, these cloths feel very different from medieval books. Unlike the strong skins of animals or the pressed fibres of paper booklets, these threads felt risky to touch, breakable. I felt how easily they could fall apart in my hands – the result of the way in which they had been worn-out and discarded.

In *Emaré*, the Emir's daughter's cloth was looted, brought from 'hethenesse' to Sicily, before being cast adrift and washing up in Wales. Abro taughe Emaré to make silks, and Emaré then teaches silk-making to the Welsh. These fictive Welsh-made silks can be seen as pseudo-Arabic cloths, inauthentic, hovering between unknown places. When Emaré weaves her own silks, she aspires to reproduce the products of an Arabic-coded elsewhere which she has never visited. The silk which Emaré wears is unavoidably precious: bright, dazzling. The silks which she makes are never described within the text: the unremarkable products of local craft. Emaré never makes herself a gown like the Emir's daughter's stolen creation. Appropriated and deconstructed, these cut and recycled cloths haunted the coasts on which they are found, preserving alternative narratives from within their new frames.

Dreaming of Crusade, Funding the Silk Trade

In the romance *The Squire of Low Degree*, the King of Hungary is still trying to comfort his daughter, who grieves her low-born lover. The Squire – as the reader knows – has made his way to Jerusalem, but the Princess is unaware that he is alive. She sobs while her father promises that she can ride to church on a red velvet chair, with cloths of fine gold wrapped 'all about your head', with white and 'asure blue' damasks all 'dappled' with 'lilies new'.[55] The lilies dappled across the surface of the damask cloth recall the fleurs-de-lys used in English crusading and nationalist iconography from the time of Edward III. The Hungarian court is inflected with the medieval English context in which the story was performed.

The King tells his daughter she shall go to evensong, to see priests dressed in 'copes of damask bright', to witness ceremonies performed at an altar clothed in 'taffata'.[56] Like those preserved in historical records, this chapel is presented as a site of luxury, strewn with precious Eastern fabrics. The quantity of stuff is used to emphasise the financial power of the Christian court. Although the scene is of religious ritual, the gaze is on the material. The expensive accoutrements of the royal priests are themselves the focal point and source of comfort. The reader is invited to dwell on the surfaces of these fabrics. In church – both in private wills and in popular romance – the imagination was drawn towards the marketplace.

The will of Elizabeth de Burgh, lady of Clare (1295–1360), provides a vivid document in which the dream of crusade coexists with the realities of the silk trade. Elizabeth was the niece of Edward II and founder of Clare College, Cambridge.[57] In her will, made on 25 September 1355, Elizabeth dispersed her extraordinary collection of silks around the churches of the South East of England: bequeathing more than thirty cloths of gold, camacas, samites, and satins in bright hues of indigo, gold, red, blue, and white.[58] She also included the following challenge:

> Item I bequeath 100 marks in order to find five men-at-arms for the Holy Land to be given to anyone who would be faithful and suitable who wishes to take up the duty, if a common expedition is mounted within seven years of my death, to be devoted to the service of God and the destruction of His enemies, for the souls of my lords, Sir John, Sir Theobald, Sir Roger, and mine.[59]

Militarism is tempered by scale: five soldiers could not recapture the lost territories. The primary aim, as with the squire's mission in *The Squire of Low Degree*, must be the deaths of individual non-Christians. There is a grim fascination in the details of Elizabeth's plan: the specification of a time-limited offer; the vision of the crusade as possessing direct salvific potential for four solitary, named aristocrats. The logic of resettlement is abandoned in favour of these scattered deaths. The silk-strewn chapel was a site in which these missions were planned. The explicit ideology of her will reframes these objects as imagined loot or relics as surely as embroidered symbolism could do. The value of Elizabeth de Burgh's silks points towards the essential contradiction inherent in her bequests, in which silks are presented as salvific, whilst the makers and traders of those silks are called to be murdered.

Elizabeth's understanding of the position of her Christian silks in a wider marketplace is visible in her bequests of church vestments as settlements of private debts: a long list of camacas and silks are recorded for this purpose.[60] The movement of church silks out of the chapel and into the bank recalls the circulation of Elizabeth's considerable finances within interfaith networks of trade and exchange. Elizabeth herself was undoubtedly aware of these networks. She moved to cosmopolitan Aldgate from the 1350s, and personally employed Bartholomew Thomasin, a Luccan-born spice merchant.[61] Her will sustains the hypocrisy of her ideology and her expenditure. Crusade and trade, salvation and wealth, dialogue and religious-racial division coexist in continuous contradiction.

The silks of the Holy Land became part of the texture of English Christianity, their rituals flooded with these imported fabrics. In other late medieval wills, gifts of silks to churches continue to figure, divorced from the explicit desire for crusade. In 1438, Richard Dixon left 'to the said chapel of *siscestre* . . . a *blak* cloth of Damask *sengill*'.[62] The Countess of Warwick in 1439 left 'all my *clothis* of gold, and *clothis* of *silke* . . . everyone I will the house of *Tewkesbery* have them, save my *Russet vellewet*, I will saint *Wynfryde* have'.[63] The gift of silks was one of the material ways in which the laity could leave their mark on the medieval church: especially significant in the case of laywomen, whose wider involvement was limited.[64] These silks record individual lives within regional English church communities, expressing the desire of the self for survival.

These were the economies of salvation. These personal collections were left to clerical treasuries in order to bring their original owners closer to God. Through the arbitrary survival of records, these now lost fabrics become verbal traces which memorialise their owners and the world in which they lived: not only the local spaces in which silks were displayed and acquired but the wider world from which those silks had travelled, remade into signs which could save the English soul. In private wills, these bequeathed silks remember acts of self-fabrication.

Continuing her commitment to Christian Syria, Elizabeth de Burgh's will records another gift: 'Item I bequeath to the Holy Land to help Christians to maintain the law of God, 6s. 8d.'[65] The bequest is farcical, so vague as to be impossible, meagre beyond belief in comparison to her huge possessions of international-profiting silks. The shillings and pennies are tokenistic: no recipient is named to act on behalf of 'the Holy Land'. The dream of crusade in Elizabeth's will is, in the end, in the service of her own salvation: an individual aim which might be fulfilled even if the Holy Land was out of reach.

Sleeping on Silks

As Elizabeth de Burgh dreamed of a futile crusade, she rested her cheek on silk sheets. Alongside the silks found around medieval churches, another site in which imported silks are frequently recorded is the bedroom. In her will, Elizabeth de Burgh left to her daughter Elizabeth Bardolf 'my bed of green velvet striped with red with . . . 1 kerchief of indigo samite . . . 1 great hall of worsted [*hangings*], the field tawny, with parrots and blue cockerels'. The scene is of secular luxury: a green and red striped velvet bed, set within a bedframe hung with indigo and tawny cloths, embroidered with multi-coloured parrots and cockerels. Elizabeth left two more silk beds to her granddaughters: 'Item I bequeath to my young daughter, Isabel Barfold, to help her marry . . . my bed of sendal, with a coverlet of ash-grey medley lined with minever' and 'to Agnes her sister to help her to marry . . . a bed of indigo of which the hangings and coverlet are of velveteen'.[66] The beds are dowries, but if the bribes succeed then they will become marital beds. Ash-grey and indigo silks and velveteens should 'help her marry': a worldly sounding phrase which lends an air of matriarchal candour to Elizabeth's description of her property and its benefits. Her voice echoes crisply from the page, reminding her progeny that her own death does not make her any less demanding of great-grandchildren.

Silks were slept on in religious as well as secular bedrooms. The last bed bequeathed by Elizabeth was a gift to the Sisters Minoresses at Aldgate of '1 bed of black tartarin with 8 hangings'.[67] Lying on black 'Tartar silk' sheets, these Aldgate nuns were couched in the cloths of a fantasy 'East'. These nuns in their black silk bed left no recorded reaction to the bequest. The bed moved from the secular bedroom to the nunnery, from a site of reproduction to a space of officially chaste devotion. 'Tartar silk' was used to make bedclothes for religious people across the medieval period. The priest Nicholas Sturgeon, in his will of 1454, left 'to my cousin John Frowyk, my bed of *grene sylke*, with the testour and canape ther-to, pale *tartyn* white and red'.[68] Sturgeon could hardly have been closer to the centres of the English church: he was canon of Windsor and the chaplain of Henry V on his campaign that culminated at the battle of Agincourt. On his death he was buried in the North Chapel of St Paul's Cathedral.[69] The silk beds found in religious contexts can be seen as an extension of the chapel: proximate to the spaces in which silks were used for rituals. In another sense, the chapel can be seen as an extension of these bedrooms: the site of fantasy and luxury.[70]

In *The Squire of Low Degree*, the King continues his promises to his daughter, still trying to comfort her for the apparent death of her low-born lover. He will give her a new bed: 'Your curtains of *camaca* all in fold ... | Curtains with *popinjayes* white and reed'.[71] Like the bed which Elizabeth de Burgh left to her daughter, this bed is decorated with parrots, polychrome. The otherworld of the Princess' bedroom will cause her to forget her troubles in this world. The sheets of the Princess' bed will be French-made 'clothe of Rayne'.[72] These are material, traded items. In that bedroom, 'A cage of gold shall hang aloft, | with *longe peper* fair burning, | And cloves that be *swete smellyng*'.[73] Surrounded by the scent of spiced incense from a gold burner suspended above her, the Princess should feel transcendent amidst this sensory aesthetic of aristocratic ostentation. But the sweet-smelling bedroom cannot make up for her longing for the absent lover.

In despair with grief, the Princess rejects all her father's gifts, and vows to become an anchoress. She cries: 'Fy on this world's vanity! | ... Farewell velvet and satin'.[74] All the sweet wines, spices, religious and secular silks which have been listed were not the Princess' dream but her father's. She only wants her squire. Luckily for her, he returns in miraculous circumstances – he has not really died, but only been away on pilgrimage, proving his worth. Her vow to give up velvet is unrealised. She gets it all: the boy and her silk bed. The description of these fabrics as part of 'this *worldes vanyté*' hangs in the air between the Princess and the King. The romance leaves the desire for Christian salvation and the possession of enormous wealth in continued, tense relation. These contradictory elements of medieval culture were carried between spaces and into the unconscious.

The Fabric of the Dream

As well as forming the materials of the bedroom, silks are often found within medieval dreams. Chaucer's earliest dream vision poem the *Book of the Duchess* (c. 1368) begins with an insomniac's desperate plea to anyone who can help him get to sleep. He promises to give: 'a feather-bed | Rayed with gold and right well clad | in fine black satin *d'Outremer*'. Striped gold and black, the precious bed will come with pillowcases made of 'cloth of Reynes'.[75] The image is situated in a detailed sense of the contemporary cloth trade, the marketplaces of Rennes, in France and 'Outremer' – the term for the former crusader settlements in Syria, still used to refer to the region.[76] Here the crusader-era term recalls not the desire for settlement but the desire for sleep. The satin bed is offered as a site of access to dreaming: the elsewhere within the self.

Chaucer's translation of the dream vision, the *Romance of the Rose*, takes place within an enclosed garden – a 'place spiritual'.[77] Now within the space of the vision, the reader is told that the garden has been planted by 'Sir Mirthe' with trees which he brought 'from the land of Alexandria'.[78] The grass is

> *softe* as any *veluët*
> On which man might his *lemman* lay,
> As on a *fetherbed* to *pleye*.[79]

The dream garden is described as being like a featherbed, velvety green grass inviting the lovers to 'play' together. The dreamscape collapses into the real site in which the dream is being experienced, blurring the distinction between wakefulness and sleep. The simile leaves the reader unable to rest fully on the fabric, half-aware of the grass which the velvet is used to describe. The metaphoric velvet bed hovers between the world and the imagination. The mind of the dreamer is lined with silks.

In Freud's study, the couch on which his patients lay for analysis was covered in a Persian rug, a gift from his cousin Moritz, who was a trader in 'oriental antiquities'. For Freud the fabric – like the archaeological objects which he collected – gave access to the 'buried unconscious'.[80] Marina Warner writes of Freud's rug as a 'magic carpet': woven by the nomadic Ghashgha'i tribe, the fabric is the bearer of narrative traditions which were illegible to the psychoanalyst in a literal sense, but which nonetheless became the basis for his understanding of the unconscious, as a site of patterned meaning.[81] These Chaucerian scenes can be seen as prefiguring that view of the European self: as a site which is articulated through the material and narrative traditions of 'foreign' fabrics. As the location of dreams, these imported textiles prompt fantasies which invite and resist interpretation. In medieval England, silks existed on the boundaries between material and immaterial space: between heaven and earth, between consciousness and unconsciousness, between here and elsewhere.

Laws against the Free Movement of Silks

In England sumptuary legislation codified the status of silks as foreign. These laws simultaneously attempted to fossilise existing social hierarchies and advocated commodity xenophobia in the prioritisation of

English cloths.[82] There is a common pattern between these regulations and the laws which divided sweet wines from non-sweet wines: the attempt to control the use and sale of these imported commodities is a feature of English treatments of Syriana. The first English sumptuary law mentioning silks was passed under Edward III, in 1363: 'for the Outragious and Excessive Apparel of divers People, against their Estate and Degree, to the great Destruction and Impoverishment of all the Land'.[83] The law reads as the encapsulation of aristocratic anxiety, forbidding 'Grooms, as well Servants of Lords' from wearing anything embroidered in or made of silk, and 'People of Handicraft, and Yeomen' from wearing anything 'of Silk by no way'. In addition, yeomen's wives were warned to wear 'no veil of Silk, but only of Yarn made within the Realm'.[84] While the law was quickly repealed, the Commons repeatedly petitioned for the reintroduction of sumptuary legislation, with an emphasis on silk, in 1379, 1402, and 1406.[85] Similar laws were enforced in Scotland: in March 1420, James I decreed: 'with the *avys* of the *hail parliament* . . . that *na man sall weir clathis of silk* . . . *bot* only *knychtis* [knights] and *lordis*'.[86] The fictional Sir Kadore becomes the legal archetype of the permitted silk-wearer.

On 25 November 1368, a group of London '*Silkwymmen*' delivered to the Mayor and the Alderman 'a bill complaining' that 'Nicholas Sarduche, Lombard, by his crafty and evil design, embraced all the silk which he could find for sale in London and refused to sell it for less than 18s . . . to the great damage of the said women and the whole realm'.[87] Marion Turner has described the petition as the making of an 'informal guild' or union.[88] Successfully connecting their collective demands to the idea of the 'Kingdom', the silk-women's bill was sent to King Edward III. Nicholas was called for questioning at the Court, and 'confessed that he had bought the aforesaid silk from Paul and Dyne, alien merchants, for further sale or transference for sale to foreign parts'. He 'threw himself on the mercy of the Court for his trespass'. The next Wednesday, 'the defendant was committed to prison'.

The London silk-women presented themselves as precarious. However, the historian Anne Sutton has traced the interrelationship of medieval London silk-women and merchants, and has shown that many of these craftswomen were among the wealthiest in their trade.[89] When the silk-women were subject to subordination within the trade, that was typically the result of their husbands' business models.[90] As Sutton writes, London was 'the major centre of the silk and mercery trade in England throughout the Middle Ages'; silks were sent from London across the markets of

England.[91] When these women grouped together against Nicholas the Lombard merchant, these were citizens with access to financial, royal, and administrative power, who used that power against a specific, immigrant subject. Like today, medieval English hospitality towards immigrant subjects was conditional: a fact which was reiterated through the courts, the prisons, and the tax system.

In 1463, the silk-women again petitioned against 'alien' merchants, resulting in the temporary restriction of imports.[92] The silk-women's simultaneous reliance on and hostility to imported goods can be seen as another instance of the fraught and contradictory ideologies of medieval England. These silk-women were working with both 'rawsilke' such as Sturmy's ship would have brought into Bristol and imported threads from Lucca, Venice, and Cyprus.[93]

When Edward IV passed sumptuary legislation once more in 1463, the law referenced the silk-women's petition:

> ITEM, it was showed in the said Parliament . . . by the silkwomen and spinsters of silk within the city of London, that divers Lombards and other Aliens Strangers, imagining to destroy their Crafts and all such virtuous Occupations for Women within this land . . . wrought Silk, Ribbands, and Laces, falsely and deceitfully.[94]

The statute stated that England was being impoverished through the import of goods 'from beyond the sea, as well by merchants strangers'; a long series of pre-made imported goods, including silks, were restricted, with the exception that in the case of their being shipwrecked, locals were allowed to sell them.[95] While imports were restricted ostensibly to protect the silk-women's craft, the law simultaneously forbade the majority of the population from purchasing the silk-women's goods. The wearing of damasks, silks, velvet, and even imitation velvet was restricted, showing that imitative fabrics were just as much of a threat as the authentic product.[96] Acts in 1465 and 1483 reiterated these regulations.[97]

The attempt to control the wearing of silk by the lower classes runs counter to the assumption that silk was affordable only by the minority. After the Black Death, with the rising of workers' wages among the survivors, and the growth of the Venetian Empire in the eastern Mediterranean, silk started to be within the reach of a wider market.[98] In combination with shifts of fashion which seemed to obscure the visible markers of rank, the availability of silk prompted moral and social panic. The crossing of hierarchies by silk-veiled yeomen's wives runs hand-in-hand with the crossing of national borders by the silks themselves. The legal protection of English wools as the correct attire for the non-elites in fact reveals the appeal of imported products across the spectrum of social backgrounds. Negley Harte has concluded, based on these regulations, that: 'Silk came to be a symbol of social mobility'.[99] In the terms of the silk laws, it is clear that silks symbolised mobility across a variety of frontiers: between England and abroad, and between social groups within England. The bill called for silk products to be worn only by the elite, and (following the demands of the silk-women) called for the routes which brought in silk to be closed. But people of all ranks and origins continued to wear whatever silks they could access, in fragments and ribbons.

Silks Retied in Context

The archetypal silk-belt-wearing, subversive late medieval heroine is Alison, of 'The Miller's Tale', last seen sticking her arse out of her window. Chaucer's Miller introduces Alison through a detailed description of her clothes. She wears a belt 'barred all of silk' around her apron, which is '*whit* as morning milk' (I. 3235–6). Her white smock is embroidered '*befoore* ... *behynde* ... *withinne and eek* [also] *withoute*', with a collar 'of coal-black silk' (I. 3238–4). The 'tapes' (ribbons) of her white cap are 'of the same suit as her collar'. She wears a broad silk headband 'set full high | And certainly, she had a *likerous* eye' (I. 3241–44). Alison is covered with silk trimmings, from her striped belt to her white dress embroidered with black thread, to her accessories. The teasing description of the embroideries wrapped around – and even inside – her dress creates an association between these silks and her sexuality. Alison's body is temptingly half-concealed from the reader. Her silks are couched in the terms of her domestic surroundings: white as milk and black as coal. The eroticism of silks here is not the eroticism of a distant 'East', but of the proximate Oxford-dwelling woman – a threat to the social order. The silk-wearing wife of a rich carpenter was the precise target of the repealed 1363 act and its successors.[100]

The will of Thomas Bathe of Bristol attests to the possession of silk belts outside of the higher estates. In 1420, he left 'to Kateryne Lewys my servant ... another girdle of silk, of black and green and rede'.[101] The historical presence of silk belts on the waists of non-elite but socially mobile medieval women reinforces the availability of silks such as Chaucer's Alison displays in abundance. Alison's decorations are an expression not of the fantasised desire to exert Christian control over the Holy Land, but of her own autonomy. The same sumptuary legislation which prohibited non-elite silk-wearing simultaneously rejected the import of fabrics: social and cross-border mobility went hand-in-hand. Alison's aesthetic places her in an international scene, at the same time showing how silks gained new meanings for their local owners.

In Chaucer's tale Alison is never punished for her sexuality – her three male lovers all end up variously injured and humiliated, but she stays laughing: 'Tehee!' (I. 3740). Her ribbons retied, she is not exactly free – she is still married – but her body is trailing with silky fragments which move as she moves through her corner of the world.

Silken Ships and Shipwrecks

In the chests of Sturmy and Heyton's ships the *Cog Anne* and the *Katherine*, silks floated around the Mediterranean archipelago, their final destination redirected from Bristol to Libya by their new pirate captain. Late medieval texts conjure images of wonderful boats filled with silks, in romantic echoes of historic vessels. The fourteenth-century crusading romance *Richard Coer de Lyon* opens with Henry II's search for a wife. English messengers are sent out to sea, where they encounter a marvellous ship: 'such a one as they had never seen. The sail was utterly of samite, and her ropes of *Tuely* silk – all so white as any milk. That noble ship all without, with cloths of gold was spread about.'[102] The ship glows with precious fabrics, in a detailed picture of marine navigation: from sails to ropes. The boat belongs to King Corbaryng of 'Antyoche', travelling from Syria into the Mediterranean.[103] On board is King Henry II's future wife and the future mother of Richard I: Eleanor of Aquitaine, reimagined as an unnamed Syrian princess. As critics have noted, through imagining the Queen of England as a Syrian Princess, the text lends a reproductive genealogy to Richard I's crusading campaigns.[104] Draped in fabrics, the Syrian ship appears as a silken promise of the lands from which it has travelled. The white silk ship offers a vision of Syria travelling towards England as an array of irresistible fabrics, peaceful and available rather than militarised in impossible opposition.

In Malory's fifteenth-century *Morte Darthur*, a popular series of prose narratives about the Knights of King Arthur's Round Table, there is a comparable image of a silken ship, travelling unsolicited towards the Christian hero. In Book XIV of the Sankgreal quest, Sir Percival is travelling across '*the see*' when '*com a shippe saylyng toward hym*' and Sir Percival 'went unto the ship and found it covered within and *withoute* with white *samyte*. And at the bord stood an *olde man* clothed in a surplice, in likeness of a priest. . . . *What ar ye?* said Sir Percival. *Sir*', the old man replies, 'I am of a strange country, and hither I come to *comforte* you'.[105] Both the ship and the vestments of the priest-like man assert the affinity of these fabrics with the Christian knight. The image recalls the appearance of the Holy Grail itself, which presents itself invisibly to the gathered Knights of the Round Table: 'Then entered into the hall the *Holy Graile* covered with *whyght samyte*, but there was none that *myght* see it, nor whom that bare it. And there was all the hall *fulfylled* with *good odoures*.'[106] The grail manifests as a relic emitting incense, with the fabric as reliquary. These spiritual associations overlay the arrival of the ship, which blends material and immaterial implications. As with King Corbaryng's ship in *Richard Coer de Lyon*, this silken ship sails towards the Christian viewer, approaching of its own accord with promises of unsolicited aid. The man from 'a strange country' does not specify his origins. The image is that of a simultaneously commodified and transcendent sympathetic stranger, who will aid the Christian knights on their quest.

Silks from Coast to Coast

In *Emaré*, silks travel across the seas and back, new journeys overlapping with previous voyages. These multidirectional paths echo with the routes of the silk trade, revolving around one another. In Wales, Emaré's new mother-in-law conspires against her, and she finds herself once more at sea, now with her child beside her. Lying on the planks of the boat, Emaré buries her face in her sleeves, her 'wide' tunic.[107] These material details make the repurposed cloth of gold visible, in its medieval European style. The details of the planks remind the reader of the dangers of the journey: the water is 'wild' and she is 'afeard of the sea'.[108] She puts her breast in her child's mouth and sings to comfort him, praying – a Marian scene, as in Chaucer's lawyer's version. After seven nights, her boat 'was driven towards Rome'.[109] The boat washes up in Rome at the 'sea side': in the imagined geographies of this story, Rome is on the coast. The pull towards Christian resolution overwhelms known coastlines.

Emaré and her gown are recurrently imagined at the 'brymme': the edge-lands, ports, and harbours which were crucial contact zones for trade and migration. A merchant, Jordan, is walking alone along the Italian beach. Directly echoing Sir Kadore's discovery of Emaré in Wales, Jordan is shocked by the 'boat he found by the *brymme*'.[110] The replicated image creates a commonality of experience between Wales and Rome, through these brief, vivid snapshots of everyday life on the Welsh and Italian coastlines. Emaré is immediately welcomed into the home of the merchant,

Jordan, and his wife, and for seven years, she lives with them – as she did in Wales – sewing 'silk work' in her bedroom.[111] If the merchant Jordan buys her threads and sells her wares, the economies of production are not mentioned. The biblically named Italian silk merchant would have been a familiar figure to the English merchants among whom the tale was read. The Christian heroine is pulled around the seas in her marvellous silks – and is met by a realistic inhabitant of the late medieval trading networks. These scenes ground Emaré's journeys from shore to shore: a fragile object in a boat. Collapsing the difference between Wales and Rome, both are the sites in which silks arrive, are traded, and are remade.

Emaré's gown is a constructed garment and a silken ghost, a stranger which seems to use its powers to aid the Christian heroine but which remains a 'ferly', a marvel, not necessarily reassuring in its presence. The tale draws towards its conclusion. In Wales, the King still grieves his absent wife – 'his lady white as foam', a metaphor which recalls both an emergent racial discourse of whiteness, and the journeys of the sea-washed heroine.[112] He hires shipmen to take him to Rome for penance, and the Welsh set off: they 'drew up their tackle', a technical phrase which acts as a reminder of the tale's performance in houses around harbours.[113] For this providential journey, the wind is calm: they 'sailed over the salt foam | Through the grace of God in throne'.[114] Described as '*fome*', the surface of the sea is less threatening than the depths, a shifting, light texture. In Middle English, the word is associated with instability, a transitory object – the shore. Silks and coastlines alike are foamy, frothy, and shifting.

Gathered in Rome, the cast are unanimously reconciled. The King of Wales takes his lodgings at Jordan's house, where Emaré has been living. A joyful meeting! Finally her father the Emperor – now an old man – repents that Emaré, 'so bright of skin', had been 'put into the sea', and he too determines to go for Rome, where he is forgiven.[115] Although the tale draws towards Christian unity, the resolution of the tale is swift, the action brief in comparison to the scenes of travel, and the wonder of the silk cloth. It is the gown, glittering and dangerous, which is preserved in the reader's mind.

The difficulty of reading silks caused some English viewers to transform their bright surfaces into mirrors, seeing their own desires reflected back to them: from the Christian resettlement of Syria to self-understanding. Settling in coastal spaces, medieval silks resist being bound to one stable location – they remained relics of the past and witnesses of the present.[116] The Syrian fabrics which crossed the Mediterranean to reach England floated alongside Syriana and Pseudo-Arabic textiles. These silks spoke their own languages and no languages, embroidered with an unintelligible script which reaches towards an imagined elsewhere without the option of return. These fabrics continued to fray and unravel as they travelled across cultures – and continued to unravel the contexts in which they arrived. Tied around Alison's waist, washed up on the imagined coastlines of Wales and Rome, medieval silks were signs on the move.

Coda: Medieval Silks in Postcolonial Museums

Westminster Abbey now has a museum space: the Queen's Diamond Jubilee Galleries, located in the thirteenth-century triforium. The objects on display include the *Liber Regalis*, a fourteenth-century guide to royal funerals and coronations, and surviving medieval funeral effigies, as well as the Westminster Retable. The Retable was the altarpiece in Henry III's Abbey. After the Reformation, it was discarded – and was eventually found on top of a cupboard in 1725, after which it was kept in the Jerusalem Chamber until 1902. There are also medieval silks and jewels on display: a few thirteenth-century taffeta seal bags; a scrap of red silk made c. 1377, from Edward III's funeral effigy; a piece of purplish-blue silk from Henry V's saddle, c. 1422; a piece of yellowish-brown silk damask, c. 1500, woven with sunrays and flowers, of Italian origin, imitating Islamic designs.[117] These fragments witness the monarchy and church self-fashioning its identity and its rituals from transnational cloths, precious commodities from economic and political centres located elsewhere. These objects look out of place in the present-day Abbey, which self-articulates as a national and global centre: the site of Nelson's effigy. These remains tell a narrative which is difficult to piece together in this space. They recall a history of premodern marginality, imitation, and appropriation, failing to provide a stable lineage for the nation, but presented as if they do.

The architecture of the Victoria and Albert Museum recalls its origins as a governmental state department, part of the project of the British Empire. In the nineteenth century, the display of objects from the colonies became a public way of confirming the idea of the capital as the centre of the Empire.[118] The 'Islamic Middle East' gallery is on the ground floor, adjoining 'Asia' and the gift shop – while the room for the European 'Medieval and Renaissance' is in the basement. The segregation of the galleries speaks to the Orientalism of the museum's design – dividing 'East' and 'West', 'Europe' and 'Islam'. The medieval collections are badly contained by these labels – mobile silks resist their categorisation in either room.[119] One Christian chasuble made from Mamlūk silks is kept upstairs – while the 'Clare Chasuble', which is made from Iranian *kanzi* fabric and with a similar border of green leaves, is downstairs – so that they cannot be seen side by side.[120] These premodern objects remember overlapping routes and transnational histories which now have to flow through the gift shop and down the stairs, against the narrative of the museum.

CHAPTER 4

Jewels / English Possession and the Unpossessable

The 300 chests which Sturmy used to transport fabrics also held '*rynges* and precious *stonys*, coral'.[1] Physically and conceptually, these commodities were wrapped with silks, gleaming within Sturmy's collection for sale. In the list of lost goods, Sturmy's stones appear in the middle of the sequence of textiles, following 'baudekyns, purses' and immediately preceding 'rawsilke'. Imported jewels were often sewn to silks. On arrival in England, these fabrics and stones formed a glittering scene. Jewels were both revered as relics themselves, and used as the adornments of reliquaries.

The geological origins of stones meant that Christian claims to their ownership became implicated in the idea of the Holy Land as physical, possessable land – not unlike the way in which archaeological evidence continues to be implicated in colonial claims to settlements today.[2] Medieval fantasies of the extraction of jewels from imagined non-Christian owners – whether griffons or Jews – reveal the desire at the foundations of the 'Englished' category of Syriana: the desire for Syria, as lost territory. Found in dream visions, lapidaries, travel writings, saints' lives, poetry, and drama, Syrian-traded stones became surrogates, fragmentary debris of vanished control.

As seen in Sturmy's inventory, the category of medieval jewels also included non-geological substances, like coral and pearls. Pearls were part of a category of medieval stones which were viewed as animalistic. Such stones were described as sexed, able to procreate and give birth, and even as having souls.[3] The Mandeville author describes diamonds reproducing, like mammals.[4] A pearl is featured in the Aberdeen Bestiary.[5] Acting of their own accord, these stones articulate alternative narratives. Looted and sold, jewels continually evaded English possession.

O Pearl! Art Thou My Pearl?

Pearl, an anonymous fourteenth-century poem written near Chester, opens with a man looking for a lost jewel. 'Alas! I lost her in a garden' – the narrator tells us sorrowfully how the stone dropped 'through the grass into the ground'.[6] Often read as an allegory for a father who has lost his child, the poem is suffused with feelings of grief and longing for the absent object. Seen in the context of the aftermath of the crusades, the poem also dramatises English desire for the lost Holy Land. The narrator's feelings are at the surface of the text, expressed through verbal and body language. *Pearl* allows us to enter the state of post-Acre melancholia not just as an intellectual or political position, but as an emotional state: the painful limbo of unresolved mourning.

The narrator tells us how often he has waited in that spot where the pearl – 'my own' – sprang into the earth. Tormented, with a burning heart, he imagines the pearl is imprisoned and rotting. But the garden is warm – it is August, harvest season, and there are fragrant plants seeded throughout the grass, ginger and gillyflower. Suddenly taken with the perfumed air, the narrator '*slode*' – slid – into sleep, at the exact place where the pearl fell.[7]

The scene shifts from the flowering garden to a dreamscape: crystal cliffs, indigo-blue trees with burnished silver leaves, gravel made entirely of pearls. There is a sci-fi aesthetic to the colour combination of bright blue and silver – or at least it looks like that now. The dreamer enters a new world, where the usual rules don't apply, and nothing is exactly as it seems. Walking through the glowing blue forest, he arrives at a riverbank made of beryl, with a riverbed made of emeralds, sapphires, and other gems, glittering, he says, like stars in the night sky.[8] The water runs over these precious stones, untouchable. The trees and banks are transparent, like glass.

Pearl is by the same author who wrote the now more famous *Gawain and the Green Knight*; both texts are found in the unique Cotton Nero manuscript, now in the British Library. The manuscript contains four illustrations accompanying the text of *Pearl*, all of which include a representation of the river [Figure 4.1].[9] Using two contrasting hues of blue, the illuminator has drawn bold waving lines across the page, rendering flow. The artist also draws attention to the marvellous spice-plants growing in the garden, which are shown large beside the river. Located in a moving river, the jewels recall their journeys, like the silks previously seen in ships and strewn on coasts. The landscape is described like a textile: the crystal cliffs are compared to '*webbez* that wives weave', while the beryl riverbanks are called the '*dubbemente*', a word usually used to describe adornments on cloth.[10]

The dreamer's grief is gone, replaced with blissful gladness at having arrived (surely!) in heaven. But his desire remains – now, a desire to cross the river. Then a girl appears, dressed in a bright white dress. 'I knew her

Figure 4.1 The *Pearl* riverbank. Source: British Library, London. Cotton MS Nero A X.ii, fol. 42 r. Printed with permission of Bridgeman Images.

well, I had seen her before', the narrator confides, but can't immediately remember where.[11] He stares, open-eyed, lips pressed together, captivated by the sight. Her dress is embroidered with pearls from hem to sleeve, she wears a pearl-encrusted crown and – best of all – a 'wonder pearl' is set in the middle of her breast. Gazing at that perfectly round, spotless, and pure jewel, the dreamer is certain there has never been a 'gladder *gome*', a happier man than him.[12] '*O perle*', he says, 'Art thou my pearl?'[13]

As well as being interpretable as a bereaved father, the narrator of *Pearl* is repeatedly described within the text as a 'jeweller'. When describing his lost pearl, he tells us that it is superior to any 'out of the Orient' which he has seen when, at work, he '*jugged* gems' – when he weighed them, to test their value.[14] In a medieval context, the term 'jeweller' can refer either to the goldsmiths who worked with gems or to the merchants who traded them. As such, the critic Helen Barr argues that the narrator is 'cast as a mercantile figure'.[15] *Pearl* is explicitly set in the world of the jewel trade – but these financial contexts are combined with an intensely spiritual imagination of jewels. The question of whether or not jewels can be owned is central to *Pearl*, as the narrator attempts to reconcile economic and transcendent value.

So is the girl in his dream the pearl he has been looking for? 'That jewel' draws herself up, straightens her crown, and addresses the narrator 'soberly'. 'Sir', she tells him, 'You have misspoken, to say that your pearl is gone away – that is in this coffer so *comly* enclosed.'[16] Yes – she is his pearl! And thank God – she is safe, in a casket, in a collection, just like pearls should be kept. She rebukes him, 'gentle jeweller', for his earthly concern: all his grief has been for a 'mad purpose', a 'reason brief'.[17] He should not have concerned himself with worldly loss: he should have kept his mind on the eternal, where she is. She is now married to Christ.

In *Pearl*, the 'wonder pearl' is symbolic, said to be 'like the realm of heaven': a reference to Matthew 13. 45.[18] The girl reminds the dreamer of this biblical parable which, in her version, is about a 'jeweller' who 'sold all his goods, both wool and linen, to buy himself a pearl which was flawless'.[19] The retelling sets the parable in medieval English economic contexts. The merchant exchanges the primary English export good of wool for one imported pearl – just as Sturmy filled his ship with wools to exchange for goods in Chios.[20] This awareness of traded realities introduces a complexity to the passage, as commercial goods are exchanged for spiritual wares.

After the loss of his best pearl, the dreamer has been stuck, unable to accept the absence. The dreamer's desire to possess the pearl on earth sustains his search – from a rightful Christian perspective, this desire is shown to be futile.[21] The mercantile ownership of jewels is contrasted with their spiritual transcendence. But simply telling the dreamer to stop wanting to possess the pearl is not that effective. He calls her 'my sweet', 'that *lovesome*'. He experiences '*luf-longing*', love-longing. Even though he knows he should let her go – should accept that she is better kept within a divine treasury – should acknowledge that he could never really own her – he is still filled with desire to have her back in his own collection.

Medieval Treasuries

Before the Fall of Acre in 1291, the high-status pearl markets in Acre had been commonly visited by European travellers. The European fashion for pearls has been linked to cross-cultural contact in the Kingdom of Jerusalem.[22] Eleanor of Castile (1241–90), Queen of England as the wife of Edward I, recorded payments to Palestinian jewel merchants in her expenditure records of 1285–6.[23] Stones continued to travel to Europe from

Syrian marketplaces long after 1291: '*perles de Damascho*' appear in the 1377 Genoese customs records.[24] Sapphires, rubies, amethysts, pearls, and diamonds travelled from countries including Sri Lanka and Afghanistan, through Syrian jewel markets onto pilgrim vessels and merchants' ships, via Cyprus and Venice.[25]

Jewels were often imported to England by merchants who were themselves immigrants, such as the fifteenth-century merchant George Morsteyn of Kraków, who received a licence to import a ruby of 214 carats; Italian and Jewish merchants were equally crucial intermediaries in trade with the Levant.[26] First-hand knowledge of the jewel routes could be found in the goldsmiths' workshops of London and York.[27] In addition to these centres, gems were brought into Southampton: for example, sapphires are recorded in the port records for 1435–6.[28] Returning pilgrims also brought back traded items: Henry of Derby purchased a Balais ruby ring in Paris, in 1393, on his way back from Jerusalem.[29]

In England, these precious objects were collected in churches and the residences of the nobility. One of the most prized treasures of Westminster Abbey was the Ring of St Edmund: a relic 'decorated with one sapphire and eight ruby gems'.[30] Such jewelled rings were designed for personal touch and intimate possession.[31] Some jewelled rings were used to contain relics. The Thame Reliquary Ring (c. 1301–1400), found in Oxfordshire, is one such example: a large amethyst cut into the shape of a double cross, set over a one-inch box with an opening mechanism, originally used to hold a relic, engraved on the gold underside of the ring with a scene of the crucifixion.[32] Being engraved on the inside of the ring, the image was designed to be in direct contact with the wearer's skin. The power of the relic, and of the amethyst, is witnessed in this experience of touch.[33] Certain jewels were reserved for Bishops: one gold ring set with a sapphire is inscribed with the name William Wytlesey, Archbishop of Canterbury (d. 1374).[34] The Christian associations of jewelled rings are multifaceted, laden with ritualistic and personal significance.

In her will of 1355, aside from her bequests of silks, Elizabeth de Burgh left a goblet of beryl to Sir William de Wykkewane, and a cup of jasper to Richard de Kyngeston. To the Black Prince – the brother of John of Gaunt – she left a gold ring with a ruby. To the Countess of Pembroke, she left a gold cross with a sapphire in its centre, and a gold ring with a diamond. Above and beyond these gifts, to the Minoresses at Aldgate, she left a crystal reliquary, together with three clasps with a thousand pearls.[35] In 1439, the Countess of Warwick left her Balais ruby, stones, and pearls to be auctioned and the profits given to the church.[36] John of Gaunt – the father of King Henry IV – left his 'good ruby, and his best necklace with all the diamonds' to his wife in his will.[37]

The imaginative Christian possession of gems was reinforced by these historical instances of tangible Christian ownership in England. Stone-set rings, small and overtly precious, are one of the main survivals of medieval jewellery, in archaeological finds and museum collections.[38] But unlike silks, where imitative fabrics and scraps of ribbon made these items more accessible, instances of private gem-ownership beyond the monarchy and the church remained markers of the greatest wealth and status. In Chaucer's 'Miller's Tale', while Alison, the heroine, is decked with silk ribbons and belts, her purse is described as '*perled with latoun*', pearled with brass: there is an ironic emphasis on the contrast between the desired pearls and the actual embellishment (I. 3251). Glimmering treasuries juxtaposed jewels and saints' relics. The spiritual status of jewels was affirmed in these Christian collections. Gems allowed proximity to the divine, for those who could afford it.

At the same time, the jewels and silks which were on display in medieval churches across Christian Europe were presented as offerings to saints: not intended for earthly ownership. In twelfth-century France, Abbot Suger documented the renovations at St-Denis church, describing how so many jewels 'were brought to us for sale from nearly all the parts of the world (and, by the grace of God, we were also offered wherewith to buy them) that we should have been unable to let them go without great shame and offense to the Saints'.[39] These jewels are both seen as commodities, and as beyond commodification. God gives the 'grace' of financial independence, integrating divine grace into the mechanics of the market. The purchase of these precious items was a divine transaction: an act of display which negates the idea of possession. In a similar way, the jewels and silks displayed at Westminster Abbey were justified as the creation of a sacred contemplative space, in reverence for saintly power. In these medieval churches, while there was enormous wealth on display, these silks and jewels were presented within a discourse which still officially refuted earthly possession. All of these goods belong to Heaven.

Heavenly and Earthly Jerusalem

In *Pearl*, the dreamer is confused. From the way the girl describes her new home, it seems like she has come from Jerusalem, but these riverbanks and blue woods do not look like the landscape of Judea.[40] She explains the difference between the 'New' and 'Old' cities of Jerusalem: the 'olde Jerusalem' is on earth, but Jerusalem as described in John's Apocalypse is eternal. As she said before, there are three locations from which the Passion can be viewed: 'In hell, in earth, and Jerusalem.'[41] As he listens to her, the dreamer is rewarded with a staggering vision of the heavenly city, built entirely on a foundation of gems: Jasper 'glinting green', sapphire, calcydone, emerald, sardonyx, ruby, chrysolite, beryl, topaz, chrysoprase, jacinth, and amethyst.[42] This list of stones is taken directly from the biblical text of John's Revelation. The *Pearl*-poet constantly redirects the reader to that source: the 'Apostle John' runs as the refrain line, ending each stanza in this section of the poem.

In the Middle Ages, both imaginative and physical architecture was often based on John's Revelation, which provided both aspirational and practical images. Details of the measurements of the Heavenly Jerusalem were taken by architects as their sacred archetype for earthly construction. In both Revelation and *Pearl*, pearls adorn the gates of the city. In *Pearl*, these jewels are engraved with the names of the tribes of Israel.[43] This allusion to engraved gems is drawn from the book of Exodus, which describes the engraved stones on the ephod [sleeveless priest's garment] of the First Priest Aaron.[44] The walls of the city are translucent, lit from within by a lantern which shines brighter than sun or moon.[45] Dressed for the Apocalypse, Christ appears as a Lamb with seven horns, still bleeding from his side as he leads a procession of a hundred thousand maidens, identically dressed in pearl-embroidered clothes. Legions of angels throw incense. The Aldermen of Jerusalem fall to their knees. The entire gathering breaks into song.

Although the girl tries to draw a clear division between heavenly and earthly Jerusalem, in fact the two were constantly overlapping in medieval imaginations. No wonder the dreamer is confused: the jewelled foundations of the Heavenly Jerusalem could be purchased from marketplaces in the 'old' Jerusalem, which, although being described as 'old', was actually a present-day reality.

Lapidary Geographies

Medieval English lapidaries were highly popular texts: books which describe medicinal, biblical, and folkloric understandings of jewels. The lists of stones in Revelation and Exodus provided the structure for these encyclopaedic catalogues. The fourteenth-century London Lapidary begins, as is typical, by recalling the 'names of the twelve stones that god hath named to Moses the Prophet' and the 'names of the eleven stones that Saint John named'.[46] The author goes on to detail the properties of stones, beginning systematically with the stones of Exodus, and then continuing, meandering and filling in the remaining stones listed in Revelation, and other gems not covered in either biblical text, like magnets.[47]

Medieval lapidaries record the geographies of the jewel trade, both real and imagined. Recopied around the British Isles, these texts were written by anonymous authors whose voices remain audible in their variant spellings. The North Midlands lapidary discloses that 'Ruby is *fund* in the *lond* of *leby*' (Libya) in the river of Paradise. The author refers back to their source: the '*buk* of *Moyses*'.[48] The London Lapidary author comments that Beryl 'cometh of the land of *Inde*' (India) as the 'bible witnesseth'.[49] The North Midlands lapidary goes on to catalogue stones ranging from chrysolite, which 'comes of the *lond* of *Ethiope*' (Ethiopia), to 'Ematite' (Hematite, or Bloodstone), which might be found in '*Aufryke* or of *ethyope* or of *Arabe*' – Africa, Ethiopia, Arabia.[50] These texts slip between continents, countries, and imagined lands: the global as seen from an English margin.

Chaucer considers the realities of the jewel trade in a short lyric, 'The Former Age'. The poet cries, with a touch of irony:

> cursed was the *tyme*, I dare *wel seye*,
> That men first did their sweaty business
> To *grobbe* up metal, *lurkinge* in *derknesse*,
> And in the riveres first *gemmes* sought.[51]

The mined metal and the sieved gem place the miraculous jewelled river in its economic contexts. There is a stark contrast between the darkness of the mine and the bright clear water evoked in the jewelled river. The 'cursed' action of seeking gems for profit is a far remove from their elevated, spiritual transcendence as washed from Paradise. At the same time, the spiritual significance of the gems forms the basis of their commercial value.

In these poetic and practical texts, the location of gems in rivers implies both their spiritual and their natural existence, their globalised movement and their rightful Christian possession. While these rivers gesture to the realities of jewel extraction and the mobility of the trade, the source was still thought to run from Paradise.

The Griffons Guarding the Land of Syria

The London Lapidary entry for Emerald begins: '*Emeraulde* surpasses all the *grenesses of grenehede*' – a colour beyond the greenness of greenness.[52] The finest examples 'come out of the land of Syria' – and Saint John 'saith in the Apocalypse that Emerald is the first stone under the true Kingdom'. So far as expected: green and biblical. The author goes on:

> & Saint John also tells us that beasts which are called griffons guard the emerald on the *flom* [river] of Paradise in the land of Syria; and that beast has four feet . . . two wings like an eagle & a backside like a lion; & a people who are named *aropiles*, who have only one eye in the middle of the forehead, come to seek the emerald, all armed on the water, and take them, and the aforementioned beasts come running and flying . . . and much *anguisshen* [the aropiles], & hard it is to take the emeralds.[53]

There is no biblical source for the tale of the griffons and the emeralds, although John's account of the Apocalypse is dramatic enough to make his appearance as the source of this episode believable. The North Midlands author tells the same story, also attributed to Saint John and located in Syria; the main difference is that the 'aropiles' are called 'Arimples'.[54] These one-eyed people look at first glance like premodern racial caricatures – and in a sense, they are. But they are also, the London author says, 'true Christian men. The griffons signifieth the devils to whom they fight against.'[55] The North Midlands author says that although they have 'bot one Ee, it is to Jesus Christ' and the griffons 'betoken the fiends'.[56]

The attempted theft of the emeralds by the Aropiles/Arimples is presented as sanctioned looting: the rightful repossession of Christian stones, from evil beasts. In neither text do the Christians succeed in stealing the stones – the fight is too difficult, and though the Christians are armed, the griffons are stronger. The medieval English reader is invited to identify with the Aropiles/Arimples. The vision is that of a varied, global Christianity founded on the idea that Christian property must be reclaimed. The scene reads as a melancholic metaphor for the Mamlūk 'occupation' of Syria, the griffons standing in as figures for the undefeatable Muslim Empire, guarding a region which the poor Christians cannot recapture, despite their rightful possession of both the land and its jewels. 'And al these things *mot* [must] have in mind, he that will bear any emerald', ends the North Midlands author's description.[57]

The original Anglo-Norman source for these lapidaries does not locate emeralds in Syria, but in 'Sithie' – Scythia, in Central Asia.[58] Some English translators stayed faithful to that tradition – the encyclopaedist John Trevisa states that emeralds are from '*Scitica*'.[59] But the majority of scribes changed the origins of emeralds as they copied their source into English: erasing 'Scythia' to set the scene in Syria. Besides the North Midlands and the London lapidaries, another late medieval translation of the Anglo-Norman lapidary promises that emeralds come 'from the Stream of

Paradise and from Syria. Those of *Sirie* are the best.'[60] Another late fifteenth-century translation agrees that the emeralds which 'come from Syria are better and a more gentil colour'.[61] The Peterborough lapidary locates emeralds in 'the land of *tyre* by a water of paradise', still recording the griffons as guarding the stones 'in the land of Syria'.[62] Tyre was the historic entry point to the settlements, so travelling from Tyre into Syria recalls the journeys taken by crusaders. These anonymous lapidaries show medieval scribes across England making emeralds part of their imaginative geography of Syria – along with the devils who currently stand over the river, in defiance of Christian soldiers.

Christian Jewels after Acre

In Mandeville's *Travels*, the Holy Land produces its own relics, in the form of gems. Approaching the port of Tyre, our guide discloses: 'there was sometime a fair city of Christian men, but *Sarasyns* have destroyed it in great part and they guard that haven right well for *drede* that they have of Christian men'. Sir John claims, with deflated bravado, that the destroyed city is guarded because of fear – that the victorious 'Saracens' remain terrified of the Christians whom they have defeated. It is a paradigmatic instance of post-Acre melancholia: unable to reconcile himself with the loss of the port of Tyre, Sir John dwells instead in the comforting fantasy of Christian dominance. The self-named knight goes on to reveal that: 'Upon that sea side men may find many rubies.'[63] The Christian pilgrim can find solace for the loss of the crusader kingdoms in the continued prospect of gem-gathering. The presence of rubies on the coast of Syria seems a miraculous confirmation of the true Christian identity of the land.

Mandeville's *Travels* was a significant source of information and narratives about jewels: one French lapidary was attributed to John Mandeville. Although there is little evidence to suggest the authorship is authentic, the attribution indicates that Mandeville's gem-lore was taken seriously. One fifteenth-century manuscript of this work includes a striking miniature of a gem-dealer's shop [Figure 4.2].[64] On the shop counter, jewels are being examined – and in the background, through the open doorway, a miner raises his pick-axe to chip the precious objects from the stone. Locating the jewel shop at the edge of the mine shaft, the labour of production is made part of the scene of exchange. Marvellous geographies absorbed, instead of erasing, these known realities.

In Christian tradition, the ruby held particular significance, associated with martyrdom, the Virgin Mary, and Christ. Mandeville's claim to have seen

Figure 4.2 A gem-dealer's shop. Source: Bibliothèque Nationale de France, Paris. MS Fr. 9136, fol. 344 r., detail. Image permission granted under Creative Commons Zero (CC0) Open Access License.

rubies along the coast of the former Christian territories is in line with these lapidary traditions, locating the Christian symbolism of jewels in a post-Acre imaginative geography. Making his way inland towards Acre, Sir John finds:

> The *fosse of Mynoun* . . . is all full of gravel shining, of which men maketh good, clear glass. And men cometh from afar with ships and with carts by land to take of that gravel. And though if there be never so much taken on one day, on the morrow it is as full as ever it was, and that is a great marvel . . . And some say that it is a *swolough* [chasm] of the gravelly sea.[65]

The divine agency of the sand, miraculously replenishing itself in glittering glass, witnesses its own God-given properties. The appearance of jewels in the very location of the last crusader settlement reinforces the gleaming spiritual associations of the rubies. The reference to the 'gravelly sea' is expanded later on in the *Travels*. Sir John travels through a valley in the land of the Christian King Prester John, in India, where he sees: 'a great *flode* that cometh from paradise, and it is full of precious stones and no drop of water. And it runneth with great waves into that gravelly sea.'[66] The waterless river rises in waves and runs smoothly through the hills. The constant association between gems and water has resulted in the transference of the properties of the river to the jewels themselves. Appearing as a chasm of the Paradisiac waterless sea, the fosse of Menon is simultaneously miraculous and marketable. The Mandeville author lays emphasis on the ships and carts in which the glass is transported away.[67]

After the fall of Acre, glass vessels continued to be transported by merchants and individual pilgrims from Jerusalem, as souvenirs.[68] The term 'acrische' was used in Europe to describe both glass made in Acre and glasswork imitating Acre-style craft.[69] Syria was specifically known as a centre of glass production, exporting both glassmaking techniques and finished products.[70] Damascus glass held a specific status: 'Damas' provenance became a general term for Mamlūk glass.[71] The heights of the Syrian glass industry were recorded in Arabic by Ibn Jubayr and al-Qazwīnī as well as in Hebrew by Benjamin of Tudela.[72] This fame was truly global: as well as passing into Europe through Venetian ports, a number of fourteenth-century Syrian glass objects made their way to China, leading Atil to conclude that 'Mamluk pieces were cherished not only in the West but in the East as well'.[73] The Venetian glass industry had its origins in materials and techniques transmitted from Syrian makers. The movement of glass from Venice to England is witnessed by a number of artefacts now in the Museum of London. Several fragments of glass wine beakers (dated c. 1290–1325) were excavated in the goldsmiths' quarter of London, signed by their maker Bartholomeus; there are contemporary references to a glass maker of the same name working in Venice.[74]

Mandeville's reimagination of transnational objects as relics, associated with the divine produce of a miraculous chasm near Acre, was a way of increasing their devotional status. These narratives allowed for the continued conception of the Holy Land as a self-evidently Christian territory, glimmering with naturally originating relics, only temporarily governed by powerful Others.

Judeo-Muslim Sources of Christian Lapidaries

These Christian frameworks for jewels were complicated by the fact that medieval English authors constantly referred back to Arabic sources for gem-lore: these lapidaries rested on non-Christian knowledge production.

The most widely circulated Latin lapidary was written by Marbode, Bishop of Rennes, surviving in over 160 manuscripts, at least thirty-three of which were present in England.[75] Marbode's text was translated into a range of languages, including from Latin into Hebrew by Berakhyah ben Natronai Ha-Nakdan, a twelfth-century Jewish author who lived either in England or France.[76] Marbode also composed a Christian symbolic lapidary, and a minor lapidary focusing on the twelve stones of Revelation.[77] But Marbode's most popular work begins with a series of letters, which claim to be those sent by King Evax of 'Araby' to the Roman Emperor Tiberius.[78] King Evax was a fictional authority; once fabricated, his 'letters' circulated widely in medieval Europe. One twelfth-century French edition of the letter from Evax to Tiberius made its way to Worcester Cathedral Library.[79] In the London Lapidary, the anonymous author attributes material to 'Evax, that was King of Arabie'.[80] The Peterborough Lapidary presents itself as the work of 'Evax', beginning:

> This is the book that Evax king of Arabe sent to Tiberius of Rome, of all manner of precious stones as well as of their names, virtues and of their colours and the countries that they can be found in.[81]

'This is the book': in your hand, reader – the manuscript gestures to itself as a material object, using that sensation of touch to encourage the imagination of a physical object which had travelled across the seas. Rooted in the realities of transnational manuscript transmission, the image of a book travelling from 'Arabe' to Rome sets the scene in a context of exchange and ancient dialogues. Although 'Evax' might be an error, and 'Araby' a fantasy, the figure was based on medieval knowledge of Arabic translations.[82] In the Peterborough Lapidary, the 'stones of *Avycene*' are cited as a source used to reinforce the book of 'Evax'.[83] Ibn Sīnā's theories of the formations and properties of stones were recorded in his foundational medicinal tract the *Kitāb al-shifā'* [Book of Healing].[84] Other known sources for medieval gem-lore include Jābir ibn Ḥayyān, Ibn al-Bayṭār, al-Rāzī, al-Ghāfiqi, al-Tamīmī, al-Dimashqī, and Ibn Māsah.[85]

In *Pearl*, the dreamer marvels at the flawless pearl. 'Not even Aristotle', he says, 'Described the nature of these properties'.[86] Aristotle's *Book of Stones* survives in three Arabic and two Hebrew manuscripts, as well as two incomplete Latin translations.[87] The claim that the original *Book of Stones* was by Aristotle is disputed – but the Arabic and Hebrew translators of the text are known. The 'Abbasid-era scholar Qusta Ibn Lūqa of Baalbek (820–912) translated the text: his version was one of the sources for Bishop Marbode's lapidary.[88] The Persian scholar al-Bīrūnī (973–1048) extended the *Book of Stones* in his *Kitāb fī al-jawāhir* [*Book on Stones*]. Al Bīrūnī's work was translated into Latin and exported to medieval Europe.[89] In his *Book on Stones*, Al-Bīrūnī includes a specific chapter on pearls, in which he associates pearls with virginity and purity.[90] Referencing the *Book of Stones*, the *Pearl*-poet signals their knowledge of Arabic-transmitted lapidary science.

The *Pearl*-poet claims that even Aristotle did not describe the ultimate pearl – but there was an Arabic legend which resonates more closely with the dreamer's image. In Arabic traditions, there was a world-renowned pearl, famed for its perfection: al-Yatīma [the Orphan]. Al-Yatīma was associated with the holy shrines of Damascus, and was part of the 'Abbasid royal insignia: disseminated on royal stamps which reflected and increased its fame. By the twelfth century, the legend of the Orphan stone had reached medieval Europe; Avinoam Shalem comments that reports were likely brought home by crusaders.[91] There is no proven link between the legend al-Yatīma and the 'wonder pearl' worn by the girl in *Pearl*, but the resonance is unmistakable. The imagined jewel in *Pearl* aspires to the status of the Orphan: reaching towards the shrines of Damascus, and beyond to the Heavenly Jerusalem.

'Margerye', the word often used in Middle English to mean pearl, is derived from the Greek 'margarite', which itself is drawn from Sanskrit 'maracata' or Persian 'merwārīd', and which has an extremely close companion in the Hebrew 'margalit'.[92] The multilingual 'margery-perle' was the product of an interfaith world of trade and translation, dialogue and exchange. But the awareness of these realities did not prevent the 'margery-pearl' becoming an icon of Christian control in the Holy Land.

Margaret of Antioch: A Christian Pearl in Syria

In the retelling of the life of Saint Margaret of Antioch by the Augustinian friar Osbern Bokenham, the name of the saint is used to draw out a comparison between the martyr – a fifteen-year-old child – and a pearl. He writes: 'Of saint Margarete, the virgin pure, | which likened is to a precious *margaryte*'.[93] The image of the saint-as-pearl is repeated:

> And conveniently, this virgin glorious
> May to a *margaryte* compared be,
> Which is white, little, and also virtuous.[94]

The 'virtues' of the stone become the 'virtues' of the saint, recalling the idea expressed in the London Lapidary that God 'hath put vertu in stones'.[95] The medicinal property of the pearl to amend bloody 'flux' stands for

Margaret's heavenly power to withstand torture. The ability of the pearl to be 'a comfort | to man's spirits' connects with Margaret's '*clennesse*', her curative purity.[96] The interpretation of stones as relics did not require a forgetting of their scientific contexts or traded histories, but a reimagining of these origins with Christian significance.

Imprisoned and tortured for refusing to worship pagan idols, Margaret explains to her tormentors that these 'false gods' are nothing but 'stones or tree, | That neither go nor move, speak, hear, nor see, | Formed by man'.[97] The capacity of stones or saints to act identified them as Christian subjects, carefully distinguished in relic discourse from the lifeless idols worshipped in non-Christian contexts.[98] The author establishes a binary: between agential Christian relic and passive non-Christian idol. In another narrative, Bokenham represents St Christina – born like a 'precious stone' in 'foul earth' – as a violent iconoclast: taking 'hir father's gods' she 'broke into pieces many one, | And by a window let them down fall'.[99] The inability of the idols to protest alone proves their absence of divinity.[100] The logic of repossession is clear: as soon as a stone proves its agential worth, it becomes Christian in identity – and therefore in property.

The life of Saint Margaret in Bokenham's account is followed by a detailed description of the movement of her relics from Syria to Europe, after her death: 'of saint Margarete the *translacyoun* | From Antioch was made into Italy'.[101] Bokenham's own task, in writing saints' lives, is to 'translate'.[102] Along with relics, literary translations moved from Antioch to Italy – this transference of knowledge is recalled in the subtext of this moment.[103]

In the life of St Margaret, the relics of Saint Margaret are rediscovered 'in a silver vessel, with gems freshly | Arrayed'.[104] This Syrian reliquary is the original container. Jewelled reliquaries in medieval Europe were constructed along these lines, aspiring to be taken for Holy Land craftsmanship. But in this narrative, the gem-encrusted reliquary is discarded in favour of a humbler container – to keep the relics hidden, safe from thieves. Throwing away the jewels, the saints' bones are preserved.

To visit the relics of St Margaret, Bokenham says that the reader should travel – not to Syria, not to Italy – to Suffolk, to his own local church. In the prologue of his text, Bokenham advertises that his parish church (thought to be Bookham) possesses a relic of St Margaret. Specifically, pilgrims can come to see the saint's 'one foot', which 'through a *cristal* bright and pure | Men may behold each feature | Thereof'.[105] The decaying foot can be viewed through a crystal panel – the debris of a saintly pearl presented behind holy glass.[106] He tells us that the foot has demonstrated its power through 'many a miracle'.[107] In exerting its Christian powers of healing, the foot witnesses its rightful movement from Syria to England.

The friar advises his reader that a pilgrim can 'specially' benefit from the relic of St Margaret, if 'with broach or ring | The foot men touch'.[108] Wearing a brooch made holy through touching the foot (that is, through touching the crystal around the foot), the pilgrim will protect themselves from spiritual and physical harm. Placing the ring onto their finger, the pilgrim will feel the sacred aura of St Margaret's toes: the power of the foot which has travelled from Antioch and is now kept close, worn on the hand.

In a post-Acre world, access to these prized Christian jewels was often mediated through contact with Muslim and Jewish traders. The awareness of this fact was a source of extreme anxiety for some medieval authors. The precious Christian contents were at risk of being tainted by their origins, unless those origins were avidly rejected or reframed.

Removing Rubies from Jews

Chaucer's Prioress, Madam Eglantine, is a fastidious creature: she loves jewels – and hates Jews. Chaucer introduces her in the General Prologue of the Canterbury Tales as a nun whose smile was 'full simple and coy' (I. 119). She speaks French as well as anyone in Stratford-at-the-Bow, now in East London. She eats daintily, dipping her fingers lightly in her sauce. She cries to see a mouse in a trap, and feeds her pet dogs white bread soaked in milk. Her eyes are grey and she wears a coral bracelet. When it comes to her turn to tell a tale, appropriately for a nun, she promises to increase the glory of Christ through her words.

So Madam Eglantine begins: 'There was in Asia, in a great city, | Amongst Christian folk a *Jewerye*' (VII. 488–9). The critic Sheila Delany has argued that Chaucer's 'Asia' can be read as primarily referring to the Holy Land, and specifically as inclusive of Syria.[109] There are ideological slippages in the Prioress' geographical imagination of the region. The Jewish ghetto described is drawn not from travels in the Muslim East, but from homegrown stereotypes and inequalities in Christian Europe. The Prioress' hostility towards her fantasy Jews is immediate and inescapable. The Jews of the Prioress' mind are occupied in 'foul usury and lucre of villainy | Hateful to Christ' (VII. 491–2), engaged in commerce and sin. The Prioress spits repetitively against the 'cursed Jew' (VII. 570), the 'cursed folk of Herodes' (VII. 574), the 'cursed Jews' (VII. 599).

The Prioress draws on well-worn traditions, summoning the bloody myth of Jewish child murder. In her story, a Christian boy is killed for singing a Marian hymn. The Prioress exclaims:

> This *gemme* of *chastite*, this emerald,
> And also of *martirdom* the ruby bright,
> Where he with throat y-carved lay upright,
> He *Alma redemptoris* began to *synge*. (VII. 609–12)

The child is presented as a miraculous jewel. The tone of these lines marks an elevation from the base slurs used against the Jews: the Prioress' language lifts in contemplation. Her pace is slowed through repetition and caesurae, allowing the miracle to assume its due reverence on arrival. The reader is invited to linger over the image. Chaucer draws on lapidary traditions, both in the associations for the Eastern location of emeralds and rubies, and their Christian symbolism.[110]

In the London Lapidary, the author chastises his reader to recall this symbolism: 'though we take no heed to the significance of the ruby and of his blissful colour, yet | Moses says that it signifies *Jhesu Xrist*'.[111] Here, Moses is imaginatively transformed into a Christian contemporary of Jesus – a historical slippage. In fact, Moses is frequently Christianised in the lapidaries. In the London Lapidary, which draws on both Old and New Testaments, the author comments of jasper that: '*Moyses* says that this stone is very good against the temptation of fiends, of Jews, and *sarazins*'.[112] The transformation of Moses into the source of information on anti-Jewish and anti-'Saracen' talismans is not unique, but provides an emblematic instance of a medieval Christian attempting to reframe imported items and their contexts. Like the Prioress, this lapidary author is keen to extract this jewel from its association with Jews.

While the Prioress was telling her tale to the gathered group on horseback, Chaucer's pilgrims were travelling towards the shrine of Thomas Becket in Canterbury. In so doing, they were travelling towards one of the most prominent sites of relics and Christian jewels. The shrine was set with a jewel-encrusted reliquary, above which a gold statue of an angel pointed to the largest jewel: a ruby, the 'Regale of France', bequeathed by the King of France.[113] Pilgrim badges replicated this scene, disseminating knowledge of the ruby across England: one such late medieval badge is to be found in the collection of the Museum of London.[114] Although the badge itself is pewter, the figure of the angel and the jewel to which it pointed are clearly rendered.[115] The ruby was fundamental to pilgrims' experience of the shrine. Hence the associations of the ruby with martyrdom combined with the imagination of its movement from the Holy Land to render it an essential element of worship. The contemplation of the ruby allowed the pilgrim to come into contact with the spirit immanent in the shrine. The Prioress' speech draws on the rich associative traditions of rubies with martyrdom and worship. The Prioress' narrative adds motivation and momentum as the group travel to pay worship to a shrine of a martyr, bearing a real jewel.

In her tale, the Prioress repeats a sequence of common medieval Christian images: an idealised Christian 'East', a powerful jewel, and the Jews, who are to be vitriolically rejected. The backlash against the child's murder, in the aftermath of the miracle, is swift and brutal: the Jews are condemned 'With torment and with shameful death each one' (VII. 628).

Although she is so sensitive that she can't bear to see a mouse bleeding, and hates it when men beat their dogs, Madam Eglantine dwells without flinching on the deaths of the Jews. She describes the executions in detail – the convicts are pulled apart by wild horses, before being hung, she says, 'by the law' (VII. 633–4). The Prioress' speech does not make her an outlier. In medieval England, a hundred years after the expulsion of the Jews, the idea that a Christian jewel should be allowed to stay amongst the Jews would have caused widespread discontent. Madam Eglantine tells her tale to the group of pilgrims expecting – and receiving – no objection.

There is no doubt about it: the appearance of a Christian jewel amongst the Jewish community is bad news. The Jews are brought into contact with the image of the gem only in order to allow that gem to enact its miraculous power against them.

Jews under Siege

Viewing their contemporary Jews as unworthy owners and mercenary idolaters, medieval English Christians dreamed about the historic destruction and looting of the Jewish Temple of Jerusalem. According to Jewish tradition, the Temple was destroyed twice, during the Babylonian siege of 587 BCE and the Roman siege of 70 CE, which are said to have occurred on the same day. In 1290, King Edward I used the shared anniversary of the Babylonian and Roman destructions of the First and Second Temples as a platform to announce his expulsion of the Jews from England.[116]

In the fifteenth-century anonymous English poem *The Siege of Jerusalem*, set in 70 CE, the governor of Syria sends the merchant-sailor Nathan to Rome, on 'an errand from the Jews'.[117] The ambiguously ethnic Greek-Syrian-maybe-Jewish biblically named Nathan takes to the seas. He voyages through 'grim waves', setting his sail high over the salt water. He travels in a '*drummond*', a large ship, driving over the deep. The sky dims and the water grows dark. Clouds clatter above as if they would crack. The storm breaks with a '*rede wynde*', a violent gale, which blows on the broad sea and surges. Nathan's ship is driven to the north. Rain and wind meet on the water, hurling everything in a heap. Nathan '*flatte for ferde*', he falls flat in fear and hides under the deck, as the ship swerves towards the shore, shooting towards Rome, towards unknown coasts, riding on the waves, rushing around '*ragged tourres*', rising waves. The mainsail at one tug '*tobresteth*' – it bursts in two, so that one end of the ship rises '*ay*' towards heaven and the other dips in the deep, as if it would drown. Over wild waves Nathan goes where any boat should overturn, dashed through rapids in the storm, until at last, with much misery, as our lord willed, he is borne into harbour at the port of Bordeaux. 'Sir', he says, addressing the Emperor Titus, 'Out of Syria, I am come'.[118] Nathan delivers his message 'from the Jews': they will no longer pay tribute to Rome.

Nathan comes from Syria bearing a Christian relic: the veil of Veronica, a cloth on which the face of Jesus is imprinted. When it is carried through a pagan church: 'the *mahound* [idol] and the *mametes* [idols] *tormortled* – shattered – to pieces | And all *tocrased* – smashed – as the cloth passed through the church'.[119] Although the idols described in these scenes are apparently pagan, the terms 'mahound' and 'mamet' both derive from an Old French corruption of the Prophet's name, 'mahomet'.[120] The Christian opposition to 'mamets' was articulated through the vocabulary of an inaccurate conceptualisation of Islam. The scene of iconoclasm combines a rejection of sacred pagan spaces with a hostile language of anti-Muslim violence. The discourse groups non-Christians together: 'pagan', Muslim, and Jewish identities are collapsed. The action of the relic against non-Christian objects in Rome prefigures the scenes which follow in Jerusalem.

The Roman reaction to the Jewish rejection of their tribute is catastrophic. The Romans arrive 'at port Jaffe in *Judees* land'.[121] The poet can almost be heard to cackle with glee: 'Now is Bethlehem – thy boast! – brought to an end, | Jerusalem and Jericho *forjuggyd* – convicted – wretches'.[122] The invasion is described again in brutal terms: 'they set upon each side Syria within'.[123] The Jews flee to Jerusalem for safety, whereupon the siege begins: the troops drive 'With engines to Jerusalem where Jews were thick'.[124] The non-Jewish Syrians are depicted as allies of the Romans, as befits the status of Syria as an Imperial province: 'Sire Sabyn of *Surrie*' is amongst the leaders of the Roman attack.[125]

In the *Siege of Jerusalem*, the Jews ride elephants and camels on bejewelled chairs, studded with '*charbokles* fine'.[126] One Jewish prince wears a breastplate with 'many precious pearl and cut stones'.[127] These stones, previously seen enacting miracles and curing the sick, do nothing to protect their owners, glimmering uselessly on the chests of those of 'Moses' law'.[128] Compared to the Christianised Moses of the lapidaries, here Moses is definitely Jewish. Like Moses, these Jews are also definitely not European.[129] In the *Siege*, Moses' people '*schrynken*' – retreat under attack.[130] The lack of agency exhibited by the jewels to save the Jews recalls the distinction made in 'The Prioress' Tale'. The presence of Christian gems, if anything, renders the Jews more vulnerable to attack. The Romans are ordered to loot the defeated community: 'the dead bodies on the bank bare for to make: | To spoil the spilt folk, none should be spared'. The repetition both of sounds and sense hammers home the command. The bodies are picked for 'gold and good stones' and '*hamberkes* noble'.[131] The armour worn by the Jews is useless to provide defence, becoming instead the spoils of war. The scene evokes layered histories, medieval and modern, of the theft of artefacts in times of military conflict. The treasuries of museums across England are filled with objects taken from the bones of the looted dead.

Titus picks his way over the bodies to marvel at the jewels of the Temple of Jerusalem. The poet deliberately tempts the reader to do the same, to forget the human tragedy. The temple is directly juxtaposed with an unflinching description of '*enfamyned*' women dying on the street.[132] This forgetting is integral to the treatment of jewels in the text, as we encounter the Temple: where even the rails under the roof were made of '*rebies grete*' (great rubies). There were so many '*perles and peritots*' that all the place seemed like '*glowande gled-fure*' – to glow, like live coals. The doors were '*dryven*' – studded – full of '*dyemauntes*', and made marvellously light with '*mergeri perles*' which '*ay lemaunde*', always gleamed and shone like a '*lampe*'.[133] The margery-pearls and rubies proclaim their own holiness through their agential emission of light, and in so doing distinguish themselves from the community which produced them. The soldiers, who needed no encouragement to lay waste to people, now, 'wait on their work, wary of the time | that so precious a place should ever perish for sin'.[134] The hesitation of the troops allows the reader to wait with them, our sympathies drawn to the gleaming jewels. The men are relieved by Titus' command that they should remove 'the treasure' before they 'burn it to the ground', which they go on to do.[135] The poet continues: 'there was plenty in that place of precious stones' and 'polished vessels'.[136] The reader follows the extent of the looting: the soldiers roam through the city in the same manner until 'Tell could no tongue the treasures that they found: | Jewels for *joly* [merry] men'.[137] The Jewish quarters of Jerusalem are figured as an endless treasure trove for the Roman troops, eventually exhausted with their findings. The richness of the Jewish people is constantly evoked, in the immediate aftermath of their desecration.

In *The Siege of Jerusalem*, the Jews are placed on the scales. After the Temple is burned, Titus establishes himself as an authority 'All Jews to *jugge* as justice himself'.[138] Although the attack was initially framed as a response to the Jews' rejection of the tribute to Rome, the trial is for the crucifixion. Pilate himself 'appeared at the barre'.[139] Titus' response is unremittingly termed in mercantile language: 'Now cursed be he', said the king, 'that the *acate* [purchase] made | He was a *merchaunt amys*', a false trader, who '*fended*', saved the money, '*to sille so precyous a prince for penies so fewe*' – to take so precious a prince to market, for so few pennies.[140] Titus characterises Pilate as a fraudulent merchant – but the Jews are the ones whose value is at stake. The association between the crucifixion and commercial exchange is a common anti-Judaic trope, previously seen in connection to the Jewish purchase of the Eucharist in the *Croxton Play*. Titus announces the punishment: 'I shall merchandise make in mind of that other.'[141] Already stripped of their jewels, the Jews themselves are transformed into objects, explicitly worthless in comparison to those treasures. In one thirteenth-century Latin commentary on the Apocalypse, the language of this scene is represented literally, with Titus shown standing with a weighing scale in his hand. The blue rod of the balance stretches flat across two folios. On the left-hand page, bowls hang from the rod in shades of green, red, pink, and blue, holding five Jews apiece, with only their heads visible above the rims – curly-haired, some clean-shaven and others bearded, all with pink cheeks and red lips, and wearing identical conical hats. On the right-hand page, the balance holds a single dark-grey coin.[142]

The deliberate use of trading language makes for an unavoidable contrast between devalued people and desired commodities. Titus sells Jewish 'bodies' as 'bargains' – 'by lower price for to pass than they the prophet sold'.[143] The price of Jewish bodies is deliberately lowered until all are 'bargained and bought and brought out of the land'.[144] The unprofitable slave auction undermines the semblance of financial rationale to reveal a pure motive of dehumanisation. The reiteration of the idea is uncompromising: the words 'price', '*bargayn*', '*marchaundise*', 'bought', and '*solde*' build on one another with grim effect. The objectification is absolute, bereft of sympathy through its phrasing as an act of divine justice enacted with self-conscious literalism.

In its associations, the scene moves between time periods: bringing Roman and Mamlūk slave markets into view, with the fate of enslavement presented unambiguously as catastrophe. The religious-racial difference between trader and slave is key here – as it was in the historical reality of the late medieval slave trade, which was organised around the principle that a person should not own or sell slaves of their own religion.[145] The original position of precious gems amongst the devalued community is presented as an unhappy accident of fate: an error.

The Mask of the Judeo-Muslim Trader

In light of these scenes of looting and destruction, it is evident that the knowledge that jewels could still be owned and traded by Jewish merchants was problematic for the medieval Christian.[146] The construction of the Jewish jewel merchant, blind to the true value of his own wares, allowed Christians to acknowledge the origins of their goods whilst still repudiating the trader. In the *Croxton Play of the Sacrament*, the merchant Jonathas – seen previously selling spices and having his hand blown off – is introduced as being from 'the city of Syria (this is full true!) | which had great plenty of precious stones'.[147] The promise is reiterated within Jonathas' speech: 'I have clothe of gold, precious stones, and spices plenty'.[148] As a Syrian-Jewish merchant, Jonathas operates within the codes – legal and social – of the Mamlūk Empire.

The identification of jewels as the source of Syrian – and so of Jewish – wealth invokes the image of the Holy Land dazzling with gems, and plays into anti-Jewish stereotypes. Jonathas lists his cargo of jewels:

> I have amethysts rich for the nonce
> And beryls which are brightest blue
> And seemly sapphires – I can show you, at once,
> And crystals, clear for to see.[149]

Jonathas draws the audience's eyes to the surface of his jewels, repeatedly encouraging us to '*se*' how '*bryght*', '*semely*', and '*clere*' they are. His adjectives focus attention on the cost of the jewels as commodities. He praises the 'degree' of his emeralds. 'I have diamonds *derewourthy* [desirable] to dress', he says – establishing the scene of the jeweller setting his gems in fixtures.[150] He goes on to describe his emeralds, onyxes, agates, topazes. He has 'pearls precious, great plenty' and 'rubies rich' which have brought him 'renown': toadstones, chalcedonies, and '*curyous*' (an adjective used here to mean costly) carbuncles.[151] Except for toadstones ('*crepawdys*'), the twelve stones in Jonathas' store are found in the biblical lists. The number itself aligns his list with the twelve stones of Exodus and Revelation. However, the order of the stones is jumbled, following neither text. The amethyst, the final stone seen in the foundations of the Heavenly Jerusalem, is promoted to first. Jasper and jacinth are left out. And above all, his jewels are '*ryche . . . ryche . . . ryche*'. The associations of richness with goodness and virtue are washed away by the cumulative impact of Jonathas' wealth. The 'lucre of money' in the play is constantly paired with the '*wyckyd*' characters of the looming Jews, bejewelled.[152] The identification of jewels as the primary source of Syrian wealth implicates these precious objects most deeply in Jewish sinfulness.

The figure of the Jewish jewel merchant continued to haunt English imaginations into the early modern period and beyond. In an echo of Jonathas' material attachment to his jewels, Shakespeare's Shylock cries out in *The Merchant of Venice* for his 'diamond gone, cost me two thousand ducats in Frankfort!'[153] Shylock's Venice draws on the medieval scene of Jonathas' Heraclea. The same spices, silks, and jewels are found still in trade there (I. i. 34–5). Portia in her judgment of Shylock is compared to Daniel, placing him on the scales and, as Titus found the Jews in Jerusalem, finding him wanting (IV. i. 339). Developed via Jonathas, Shylock proved an enduring image which is hard to shake off, bringing with him persistent stereotypes of bejewelled Jewish wealth and blindness to spiritual value.

Jonathas' commercial attitude towards his stones effectively makes idols of relics: rendered mute and material, bereft of the spiritual power located elsewhere in the play in the explosively agential Eucharist.[154] In Chapter Two, I discussed Jonathas' opening prayer to 'almighty *Machomet*' in the context of medieval Judeo-Arabic records which show the re-use of Muslim prayers within transnational Jewish trading communities across the Mediterranean.[155] Returning to that prayer now, the attribution of the wealth of jewels to '*Machomet*' brings Jonathas' jewels towards the category of 'mammets': the corruption of Mohammed's name which was used by medieval Christians to describe idols. Jonathas' jewels – like his spices – are fragments of the buried histories of Jewish gem-traders in Syria. The local lives of Arab-Jewish communities can be seen, as if through a prism, in the fractured edges of these despised gems.[156] Jonathas is doubly situated: he lives in Syria and travels through the Mediterranean, like others in the diaspora who move in both directions. He speaks in the phrases of the Muslim culture within which he inhabits, while maintaining a Jewish identity – these aspects together make him threatening, make him vulnerable to Christian violence, as a Jewish merchant who has access to the cultural capital of a Muslim-ruled Empire. When Jonathas is converted and begins to speak in liturgical Latin, both his Jewishness and his Syrianness are diminished: he is made both Christian and European, as he has not been until that moment.

Remaining with Jonathas and his jewels before that moment of conversion, perversely, in condemning both Jonathas and his jewels, the *Croxton* author allows these gems to remain part of an ethno-religiously foreign vision of Syria. These repudiated jewels are allowed to remain un-Christianised: owned by assimilated Syrian Jews. Left on the ships of the newly converted merchants, the jewels in this English text exude a condition of displacement, resonating with multiple exiles.

At its peak before the 1290 expulsion, the Jewish community in medieval England numbered around 3,000–4,000 people: 'there are more documents written in Hebrew characters surviving from England than anywhere else in the medieval western world'.[157] The English community was a thriving centre of medieval Jewish life – until, on the anniversary of the destruction of the First and Second Temples, Edward I decreed that it should exist no more. From the expulsion of the Jews in 1290 until 1656, England was a lost Jewish homeland, the mandated absence of Jews buried in the foundations of the English nation. Jonathas remembers a Jewish community in the Mediterranean which stayed present in English minds not just through fantasy, but through encounters in harbours and marketplaces. Medieval English travellers met with Jews who were settled – like Jonathas, who says he '*wonneth*', dwells – in Syria. Jonathas repeatedly speaks his affinity in the social and verbal codes of his cultural environment.

In an episode of Mandeville's *Travels*, our guide arrives at the court of the Sultan, who rules over Syria as well as Egypt, Jerusalem, and 'Arabia'. The ruler chastises the knight's complacent praise of the Christian rulers of Europe, displaying uncanny knowledge of the malpractice of priests:

> And then I asked him how he knew and understood the state of Christian men so. And he said he knew it well, both of *lordis* and of commons, by his *messyngeris* which he sent through all the countries as if they were *merchaunts* with *preciouse stoones* . . . to know the manner of all countries.[158]

The Sultan's messengers, dressed as exotic jewel merchants, anticipate and ironise the stereotype which they know to be current in the Latin West. The emissaries are able to gain unprecedented access to Christian communities in disguise: appearing as the Christians expect them to appear, bedecked with gems for sale. The self-consciously parodic 'Eastern' costume has as its main signifier the jewel as commodity. The Sultan's messengers adopt as camouflage the flattened identity of the Other as they know it to be constructed in Europe. That camouflage is unmistakably the same mask worn by Jonathas 'the Jew'. These shared disguises are transparent from within, detachable and usable – ownable, like the jewels which these stereotyped traders sold back to the Christians who met them.

The *Pearl*-Poet Judges the Jews

In *Pearl*, having recounted the parable of the Christian merchant and his flawless pearl, the girl retells the narrative of the Passion to the dreamer. She calls Christ her '*lemman*', her lover. To her, he is a 'jewel'.[159] The language of erotic love hangs over her description of her husband's death. She recounts how he was led to slaughter: 'when Jews him *jugged* in Jerusalem'.[160] The term 'jugged' builds on the initial romantic metaphor of Christ-as-jewel, to create a scene of traders weighing stones. The mis-weighing of Christ by the Jews invokes the trope of the dishonest Jewish trader, as well as the broader imaginary of Jews as essentially materialist. In describing Jesus as a gem among unreliable Jews, the *Pearl*-poet both acknowledges the Jewish origins of Christianity and rejects those progenitors. The *Pearl*-poet succinctly encapsulates the fraught and simultaneous association and dissociation of jewels and Jews. The ability to value jewels correctly – and not only for their financial worth – is presented as a specifically Christian virtue.

Towards the end of *Pearl*, the dreamer's desire to be in Jerusalem grows too intense. 'Delight me drove' to cross the river – he begins to wade into the water.[161] Christ, his prince, is highly displeased. He is repelled – not just from the river, but from the vision. He awakes back in the garden, still bereft of his pearl. Immediately 'a longing heavy me struck into a swoon'. He starts to mourn again: 'O pearl'.[162] But this time his grief is more for himself, stuck in 'this grim dungeon' while she is part of a gay garland, with Christ and his other lovers.[163] The English garden, so fragrant and warm, is no match for the crystal and fire of Jerusalem. Longing for the impossible capture of the long-lost Kingdom, medieval Christians were stuck on the fantasies of their stones – and on the fantasies of those who sold them.

Like borrowed words, relocated gems became capable of new expression, embedded, unable to return to their origins. Their fragments remained preserved in local earth, treasured and polished – while the Jewish jewel merchant remained a ghost in England, haunting the unhospitable land: the green Jerusalem of Wiltshire.

Postscript: The Treasury Is Sold Off

In 1540, Westminster Abbey lost its primary role as a Benedictine site, when Henry VIII dissolved the monasteries. Taking one last look at the Abbey, the records taken at the dissolution of the monasteries show how the medieval collections of silks and jewels were dispersed. The list reads as an auction-house catalogue: '[Sold.] 3 copes of white bawdekyn with flowers of gold and daisies'.[164] A 'basin of crystal garnished with gold, precious stones and orient pearls' is 'cracked' and with empty 'sockets' missing '3 pearls and 2 stones'.[165] Not yet sold: '2 mitres garnished with counterfeit stone and pearl'.[166] The fake jewels, aspiring to be taken as precious stones, had remained part of ceremonies, their inauthenticity no reason for exclusion. The 'counterfeit' reality became relevant only once the mitres were no longer needed by the expelled monks, once they were no longer regarded as sacred – once they tried to re-enter the marketplace without being considered holy. In the Abbey collection of Syriana, fakes and relics collided and were kept safe, prized for both their devotional and commercial value.

Sold off and broken, the objects in the Tudor Abbey returned to the condition of being commodities, now as the commercialised contents of a Catholic treasury, in the time of the English Reformation. The destinations of these items go unrecorded. The disappearance of the Abbey treasury is just one case of the fragmentary survival of artefacts from the Middle Ages. Today, excavated jewels and rescued relics find temporary residence in backrooms of museum storage units, in vaults for safekeeping and vitrines for display: not truly at home, desiring to be touched. In medieval England and now, these displaced jewels haunt their collectors, unsettling the spaces in which they were displayed, resistant to rituals but unable to stay still.

PART III
The Workshop

Robert was still – still breathing, but only just. John ran his thumb over Robert's lips to feel the soft air leave his mouth. As if for the first time, John felt the pain of his own wounds, his own injured side and arms. Shocked by the return to his own body, John's eyes stung and he placed his palm over the sore – flecked with sand. He would need treatment too, he began to realise. An alumed sponge dabbed onto the cut, to prevent infection – if he was going to live.

The final object in my analysis of Sturmy's cargo is also the heaviest: 'Item *alome foile* and *roche* to the weight of 152 tons.'[1] Alum (aluminium potassium sulfate) was imported in bulk, crucial to the physical balancing of Sturmy's ship as well as its economic momentum: boxes of alum were used as ballast. The amount of alum on Sturmy's ship would have dyed 34,000 cloths, equivalent to the total number of cloths exported from England in a year in the 1450s.[2] Sturmy's intent appears to have been to monopolise the supply of alum in England, cutting out the Genoese intermediaries who dominated the trade and controlled major alum mines from their base in Chios. Gattilusio's attack on Sturmy's ships can be seen as a calculated response to this threat to the Genoese monopoly. As well as being a pirate, Gattilusio was the owner of a number of Genoese alum mines.[3]

My final section is devoted to the cultural significance of this mineral alum, which is found throughout medieval English industrial, medicinal, alchemical, and literary practices. The shipment of alum on Sturmy's ship was fuel for the workshops where these activities occurred: spaces of making and transformation. The materials used for surgical, clothmaking, and alchemical production were made using shared apparatus. Distilleries could produce *aqua vitae*, or ink. Alum recurs in recipes from dyes to corrosive plasters, standing at the gluey border between connected crafts. As a dye fixative, alum became invisible in the final product, but remained indispensable, not least to the production of books: alum is present in the inks and text box rulings which shaped the medieval page. Literary

Figure 5.1 Alum mines. Source: British Library, London. Egerton 747, fol. 3, detail. Printed with permission of Bridgeman Images.

representations of alum draw attention to the imaginative qualities of these acts of making: the manual labour which underpinned medieval English culture.

Rock alum was obtained through mining: as shown in one fifteenth-century illuminated manuscript of the herbal *Tractatus de Herbis* [Figure 5.1]. Before the fall of Acre, prized Syrian alum was brought from mines in Aleppo. In 1248, a merchant's contract in Marseille lists forty sacks of 'alum of Aleppo' alongside Syrian brasil, Indian ginger and sugar, and 'Arabian' myrrh, all of which were brought from Syrian marketplaces.[4] Venice was preeminent in the pre-1291 alum trade, with settlements in Aleppo and Damascus; Venetian Statutes of Goods from 1233 and 1255 show the regulation of rock alum alongside precious spices and glass-making materials respectively. Alum of Aleppo or '*alum glaciale*' was distinguished from Castilian and '*alumen minutum*' at the Champagne trading fairs in 1248.[5] The historical movement of alum from Syria underpinned the continued Holy Land associations of alum in the late medieval imagination, in spite of the reported knowledge of alum mines in the Mediterranean and Black Sea.

Post-1291, Genoese industrialists (piratical or otherwise) became the primary sources of the mineral in Europe.[6] After the fall of Acre, the Genoese established settlements in 'the alum-producing lands', first on the coast of Asia Minor and then in Chios.[7] Genoese-run Mediterranean trading posts and mines were deeply implicated in the continued aftermath of the crusades, and in the development of early modern European colonialism.[8] In the *Libelle of*

Englyshe Polycye, the author describes the Genoese importing 'Cotton, Rochalum, and good gold of Genne', proximate to the previously discussed imports of 'cloth of gold, silke, and pepper blacke'.[9] In 1303 alone, 500 loads of alum were brought through Montmélian from Asia Minor.[10] The Genoese-based merchant Francesco di Marco Datini built an oligarchic trading fortune by supplying alum to the Prato cloth industry. Datini imported rock alum alongside spices and Damascus sugar: reiterating the integration of alum into the milieu of Levantine goods.[11] The Genoese traded in slaves across the Levant and Mediterranean – and also employed slave labour in their alum mines in Phokaia. The prohibition against Christian enslavement of other Christians was used as the rationale for the exclusive use of non-Christian slaves in European territories.

The Genoese conquest of Chios in 1346 looks simultaneously back and forwards in time. Designed as a surrogate for the lost Frankish territories in Syria, the calculated conquest and administration of overseas territories for financial gain by an Italian conglomerate contains strategies which would become hegemonic within European colonialism.[12] In this part I move towards the end not only of this book but of the period under consideration. The significance of the bulk trade in alum in the later Middle Ages can be seen in a continuum with these early modern industrialising economies, providing a model on which European commerce and colonialism developed.[13] The late medieval English desire to compete with the Genoese was connected with a desire to emulate patterns of economically motivated settlement and mineral extraction.

Whereas English regulations restricted the quantity of imported silks or sweet wines, large quantities of alum were imported by necessity and command. In the fifteenth-century *Liber Albus*, the regulations of the city of London demanded: 'Also, that a Merchant-stranger shall sojourn wheresoever he shall please . . . if it is pepper, cummin, ginger, alum, brasil, latten, or incense [that he brings], he must not sell less than 25 pounds at a time.'[14] In 1450, Henry VI sequestered £8,000 worth of Genoese-imported alum, offering compensation to the affected merchants John Ambrose, Leonard Catane, Catane Pynell, and Ambrose Spynull, in the form of freedom from duty on transactions up to the same value. The action, codified in the Parliamentary Bill '*pro venditione aluminis*' [for the sale of alum], signalled an intent for alum sales to be a royal prerogative within England: that the King 'have to his use, all the *allome foyle* belonging to the *marchauntes* of *Jene*'.[15] Whereas with silks, jewels, and spices, royals were content to possess individual items, with alum we see additional moves towards ownership of the supply chain.

By the late fifteenth century, the control of alum was entangled in the conflict between the Ottoman Empire and Christendom. In 1462, alum deposits were discovered in the Papal territories at Tolfa, near Rome. The news was announced to the Pope as bringing 'victory over the Turk': alum was seen as a 'providentially discovered' mineral placed in Vatican lands under God's influence.[16] The scales appeared to be tilting in favour of Christian expansionism; the divinely sanctioned economic profits from the alum mines would prove highly useful in funding overseas missions. Although in one sense the Tolfa mines distanced alum from its Syrian associations, in another sense, the view of the event as a miracle returned the mineral to a crusading fantasy. The goods of the Muslim-controlled Holy Land had miraculously manifested themselves in Christian Rome.

Medieval Christians resisted repeated papal attempts to create an alum monopoly. A series of papal legislative bills culminated in a 1506 bill of excommunication against those who bought or sold 'infidel' alum – but cargoes of Ottoman-mined alum continued to travel to England into the sixteenth century.[17] It appeared that it was not only essential for the English to import alum in general, it was essential to import alum from the East. The miraculous Italian mines produced inferior minerals.

Alum both extends and deviates from the themes of this book. Instead of the rare, luxurious, and sweet objects seen hitherto, alum is bought in bulk, industrial and foul. Alum was a product of the medieval 'middles': the sites in the Mediterranean through which minerals and other commodities travelled alongside new vocabulary. In the Middle Ages, pilgrimage and trading zones across Greater Syria and the Mediterranean were midpoints through which English travellers were brought into contact with other cultures, and particularly with those Arab-Muslim and Arab-Jewish cultures which were apparently excluded from post-crusading England. These 'middles' remained sites of exploitation and conflict, witnessing free and forced movement across the Mediterranean. Alum is a material trace of these complex histories, a record of early industrial systems of labour and settlement.

The manuscripts which contain traces of alum are vivid evocations of the complex world of medieval workshops. Stained, burned, and annotated, these books recall their existence in vocational spaces, marked with the traces of their readers' physical engagement in the activities described. Just as one manuscript was designed for multiple spaces, so alum slips from the alchemist's den to the scriptorium and back. The workshop was not a space in which fantasy was left at the door, but a place in which the desire for Syria was put to work.

CHAPTER 5

Alum / The Demand for Sodomite Salt in England

Sturmy's ship held: '*alome foile* and *roche* to the weight of 152 tone to the value in *Englond* of . . . £3040'.[1] In Sturmy's cargo, alum is second only to sweet wines in financial cost: approximately £1,954,749 in today's terms.[2] Sturmy's alum would have likely been extracted from Genoese-run mines in Phokaia, modern-day Foça, on the Aegean coast of Turkey. These origins unsettle the authenticity of this product – alum was another interpolator in merchants' cargoes of Syriana, alonsisde Italian-made Damasks and Mediterranean wines. Like these more luxurious items, the Holy Land associations of alum persisted in the medieval English imagination. These associations were based both on recollection of the pre-1291 sources of the mineral and on the vivid mythologies of alum as the product of the Dead Sea. The Dead Sea itself was seen through its biblical origin narrative: as the remnants of the cities which collapsed through their sin.

The previous commodities considered tended to be grouped together, forming a luxurious imaginary of relic-like Syriana in medieval England, as in spiced wines or bejewelled silk copes. I consider alum alongside asphalt and bitumen: associated mineral salts in literary, biblical, scientific, and geographical accounts. The connection between alum and other examples of Syriana remains present, with an altered resonance. Instead of being displayed alongside silks in treasuries or at altars, alum was actively brought to bear upon those other imports. 'Alum de glas' was used to turn red wine into white or Spanish wine into sweet Romeney, as well as to cleanse pearls and dye silks and sendals.[3] The processes of dye making and medicine saw alum treated as a debased substance, ignominiously mixed with substances like old urine and common plants. In contrast to the devotional preservation of relics, alum appears as a material designed to be tampered with and to change in aspect. Alum was used in the process of sugar production in Palestine – as the plantations and mills were near the Dead Sea, the mineral could be brought from the water to the mills on the banks.[4]

As an industrial and foul mineral, alum pervaded medieval English culture – but has been invisible as an object of cultural analysis. In this chapter I restore Sodomite salts to view, as they appear scattered throughout the moralistic poem *Cleanness*, Mandeville's *Travels*, Chaucer's 'Canon's Yeoman's Tale', dyers' manuals, surgical texts, and Chaucer's dream vision *The House of Fame*. Transformative and transmutational, alum was alchemical, healing, and polluting, the signs of its agency deeply ambivalent. In the medieval imagination, alum is characterised by a cursed fluidity. The shifting nature of alum is integral to its representation and function, alternately being employed in dissolved form as 'alum water' for the dying of cloths, in crystalline powders of 'alum rock' for the production of inks, in pastes to prepare manuscript pages for inscription, in corrosive plasters to heal surgical wounds. These protean and transformative qualities can be seen in relation to the imagined origins of alum in the antinatural waters of the Dead Sea, laced with the lifegiving ashes of the destroyed communities of Sodom and Gomorrah.

The Sodomite Origins of the Dead Sea

The Dead Sea was formed when Sodom and Gomorrah collapsed, first into flames and then into a mineral-rich lake.[5] The episode is retold in the fourteenth-century moralistic poem *Cleanness*, which appears in the same manuscript as – and is considered as the work of the same anonymous author of – *Pearl* and *Gawain and the Green Knight*. In *Cleanness* – unlike in the Hebrew Bible – the acts which take place in Sodom before its destruction are explicitly sexual.[6] The poet condemns the participants to a pathological degree, repeating that the city of '*Sodamas*' sinned in the 'fault of this filth'.[7] The 'great sin' of Sodom is alliteratively paired with the 'guilt of *Gomorre*', although the sexual practices of Gomorrah (traditionally understood as relations between women) are undescribed within the text.[8]

The beginning of the end of Sodom is signalled by the arrival of two angels, who have been sent to spy on the Sodomites by their divine master, God. Lot here is called the 'dear brother' of Abraham – according to biblical tradition, Lot is Abraham's nephew.[9] Lot is eager to play host to the '*swete men*' who arrive unheralded at his door, with their hair like '*raw sylk*'.[10] The pretty femme angels, in what looks like the first (and only God-ordained) police sting, prove irresistible to the people of Sodom. Soon there is a crowd at Lot's door demanding to be allowed to come in and introduce the '*outcomlyng*' to their ways. '*Oo, my frendes*', Lot replies – the *Pearl*-poet's dialogue bringing his voice from the page – '*Avoy*!'[11]

The rejoinder from the group of Sodomites is immediate: '*Who joyned þe be joystyse oure japez to blame*': who made you the Judge, to blame our games?[12] There is a dramatic irony here, in the presence of two divinely appointed judges, the very angels whom the Sodomites wish to seduce. Unaware of the angels' ulterior motives, the Sodomites reasonably remind Lot that – as he knows – whenever a 'boy' comes to '*þis borȝ*' (this town) everyone is invited, so why should Lot prevent them from visiting the 'boy' in his house, just because he is a '*burne ryche*' – a rich man?[13] To the Sodomites, Lot is the greatest hypocrite, selfishly keeping his boys to himself, using his wealth to keep an unfair privilege. These pretty guests should not be shut away in a private home: they should be welcomed by everyone, as is proper. The Sodomites configure their community in public spaces, with the act of group sex defining them as a social organisation. To be a Sodomite is to be resident in, and to participate in, these collective 'japes' – these playful gatherings. That is why guests are typically invited by everyone: because Sodomy is not a private act.

The *Pearl*-poet punctuates this account of the Sodomites' ways with an exclamation – 'What!! . . . What! . . . What!' – distancing the text, but not quite successfully distancing Lot from suspicion.[14] As he listens, Lot is washed with '*schame*' – recalling the fact that 'he knew the custom' himself.[15] It is unclear as to whether the knowledge of the 'custom' causes Lot shame because of his regret at participation – or simply because he knows that his failure to share his guests with the community has broken the rules of Sodom. The ambiguities in the *Pearl*-poet's representation are too tempting, even though the poet revels in the destruction which follows.

The angels, at least, are convinced that Lot is not a true resident of Sodom. They warn him and his family to leave. The cities begin to burn: 'flakes of sulphur | All in smoldering smoke *smachande* full ill | *Swe* about *Sodamas*': the smack, the stench of the smoke was bitter as it groaned about the city.[16] The smoke is multisensory, smelling and moaning, evoking the cracking of the buildings and their inhabitants. Hell, personified, is '*ferlyly fayn*' – wonderfully glad – at the destruction, and cracks open the ground.[17] All '*birolled* with the rain, roasted and burned | so that all the region *torof* in *riftes* full great'. By the time that the 'breath of the brimstone' had faded, 'all the cities and their sides *sunkken to helle*'.[18] The quick horror is complete.

The appeal of Sodom and Gomorrah before their decimation swirls around the boundaries of *Cleanness*. Afraid for Lot, Abraham has been unable to sleep while the cities are burning. He rises early the next morning and walks out to look over the ashen landscape. He 'sent towards *Sodomas* the sight of his eyes'.[19] Sodom '*þat ever hade ben an erde of erþe þe swettest*' – which had 'ever' been a yard of the sweetest earth 'as *aparaunt* to *paradis*', like a settlement of Paradise – now is 'plunged in a pit like of pitch filled'.[20] Abraham's view of Sodom as Paradisiac draws on Genesis 13. 10. It might be assumed that Sodom ceased to be Edenic at the moment in which sexual sin was introduced to the land, but that is unspecified here. Abraham, in high anxiety for his friend, who he assumes has been burned with the other Sodomites, believes that Sodom has been a Paradise 'ever', always: right up until the instant of its God-mandated destruction. At that point (and only then) it was plunged from sweetness to hellfire. The nostalgia for Sodom at the moment of its descent into smoke and brimstone tugs the denied subtext ever closer to the surface. Lot knew the custom when he invited in those boys. The pit of pitch lingered on as a sign of the burned Paradise which once stood on that site.

The Production of Sodomite Salts

At the site of the Dead Sea, bodies turned into rocks, their ashes became salts – the dissolving edges of rocks melt into a body of water. Geological details of the landscape were integrated into a reading of scripture. The minerals which were associated with this site could not easily be extracted from those narratives. The idea that alum had been brought from the site of Sodom persisted throughout the Middle Ages. The ashes of the sinning cities remained, crystallised and bitter. These salts clung to the banks near the site of Lot's wife's transformation into a pillar of salt. That disobedient woman – she turned to look at Gomorrah falling, and was crystallised. There is a gynomorphic rock structure beside the Dead Sea which in the Middle Ages was seen as proving the truth of Lot's wife's fate.[21] Lot's wife is present in the *Pearl*-poet's account: she became 'all so salt' and 'so she yet stands'.[22]

The scene of Lot and his daughters fleeing Sodom was a common subject of medieval illuminations, as in one late fifteenth-century manuscript of the *Speculum Humanae Salvationis* [Figure 5.2].[23] In this image, the blue hills of the Holy Land contrast distinctly with the smoking spires of the damned cities. The cloth of gold and turbans worn by Lot and his daughters situate these biblical Jews in their lands of origin. The chess-piece-style salt pillar into which Lot's wife has turned stands out curiously in this geographically detailed landscape, a gleeful goat playing at the side of a rearing beast, about to lick the salt. In this image, Sodom can be seen sinking into the pale lake of the nascent Dead Sea. Salty minerals: traces of disobedient bodies. The rock structure seen as Lot's wife and the salts in the

Figure 5.2 The destruction of Sodom. Source: British Library, London. Harley MS 2838, fol. 34, detail. Printed with permission of Bridgeman Images.

lake are observable realities. The sulphurous rocks on the shore erode into the water, dissolving and preserving narratives.

The recollection of Sodom remained part of the present mythologies of the Dead Sea salts, in *Cleanness* and in other late medieval imaginative geographies. The *Pearl*-poet calls the lake 'the dark *Dede See*', and explains: 'as it is cursed of *kynde* [nature]', both in its depths and along its coasts, the 'clay that clings thereby are corrosives strong', that is: 'alum and *alkaran* [bitumen] which are *angré* [bitter] both'.[24] This understanding of the Dead Sea as the source of mineral salts echoes the Hebrew Bible. In the book of Genesis: 'the Valley of Siddim was riddled with bitumen pits, and the kings of Sodom and Gomorrah fled there and leaped into them'.[25]

In his fourteenth-century encyclopaedia, Trevisa writes that 'Judea is a part of *Siria* . . . also in the end thereof is the Dead Sea, which is called *lacus Asphaltus* . . . therein is glue and nothing liveth therein . . . And this *Deede See* swalloweth the river of Jordan and spoils good water, y-meddled with water of *pestilence*.'[26] Trevisa's account drew on Classical sources – in his Latin *Etymologies*, Isidore writes that: 'Bitumen comes forth in the lake Asphaltites in Judea; sailors in skiffs collect floating clumps of it as they draw near. In Syria it is a mud that boils up from the earth.'[27] The minerals

Figure 5.3 The Burchard map. Source: Bodleian Library, Oxford. MS Douce 389, detail. Photo: © Bodleian Libraries, University of Oxford. Image permission granted under Creative Commons 4.0 International Public License (CC BY-NC 4.0).

found in the Dead Sea are located in a biblical landscape which is still experienced in the present moment.

On medieval maps, Sodom and Gomorrah were frequently depicted as standing visibly beneath the transparent waters of the Dead Sea, as seen in one fourteenth-century map based on the text of Burchard of Mount Sion's *Descriptio Terrae Sanctae* [Figure 5.3]. This 'Burchard map' has been associated with William Wey's lost '*mappa* of the *Holy Lond*': a similar map can be assumed to have hung in his Jerusalem-imitative Wiltshire chapel, a devotional object.[28] Instead of holiness and fertility, the noxious minerals in the Dead Sea, with their strange transformative ways, evoke anti-natural perversions. The aridness of alum, asphalt, and bitumen were seen as traces of Genesis hellfire – even while these substances originated in Genoese pits.[29]

The *Pearl*-poet goes on: 'and there *waltez* [foams] from that water in *waxlokes grete* | The *spumande* [frothing] asphalt, which Spicers sell'.[30] The 'waxlike curls' of asphalt miraculously generate from the dingy waters, imaginatively associated with flowing locks of hair. While alum and asphalt are ostensibly condemned as signs of the anti-sacral, the *Pearl*-poet in the same instant recalls the availability of asphalt in Spicers' shops. This reference to the trade in asphalt draws attention to the paradoxical commodification of a cursed mineral, contextualising the biblical produce of Sodom in its contemporary trading networks. The reader is reminded of the desirability of Sodomite minerals in the late medieval world.

In the narrative of *Cleanness*, moral and economic values collide, with a tension between the unholy product and its known financial value. The late medieval marketplace of goods in circulation and the preserved moment of the biblical past collide and oscillate in alum and asphalt. In the case of sweet wines, spices, silks, and jewels, it was seen that the divinity of a product was often inseparable from its marketability. Here the trace of damnation was not enough to stem the sale of goods. The Dead Sea is transformed from a space where life is suspended into an active trading zone. The medieval reader is encouraged to visualise the agential minerals of the Dead Sea in their local shops, that proximate scene layered over the vision of Sodom and Gomorrah still sinking into the depths.

Sir John's Guide to the Dead Sea

The origins of alum in the Dead Sea were recorded in Mandeville's *Travels*, which has been identified as a source for *Cleanness*.[31] Although the *Travels* survives in around 300 manuscripts, this episode is not found in every version. In one edition known as the 'Cotton Manuscript', the text reads: '*Of the dede See; and of the Flom Jordan*'. The scribe records that 'from Jericho, three miles, is the *dede see*. About that sea groweth much *Alom* and *Alkatran*.'[32] The term for bitumen, 'alkatran', is an inexact echo of the Arabic 'al-qār' – used to describe bitumen or tar. As is later found in *Cleanness*, the Mandeville author here describes how the Dead Sea 'casteth out of the Water a thing that men call *Aspalt*; also in great pieces, like the *gretnesse* of an Horse, every day, and on all sides'.[33] The daily production of asphalt from the Dead Sea in huge, horse-sized swathes recalls the wonderous production of relic-like glass from the opened chasm of the 'gravelly sea' or fosse of Menon and the plentiful presence of rubies on the seashore near Acre, previously discussed in the *Travels*. The scene becomes another instance of the marvels of the Holy Land: 'And from Jerusalem to that Sea, is 200 Furlongs.'[34]

The biblical story of Sodom and Gomorrah is a transformation miracle. Human and architectural forms become minerals. Solids become liquids, yet those liquids remain ambivalent in nature, refusing to act within the boundaries of natural law. The Mandeville author writes:

> It is called the Dead Sea, for it runneth not, but is ever unmoveable. . . . And no man may drink of that Water, for *bytternesse*. And if a man casts Iron therein, it will float above. And if men cast a Feather therein, it will sink to

> the bottom . . . these things be against *kynde*. Some men call that Sea, the *Lake Dalfetidee*; some the *Flom of Develes* . . .. And into that Sea sunk the five cities, by Wrath of God, that is to say, *Sodom*, *Gomorre*, *Aldama*, *Seboym* and *Sedor*, for the *abhomynable synne* of *Sodomye*, that reigned in them.[35]

The naming of the Dead Sea as 'the Lake Dalfetidee' embeds the Arabic definite article 'al-' in the word, in combination with the abbreviated French possessive 'de' and the Anglo-French 'fetide' [the stinking place]. Other manuscripts of Mandeville's *Travels* name the Dead Sea as 'Alsiled', combining 'al-' with the Middle English 'sile' [bog].[36] These multilingual Arabic-Anglo-French neologisms are tethered to the scientific texts which formed the foundations of the medieval English understanding of these minerals. While the multilingual 'Lake Dalfetidee' was the title used by some, others prefer 'the Flom of Develes' – the devils' river. The morally loaded term is offered as a balanced alternative to the previous label. The Dead Sea reveals the submarine presence of the destroyed cities. The dense salted water which caused iron to float and feathers to sink witnessed the historical presence of Sodomite acts: the water itself continually replicating the defiance of the Sodomites to the prescribed laws of God.[37]

Pilgrimage to the Site of Sodom

The Dead Sea is a place in the Holy Land which is taken as authenticating scripture. Although the events which were authenticated were said to be sinful, it was often difficult for medieval authors to depict such a space in a straightforwardly hostile manner. As Blanch and Wasserman have noted, when medieval theologians attempted to define the boundaries of acts against nature ('*kynde*') they were aware that divine miracles could easily be absorbed into that critique.[38] In Caesarius of Heisterbach's *Dialogue on Miracles*, a miracle is defined as being 'anything contrary to the course of nature at which we marvel' – as such, miracles had the potential to be performed by 'evil spirits as well as through saints'.[39] In the works of the *Pearl*-poet, what it means to be 'against *kynde*' is supposed to be unambiguous: to be '*unkyndely*' is to be like Satan.[40] When nature is disrupted by man, that is sinful – when nature is disrupted by God, that is divine. When the Dead Sea continues to violate nature, that is read as a direct trace of the original human violation which – through the curse of God – has remained present in the body of water. The boundaries between the human, the divine, and the natural are deeply troubled.

Through their histories and narratives, alum and bitumen remained part of the spiritual geography of the Dead Sea: the sensory foulness of these minerals proved their biblical origins. These minerals became the material traces of anti-natural acts which perversely asserted the sacrality of the landscape through their sensory confirmation of their cursed history. The corrosive properties of alum, as well as its sensory stench, were directly read as signs of the biblical prohibition which consequently placed those unclean salts among the clearest symbols of the sacred land.

As Nicole Chareyron writes: 'To relate the realm of visible, palpable realities to the biblical world . . . such was the pilgrims' hope.'[41] In the Hereford Mappa Mundi, the seas were painted with corrosive copper-based ink, with the result that Sodom and Gomorrah now stand out from the site of Dead Sea in parchment ridges.[42] The ink which was used to represent the water shared its properties with that self-same liquid, flattening the distinction between the artistic materials and the subject of representation. Like the Hereford map, the Dead Sea in the medieval imagination was a corrosive lake, whose properties were received through both materials and representation – through touching the corrosive water, and through visualising its origins.

As the subject of contemplation and strange devotion, the Dead Sea was a common late medieval pilgrimage destination, found in the recorded visits of European travellers including Giacomo da Verona, in 1332, Louis de Rochechouart, in 1461, Santo Brasca and Pierre Barbatre, in 1480, and Denis Possot, in 1533.[43] Yet the Dead Sea remained a destination conceptually far removed from the sacred Jordan river nearby: 'O abominable', cried Nicolas de Martoni as he stood on the banks in 1394.[44] Instead of evoking wonder at divine grace, the Dead Sea invited pilgrims to recall the disruption of God's law by man. In a sense, the Dead Sea was an inverted pilgrimage site of continual disrepute, the preserved moment of Genesis punishment offering an inlet into the fumes of hell.

Transported in bulk, Dead Sea minerals were not worshipped like relics, but remained crucial to late medieval spirituality. These Sodomite salts were proximate signs of biblical scripture which were desired and absorbed. As will be seen, these materials of devotional culture then became the industrial elements of cultural production.

Sodomite Salts Create the Elixir

Seen through the lens of its Sodomite past, the Dead Sea was a fundamentally alchemical space: an anti-natural natural body which

Figure 5.4 Flasks by the Dead Sea. Source: British Library, London. Harley MS 658, fol. 39 v., detail. Printed with permission of Bridgeman Images.

challenged the fixity of the order of things. In one late twelfth- or thirteenth-century plan of Jerusalem, the Dead Sea is depicted as a circle, labelled '*fluuius diaboli*' [the devil's river].[45] Beside this minimalist representation are two smoking flasks [Figure 5.4]. Moving away from submerged cities or gynomorphic rocks, the Dead Sea here is represented by two scientific vessels. As recognised in this image, the site of biblical transformation provided the raw materials required for the Arabic-transmitted medieval sciences of medicine and alchemy. These minerals retained their origin narrative in active use: Sodomite salts whose agency derived from their anti-natural past.

Alchemy was an art of transformation: cultural and material. This sense of alchemical practice is found towards the end of Chaucer's unfinished narrative collection *The Canterbury Tales*. The Canon and his Yeoman race to catch up with the group and seek to join the party, their arrival figured in alchemical terms: sweating, the Canon's '*foreheed* dropped as a *stillatorie*' – a distillation vessel (VIII. 580). With the arrival of these new alchemical pilgrims, the shape of the project of the tales is made to shift. The drops on the Canon's brow seem to signal the transformation of the *Tales* into a project which will never reach its resolution but always remain in motion. The Canon states his desire to be allowed to ride with the group not as a devout pilgrim but, as his Yeoman says, 'For his *desport*; he loveth *daliaunce*' (VIII. 592). 'Dalliance' can mean conversation, platonic or sexual play. Here, 'dalliance' is the Canon's view of the 'game' of telling tales. These alchemists love to play – whether with alchemical materials or with language.

The Canon and his Yeoman are invited to join the group and tell a tale. When the Canon realises that his servant is about to reveal all his secrets, he flees in shame – but the Yeoman stays to speak his truth. Playing to his crowd, the Yeoman promises to reveal the scientific terms, which are 'so *clergial* and so *queynte*' (VIII. 752). The word '*clergial*' means scholarly, clerkly. The adjective '*queynte*' can mean strange, cunning, supernatural; as a noun, the word '*queynte*' was also used to refer to genitalia. So this *cunty* clerk lists the materials required for alchemy: '*curcubites* and *alambikes* . . . arsenic, *sal armonyak*, and brimstone . . . *sal tartre*, alkali, and *sal preparat* | And *combust* matters and *coagulat*; clay made with hors or man's hair, and oil | of tartre, *alum glas*' (VIII. 794–813).

In the Yeoman's catalogue, the imported mineral 'alum glas' appears in a long sequence of complex borrowed words. The word 'alembic' derives from the Arabic *al-anbīq*, which itself derives from the Greek *ambix* [cup].[46] The term 'arsenic' derives from Anglo-Norman *arsenik* and Middle French *arcenic*, which themselves derived from the Latin *arsenicum* and Greek *arsenikon*; the *Oxford English Dictionary* identifies the original root as 'an unattested Middle Iranian word (probably transmitted via a Semitic language)'.[47] The words trace the same paths of cross-cultural contact as the science which framed their use, the extension of Hellenistic science through Semitic translations in Arabic, Hebrew, or Syriac before these ideas entered Latin and European vernaculars.

Alum was an essential component of alchemical practice in Hellenistic, Jewish, and Muslim traditions – traditions which were integrated in Arabic texts, and received in England through Latin translations of those Arabic versions.[48] The cross-cultural origins of alchemical science were foregrounded in England: the fifteenth-century Bristol-based alchemist Thomas Norton wrote in his *Ordinal of Alchemy* of 'our stone | which the *Arabies* call the Elixir'.[49] The vocabulary, apparatus, and constitutive raw materials of alchemical science in medieval England were explicitly translated from Arabic sources. As with pseudo-cloths whose lettering recalled their imported origins, these textual traces of Arabic strengthened the association between alum and the Holy Land. Seen through biblical and alchemical frameworks, Sodomite salts were scientific and devotional objects which were in demand because they existed at the intersection of these categories. The English word 'alum' derives from the Latin 'alumen' [light]. The Arabic term for alum is *al-shabb* – but in the Yeoman's list, the context of other Arabic borrowings – alembics, alkali – causes the word to sound like 'al-um': the Arabic definite article attached to a preverbal hesitation. 'Al–um', the – what was that again?

Alum and Other 'Gibberish'

In medieval England, one of the main sources of alchemical knowledge was the *Summa Perfectionis* of Pseudo-Geber. Translated from a Latin text which was compiled from varied Arabic sources, the work was presented as being a translation from the works of Jābir ibn Ḥayyān (721–813 CE), who is often considered the founder of Arabic chemistry. Known in Latin as 'Geber', Jābir ibn Ḥayyān was celebrated as the founder of alchemy in the Latin West: sixty-three extant Latin manuscripts of the *Summa Perfectionis* survive.[50] The influence of 'Geber' was explicitly linguistic as well as theoretical – through Jābir's works, a whole new vocabulary entered English, as seen in the Yeoman's list of vocabulary.

The word 'gibberish' derives from the medieval Latin name for Jābir ibn Ḥayyān.[51] From the late sixteenth century onwards, 'gibberish' gained racialised and derogatory connotations: in that context, 'gibberish' was sublinguistic, the coloniser's way of hearing the speech of the colonised.[52] That pejorative use of the term is post-medieval. In the Middle Ages, 'gibberish' is experimental: the linguistic material for literary play and scientific innovation. It is a pleasure for the pilgrims to hear the Yeoman's 'gibberish' – they listen eagerly to his *cunty* words. In Chaucer's tale, the reader is invited to revel in these unfamiliar terms, these high-status Arabic words absorbed into English. As a material substance, the qualities of alum are unfixed and transformative. As a linguistic substance, 'al–um' and its borrowed companions – 'gibberish' – share those same qualities, unfixed and transformative within English texts, absorbed and dissolving into new literary forms.

Alum was considered as one of the 'middle minerals', which was a crucial category for the creation of the 'Elixir' in alchemical theory. Albertus Magnus (1199–1280) defined 'middle minerals' as:

> those things that seem to be intermediate in nature between stones and metals . . . that in some respects are earthy and in others watery . . .. Furthermore, intermediates are any substances that fuse by dry heat and afterward tend to solidify . . . such as all kinds of *alumen*. . . . the nature of intermediates is especially noteworthy in the transmutation of metals.[53]

Albertus' description had a long-lasting influence. Norton wrote: 'It is not necessary to name the middle minerals, | For Albert writes openly of them alle'.[54]

Albertus explicitly attributed his alchemical lore to Arabic authorities, citing Ibn Sīnā, as well as the anonymous *Book of Alums and Salts*, which was attributed to al-Rāzī and translated into Latin by Gerard of Cremona.[55] In the *Kitāb al-shifā'* [Book of Healing], Ibn Sīnā discusses the alchemical and medicinal uses of alums and sulphurs, and their status as salts; this text was translated into Latin as the *Liber de mineralibus* [Book on Minerals].[56] Alum also features as a 'middle mineral' in the works of Pseudo-Geber:

> *Of the Preparation of Middle Minerals* . . .. *Glassy* or *Roch-Allom* hath a twofold way of *Preparation*: one for washing calcined *Bodies*, and the other for subliming *Spirits*. . . . Dissolve it in clear *Fountain Water*, distill it through a *Filter* . . . so you will have prepared *Crystalline Allom*.[57]

The category of 'intermediates' with extraordinary powers is a relational category: these are most potent when acting upon and with other substances. As a 'middle mineral', alum was designed to be combined and blended, to be brought into contact with others to realise its transformative effect. In that sense alum was a relational substance: appearing in and as an emblem of the medieval poetics of Relation. Shining bright as *alum de glas* or dissolving into absence as the salts coating the banks of the Dead Sea eroded into the ashy waters, alum was catalytic, transformative, and cursed, letting out its ambivalent light across medieval England.

The Judeo-Muslim Origins of English Alchemy

In 'The Canon's Yeoman's Tale', Chaucer translates directly from a Latin version of the works of the tenth-century alchemist Muhammed ibn Umayl. Towards the end of his tale, the Yeoman recounts an anecdote about an unnamed 'disciple of Plato'. The Yeoman describes how this 'disciple' once went to his master, Plato, as his 'book Senior will bear witness'. The 'book Senior' refers to the 'Senior de Chemia', a medieval Latin version of Ibn Umayl's *Risālat al-Shams ilā al-Hilāl* ['The Letter of the Sun to the Crescent Moon']. In the Yeoman's words, the disciple demanded: '*Telle me the name of the privee stoon.*' Tell me! says Ibn Umayl. And Plato answered – 'Take the *stoon* that *Titanos* men name.' 'Which is that?' said Ibn Umayl. '*Magnasia* is the same', said Plato. 'Ye, sire, and is it thus?' Ibn Umayl replies, slightly rudely. 'What is *Magnasia*, good sir, I pray?' (VIII. 1449–58).

In 'The Canon's Yeoman's Tale', this dialogue takes place between two authors: the anonymised Ibn Umayl, as the author of the Book Senior, and Plato. In Ibn Umail's original text, the dialogue is between the figures of Qālimūs and Rūnūs.[58] In the intermediate Latin translation, the debate is between 'Solomon' and a 'Sage'. Chaucer has exteneded his translation between the lines. In Ibn Umayl's text, Rūnūs asks simply: '*mā al-maghnīsīyā*' [what is magnesia?] – Ibn Umayl's irreverent questioning of Plato is Chaucer's addition.[59] The interpolated dialogue, with its broken metre and abrasive tone, recalls the interruptive manner in which Chaucer's ventriloquised women speak. The Wife of Bath loses her train of thought in her prologue: 'But now, *sire*, let me see what I shall say. |

A ha!' (III. 585–6). These marginalised, ventriloquised voices – an English wife, an anonymised Arab poet – echo each other across the *Tales*. Inhabiting the translated Arabic text, Chaucer veers further from literal translation, in the aim of creating an audible voice, an English echo.

As heard above, in Ibn Umayl's *Letter of the Sun to the Crescent Moon*, the source of the alchemical Elixir is recorded: magnesia. Elsewhere in the *Letter*, Ibn Umayl writes that:

> *abār nuḥās* is perfect . . . for they are named inferior to *Magnesia* . . . whose bodies are masculine and feminine, collected and coagulate . . . which are called grains, & salts, & soda, & alum.[60]

In other words, alum and other salts are like magnesia – but inferior. A blend of masculine and feminine coagulate elements, alum is still unstable and transformative, glassy. Albertus Magnus describes magnesia as 'a black stone frequently used by glassmakers. This stone melts and fuses if the fire is very strong, but not otherwise; and then, mixed with the glass, it purifies its substance.'[61] In his work on alchemy, Norton writes of Magnesia that 'The price of a ounce conveniently | Is xx. shillings'.[62] Bought in bulk, alum was more accessible than the ideal material of Magnesia – and could be used for the same purposes. These poetic records of the purchase of minerals for alchemy are witnesses that these translated ideas were designed for practice. When alum was used in its crystallised form, as *alum glass*, that transparency brought it closer to the ideal substance for the making of the Elixir.

Ibn Umayl draws his doctrine of Magnesia from the works of Maria Prophetissa, the earliest historically attested alchemist of Hellenistic Egypt (active before 200 CE).[63] Known variously as Maria 'the Hebrew' or Maria 'the Jewess', the influence of Maria Prophetissa was widespread across the Islamic world for more than a millennium after her death. The inventor of a wide range of alchemical apparatus and concepts, Maria's name survives today in the still commonly used 'bain-marie' – Maria's bath.[64]

Ibn Umayl writes: 'Māriyyah has called *abār nuḥās* the "Honoured stone" & . . . Consequently it gives birth to the Perfect Gold.'[65] Māriyyah al-'Ibrāniyyah [the Hebrew], as she is known in Ibn Umayl's work, is cited by name no less than twenty times in the *Risālat al-Shams ilā al-Hilāl*, making her one of the primary sources. Raphael Patai suggests that Ibn Umayl appears to have owned a number of her books, now lost to us.[66]

In Chaucer's translation, Plato explains that Magnesia is: 'a water that is made, I say, | Of elements four' (VIII. 1459–60). Here Magnesia is characterised as an alloy of four minerals, or four elements. Maria

Prophetissa defines the 'divine water' used to make gold as a combination of sulphurous minerals, such as alum, along with the 'tetrasomia', an alloy of copper, iron, lead, and zinc. The 'elements four' used to make the alchemical water in Chaucer's tale, while evoking the four elements of earth, air, water, and fire, can also be seen as an allusion to Maria's concept of the *tetrasomia*.

Transmitted into Chaucer's work, Maria and Ibn Umayl have lost their names. 'The Canon's Yeoman's Tale' leaves us with the echoes of these foundational alchemical figures and their own deep transhistorical dialogue. Like alum dissolving into water, the original substance of Maria's and Ibn Umayl's texts has melted away in translation. When the text is held up to the sun so that Englishness can evaporate, their ashes become visible again. These salty phrases are remnants which have resisted destruction – traces of Maria's books, which are gone except in fragments.

The Dead Sea and the Alchemist's Den

In 'The Canon's Yeoman's Tale', alchemists are treacherous. The Canon who wants to join the pilgrimage is a resident of 'the *suburbes* of a town' (VIII. 657). When the Yeoman tells his narrative, which considers a group of alchemists based in London, he warns that these people are 'among us' (VIII. 973). These are settled English fraudsters, local practitioners of Sodomite transformations.

Alchemical practice was often perceived as irreligious: unsanctioned human endeavours to transform the God-made world. This anti-natural element of the craft brought out an affinity between the alchemists and the Sodomite minerals which they used. The Yeoman tells the reader how to spot an alchemist:

> Men may them know by *smel of brymstoon*,
> For all the world they stink like a goat:
> Their *savour* is so *rammysh* and so hot
> That though a man be a mile away
> The *savour* will *infecte* him, trusteth me. (VIII. 885–9)

The sulphurous stench of the alchemist's den recalls the bitter stink of the Dead Sea. In the Yeoman's words, the smell can 'infecte' from a distance. These infectious stinks are clearly immoral – signalled in the biblical language of brimstone. Similarly, the *Pearl*-poet describes the Dead Sea as a '*stynkande stanc*' – a stinking pool – the stench exuded as a consequence of that 'destroyed sin'.[67] In Trevisa's work, if a material 'stinks', it signifies that 'the substance is unclean . . . evil and horrible to *kynde* [nature]'.[68] The image of the alchemists, derisively described as animalistic, recalls to mind the grinning horned goat pictured beneath the salty block of Lot's wife – an image of the Devil.

In alchemical practice, Sodomite minerals are explosive – an action which recalls the original transformative explosion of the cursed cities collapsing into the Dead Sea. Chaucer's Canon's Yeoman comments that often it happens so: 'the pot *tobreketh*, and farewell, all is gone! These metals are of such great violence that the '*walles*' of the pot cannot make 'resistance' – even if the pot is made from 'stoon', the metals '*percen* so' – pierce – and 'through the wall they go | And some of them *synken* into the ground' (VIII. 906–12). In a blast of smoke, the pot breaks apart – in an echo of the destruction of Sodom.

The *Pearl*-poet's cities '*torof*' as the cauldron '*tobreketh*'. The inhabitants of Sodom and Gomorrah sunk into the ground, as these precious metals sink into the floor of the alchemist's chambers. Both scenes are dangerously close to Hell. The Yeoman describes how the gathered alchemists curse the 'fiend' who they cannot see, but who they assume is 'with us' – that '*shrewe*!' (VIII. 916–17). They blame the Devil for the failure of their experiment. The Devil cracks the floor of Sodom and the walls of the pot, which are both destroyed through the sudden combustion of sulphurous minerals. Alchemy and Sodomy alike take place on fragile surfaces beneath which hellfire simmers. The alchemists sweep the floor for fragments of alum and metal to be recycled in the next attempt. These glassy shards are too useful to be discarded. The alchemist's den and the Dead Sea are both places of destruction and recovery: both that lake and the collapsed cauldron are cursed sites from which useful minerals can still be sieved.

Divine Revelation and Cursed Transformations

The association between the alchemist's den and the Dead Sea gestures to the fact that – as with medieval attitudes towards the Dead Sea – alchemy occupied the troubling borderline between manmade heresy and sanctioned miracle. This paradox lay at the heart of alchemical practice, and at the centre of medieval attitudes towards alum.

Across the Abrahamic faiths, alchemy was said to be the product of divine revelation. The tenth-century Baghdad-based bibliographer al-Nadīm claims that alchemy was revealed by Allāh to Moses and Aaron.[69]

The alchemist Maria was described as a prophet by Muslim, Jewish, and Christian authors.[70] Ibn Umayl writes of how:

> Some said regarding this Art that it is from eggs, hair, dung, urine, blood, bile, sperm, sulphur and other defective combustible corruptible and perishable minerals. After they came to know that it is a perfect science of great importance which surpasses all other sciences and that it is the secret of Great and Almighty Allāh . . . they gave up the idea that it proceeds from Eggs, Hair, Arsenics, Sulphurs, and from (other) filthy and impure things . . . Allāh forbid![71]

These denied substances appear grouped in 'The Canon's Yeoman's Tale': '*Unslekked* [non-hydrated] limestone, chalk, and egg-white, | Powders diverse, *asshes*, dung, *pisse* and clay' (VIII. 806–7). Alchemical practice worked with these bodily and unclean substances: the theoretical separation between holy revelation and defective materials was not upheld in workshops. Ibn Umayl's attempt to salvage alchemy as a holy art relied on excising the primary materials of that art from its depiction.

In alchemy and gem-lore, alum was used to cleanse pearls, following Arabic texts such as al-Bīrūnī's *Book of Stones*.[72] In one anonymous fourteenth-century compilation of dye and medicinal recipes, the Trinity Encyclopaedist begins: 'For to clarify *perles* and to make them bright and shining. Take of *alum roche*.' The alum is dissolved 'in common water, that is to say in Thames water or in water of a well' and a scrap of linen is soaked in the alumed water. Then '*frote* [rub] well with thine hands that piece of linen cloth with thy *perles* therein in that water that is so *distillyd* with a *feltre* [matted felt] ever more washing and *gnoddyng* [kneading] them well between thy hands intil they be clear enough'.[73] Appearing in conjunction with the relic-like pearl, the bitter alum does not taint the transcendental purity of that sacred product – it enhances it. Alum here is used as an alternative to sweet wine: elsewhere, 'good *Malvosyn*' is also recommended to cleanse pearls.[74] Drawing on these practical traditions, in *Cleanness* the *Pearl*-poet advises that to clean pearls, you should: 'wash them with worship in *wyn*', which will cause them 'by *kynde* [nature]' to become 'clearer than before'.[75] The 'nature' of the pearl is transformed through worshipful treatment with wine, placing two divine substances into sacred contact. Meanwhile in other workshops, Sodomite salts were used to polish Christ-like pearls and to make the Elixir.

Medieval English authors who wanted to depict alchemy as divine Christian revelation faced a further challenge. In addition to the problematic nature of alchemical materials, they needed to assimilate the unavoidably non-Christian origins of their science. In his *Ordinal*, Norton warded off allegations that 'holy *Alchymye*' was first known by 'pagans', stating that 'this science was never taught to man' unless he had been proved 'perfectly'.[76]

In Chaucer's translation of Ibn Umayl, alchemical revelation is attributed to Christ: a figure who does not feature in the original Arabic text. In the Yeoman's continuation of the dialogue between the anonymised Ibn Umayl and Plato, despite the disciple's demands, Plato refuses to reveal the true root of the Elixir. Only the substances of Magnesia and the four elements are named, but not the final source: 'for unto Christ it is so dear' that he does not wish it to be 'discovered' except 'where it liketh to his Deity | Men for to inspire' (VIII. 1467–70). For either Plato (the ancient Greek philosopher) or Qālimūs (Ibn Umayl's Muslim sage, from whose script Chaucer's character of Plato speaks), the reference to Christ is a departure from context, an alteration of their voice. The critic Dorothee Metlitzki points out that this passage of Chaucer corresponds to a later moment of Ibn Umayl's text, in which he describes an agreement made among a group of philosophers. In Ibn Umayl's text, these philosophers discover the root of the Elixir but vow to conceal their findings: 'not one of them would reveal it and they referred the matter concerning it to Allāh'.[77] Through sequential translations from Arabic to Latin to English, 'Allāh' becomes 'Deus' [God] becomes 'Christ'.[78]

In Chaucer's work, the Yeoman admits that alchemy is a contravention of Christian law, unless the alchemist has specifically received divine inspiration. He advises: 'let it go. | For whoever maketh God his adversary | As for to work anything in contrary | Of his will, certainly, never shall he thrive' (VIII. 1475–8). Used as the components of a cursed practice against the will of God, the Sodomite materials of brimstone and sulphur are laced with the memory of Sodomite acts. Alchemy itself becomes a quasi-Sodomite craft both in its ingredients and its subversive framework. Even while the tale dwells on the damned aspects of alchemy, there is a sense that there may be those in the audience who remain undeterred in their own experimental practice.

Chaucer's 'Canon's Yeoman's Tale' was received as a practical alchemical text throughout the later medieval and early modern periods. The text was circulated throughout the fifteenth and sixteenth centuries as an extract, found in alchemical miscellanies designed for functional use. The idea of Chaucer as alchemist was a vivid fiction, used to create an English genealogy for early modern practitioners in the British Isles.[79] In one sixteenth- or seventeenth-century miscellany, beside a recipe for the philosopher's stone a later hand has crossed out the stated author, 'Arnoldi de villa nova', and made the marginal insertion: 'Galfeidus Chaucer his worke'.[80] The early modern attribution of the Elixir as Chaucer's 'work' testifies to generations of alchemists who read 'The Canon's Yeoman's Tale' as far from a cautionary tale – that is, as a guide. Alum exists as a witness to the practical application of alchemical texts, which show Sodomite salts as an imaginative category with a material impact.

Making English Culture with Sodomite Salt

Beyond alchemy, alum found its way into English crafts, from medicine to clothmaking to bookmaking. While alchemy was the primary intellectual framework for the use of alum, the cloth trade was the primary sector which gave the mineral its economic value. The primacy of the cloth industry, and especially the wool trade, made these Sodomite salts essential to the medieval English economy. Alum was a mordant needed for the application of dyes to linen, wool, and imported silks, used when preparing these cloths to receive dye. It was its use as a fixative which rendered alum so indispensable, and required it to be imported in bulk. In the *Etymologies*, Isidore speculates that 'Alum (alumen) is named from "light" (lumen), because it furnishes brightness to cloth being dyed'.[81]

The alchemical background of alum was not forgotten in these crafts. The Yeoman names 'verdegrees' as a material for alchemy (VIII. 790), but that substance was more commonly used for the green tints of medieval inks.[82] The capacity of alum to transform and to fix, to dissolve and melt as well as remain crystalline in powdered form, which rendered it so essential to early English science and industry, remained an extension of its protean Sodomite and alchemical identity, as a mineral beyond the laws of nature.

In medieval dyers' manuals, alum appears as both noun and verb, as in one anonymous early fifteenth-century manuscript:

> For to *alyme* thy cloth, first take thine *alyme* and make it small, and then put it in water and set it over the fire, and melt thine *alome*, and then *nym* [grasp] thy cloth and wet it . . . and then when thou *alemyst* thy cloth, take a little linen *clout* [scrap] and *alyme* it with thy *clout*, for when thou makest thy colours thou may see by thy *clout* if it be good or no.[83]

Alum changes form with each step: crushed, dissolved, melted, soaked into cloth. The method of using alum is described with clarity in this recipe, each step marked chronologically, in stacked clauses: 'first . . . then . . . then . . . then . . . when'. Frequently, dyes also contained alum: layers of the mineral building up on the cloth, each one reaffirming the necessity of the imported material. As one compiler put it succinctly, 'put alum with every colour'.[84] Another contemporary compilation for stainers describes in more detail how to make 'Scarlet water. Seth a pound of brasilwood [a red pigment] in urine that never was cold till it be *mult* [melted], then put thereto a pound of alum and stir it well till it be *mult*, then put therein gum of *Arabi*, and resolve it to a pot of earth with all the dregs.'[85] In this recipe alum is mixed with hot urine and earth: a typical combination of substances used to prepare medieval dyes. Relic-like silks were plunged into debased liquids. The combination of alum with imported acacia sap, known as 'gum of Arabi', places two imported goods together.[86] The local and the foreign are dissolved together in the process.

Both the other materials and the implements used for dying could also be sourced from the local surroundings, as in this description of polishing cloth from a late fifteenth- or early sixteenth-century household book:

> To make a cloth for to shine when it is *wroght* [done]. Take alum and grind it small, and take egg-white and put the alum therein, and let it stand and it will be water, and then make a brush of squirrel tail and glaze the cloth there-with and it will shine.[87]

Alum was integral to creating the symbolically charged dyes with which fabrics were rendered articulate in the medieval imagination. The types of cloths which required glazing were typically those high-status fabrics discussed previously as holy relics: 'For to refresh *clothe of golde* . . . take water of *alam* and glaze over.'[88] Alum creates a protective surface over these fabrics, sealing them from damage, confirming their precious identity by sharpening their reflective gleam. At the same time, alum was mixed with the everyday, egg whites and locally sourced squirrels' tails. Drawn towards its imagined Holy Land origins through contact with precious relic-like cloths of gold, alum remains grounded in the proximate world of English wildlife and produce. The imported mineral was protean in its material form, and in its capacity to settle and combine with other objects in the lands of arrival.

The style of these dye recipes is meticulous and practical, assuming the medieval reader's access to the ingredients and need to follow the instructions. These are manuscripts which belonged in workshops:

> For to make white sheep's leather, as for bags or *qwyschouns* [cushions] or what other thing that thou want . . . Take the alum and melt it . . . and then take thy *skyn* and put it in thine *alum watre*, and alum it well upon the *flessche* [flesh] side.[89]

'To make', 'to take', to put', 'to alum' – the mineral falls easily into the sequence of commands, a verb as familiar within this technical context as the other unspecialised words. Within a sentence, alum moves from solid to molten fluid to dissolved substance until it leaves the realm of nouns altogether and becomes an action. The use of alum as a verb is repeated within the Trinity Encyclopaedist's work. To make red leather, the direction is similar: 'take thy *skyn* . . . and *alumne* it in a quantity of *alum watre*'.[90] Here alum acts on animal skin, on flesh for garments or bookbindings. Within manuscripts, vellum or parchment pages were also often treated with alum before receiving alum-mixed inks. Alum becomes a verb at the moment at which it is brought to act upon skin. Itself an inanimate material which has become an active agent, alum is brushed along the remnants of bodies which have once been active and which are now inanimate material. Alum is crucial in that final stage of a process of turning what was a nonhuman agent into an object for human use. Another common command in the Trinity Encyclopaedist is to pound cloth 'until the alum be clean *drunken* into thy *skyn*'.[91] The turn of phrase curiously reverses the process again: now alum is the passive object of absorption, while the lifeless skin is imaginatively revived to drink, posthumously. Alum passes fluidly between passive and active and causes the object on which it acts to do the same. The use of alum in preparing leathers for dying is especially marked in relation to the ubiquitous use of alum in treating human skin during surgical procedures.

The Sodomite Craft of Surgery

The Sodomite salts – alum, brimstone, sulphur, and other substances associated with hellfire – were valuable medicines. In medical manuscripts, their healing properties were often recorded alongside their association with moral impurity, which has been witnessed in both the alchemist's den and the Dead Sea. Trevisa writes – having said that 'stench' is a sign of evil – 'sometime it happens that *stynche* helpeth'.[92] Following the medical lore of Ibn Sīnā and Constantine, strong smells were viewed as having potent curative properties.[93] The corrosive qualities of bitter minerals likewise were needed for their cleansing operations. Medical practice often employed the same apparatus and ingredients as alchemy: one fifteenth-century manuscript of the *Liber Medicinarum* of John Arderne (1307–80) contains an illustration of furnaces, stills, and other equipment explicitly designed for either the preparation of remedies or transmutation.[94] Accordingly, the alchemical frameworks through which

Figure 5.5 Asphalt. Source: British Library, London. Egerton MS 747, fol. 9, detail. Printed with permission of Bridgeman Images.

alum was viewed as the source of the Elixir remain proximate to these medical records of alum.

The medical uses of these salts explicitly invoked the narrative of their Dead Sea origins. In one illuminated manuscript of the medical encyclopaedia *Tractatus de Herbis* – previously discussed for its depiction of alum mines – the visual referent used to illustrate the minerals asphalt and bitumen is a dark city in flames [Figure 5.5]. The iconography in this medicinal herbal mirrors the representations of Sodom found in biblical illuminations and medieval maps. The image is labelled: the minerals 'Aspaltu-i-bitumen' are located at the historic site of 'sodome et gomorree'. Within the text, the reader is informed that these minerals are sourced from 'd'ultramaris' – Outremer, the crusader name for the Frankish settlements.[95] At this site, the lost biblical cities and the lost crusader settlements are brought together as the imagined origin points of minerals – which were in fact available in contemporary marketplaces across the Mediterranean. The appearance of imagined architecture is uncharacteristic for the book: typically, textual entries for plants are accompanied by botanical drawings, enabling the reader to identify and select the correct plant. Shifting in time and geography, the image of asphalt and bitumen would not help a reader to select these salts from a shelf in an apothecary's shop.

An understanding of their connection to Sodom did not undermine the medicinal virtues of alum and asphalt. Instead, medieval practical texts witnessed the creation of a distinct category of Sodomite salts, the properties of which were directly associated with biblical sin and which continued to prove their utility in the present moment because of, and not in spite of, those origins. Chauliac writes that '*Alume roche* is hot and dry in the third degree . . . *Aspaltum* is hardened scum that is found in the *Dede See*; it is hot and dry about the second degree; it heals ulcers'.[96] The humoural heat of alum and asphalt derives from the land in which these minerals originate – the heat of the cities turned to ash.

Chauliac cites Ibn Sīnā and Galen as authorities for the use of alum in plasters for ulcers, especially those which are 'hard to heal with a property that is hid to us'.[97] The mysterious and suspect quality of alum as a shapeshifting, transmutational mineral enables it to deal with the invisible, elusive causes of disease. When Chauliac provides a list of medical '*corrosyfes*', the catalogue replicates the corrosive minerals represented in *Cleanness* as the trace of biblical sin.[98] These medicinal uses do not erase the hellish connotations. According to medieval understandings, brimstone was capable of being at once a terrible reminder of God's wrath and a virtuous substance. The term 'virtue', which was used to describe the properties of relic-like stones, was also used to describe the properties of Sodomite salt. As Trevisa writes: '*brymston* . . . hath *vertu* of tempering . . . of consuming and wasting, and of . . .. restoring'.[99] The virtuous strength of alum, asphalt, and brimstone was paradoxically intertwined with the sense that those properties originated in acts which contravened divine law.[100] That which was antithetical to spiritual 'cleanness' in the works of the *Pearl*-poet could, without alteration, be used to cleanse the body from infection.

In the anonymous Middle English translation of Guy de Chauliac's *Cyrurgie*, the author comments that his advice for surgery is written 'after the lore of *Albucasis*, the which all *leches* [doctors] know'.[101] 'Albucasis' refers to the Andalucian physician Abū al-Qāsim al-Zahrāwī (936–1013) whose *Kitāb al-Taṣrīf* [Book of the Method] had been translated into Latin in the twelfth century by Gerard of Cremona, and whose encyclopaedic works provided the model for Chauliac's own.[102] Following al-Zahrāwī, the English author describes how to treat inflammation: 'forsooth . . . take up the *skyn* with shears . . . and that which is above the skin, cut it off with *scheres*'. After cutting up the skin with scissors, the procedure continues: 'on the first day, dress the wound with cotton or such other dipped in *salte* water. I do it forsooth with egg-white made thick with *alume*.'[103] This description of the medical use of alum recalls the methods used for its application in the dye industry. In both cloth-making and surgery, alum is mixed with egg – here to create a smooth gel, cleansing and soothing. In other workshops, a similar mixture was spread on leathers: in surgery, that substance acts on the human body, drawing the human and the animal into association, with alum used abrasively on the boundaries of both.

In an early fifteenth-century English translation of John Arderne's fourteenth-century Latin treatises of *Fistula in Ano* [Ulcers in the Anus], alum appears in surgical use within the body, as well as on that boundary. Like Chauliac, Arderne writes in the first person, authenticating his text through his documentation of the patients he treated as a Master Surgeon: 'I, John Arderne from the first *pestilence* that was in the year of our lord 1349 dwelled in Newark in *Notyngham-shire* unto the year of our lord 1370, and there I healed many men of *fistula in ano*.'[104] Arderne's view is that clinical practice should be the foundation of medical lore, referring to Ibn Sīnā: '*Avicen*, forsooth, says that "experience overcometh reason"; and Galen *in pantegni* says that, "No man ought for to trust in reason alone but if it be proved of experience".'[105] These citations position Arderne as a learned reader of Arabic medical traditions in their translated editions. As with dyers' manuals, these medical works are practical in expression; these recurrent references to alum in both Chauliac's and Arderne's works assume that the reader will have ready access to the mineral for their own surgical practice.

Alum was attributed with the capacity to renew flesh. Acting to reverse the natural decay of the wounded body, the corrosive properties of alum recall its imagined origins in the anti-natural waters of the Dead Sea. Arderne states that 'powder of *alum ȝucarin combust*' – burned potash alum – has '*vertu* in regeneration of *flesch* and *cicatrizacione* [healing]'.[106] This medical term 'vertu' echoes the language of lapidaries and herbals, used to express the God-given properties of stones, minerals, and herbs.[107] Arderne describes how the doctor should take alum: 'And meddle it with the yolk of a raw egg' – echoing recipes used in alchemy and the dye industry. He goes on to say that the doctor should add 'a little oil of linseed ... if it be had, or *sanguis veneris*' – a mixture of aloe, myrrh, alkenet, and dragon's blood – 'or *melle rosat*' – rose-scented honey.[108] These products brought their own associations: roses, honey, and myrrh evoke biblical sweetness, dragon's blood is mythological, and alkenet was used to create the palette of crusader cuisine – all of these connotations are relevant here, combining with the potent mineral to create the sense of a supernatural power in the gluey cure. Then the doctor should soak the mixture 'with soft strips of linen cut small or with cotton. Be it put warily into the wound. For why? It cleanseth the wound and healeth and dryeth it well for certain.'[109] Alum cleanses, heals, dries – it is an active agent.

Ardene carried out his surgeries on elite patients, whom he records, addressing as 'your *gentilnes* and your highness'.[110] Chauliac records a recipe for 'a powder the which Master Arnold made Pope John for the redness and moistness of eyes', made from '*margery perles*', coral, and 'raw silk'.[111] In these cures, relic-like commodities are brought to bear on the ailing bodies of the nobility and the Papacy. The use of powdered pearls and silks to cure the Pope's eyes integrates relic discourse with scientific understanding: spiritual narratives were fundamental to medieval understandings of the world, underpinning medical practice as well as religious ritual. Holy cures for holy men were expected – and if the laity could access them, these same holy cures would do anyone good. Chauliac claims that he cured himself of the Black Death using a mixture of pearls, coral, sapphire, emeralds, aloe, spices, and sweetened roses.[112] The spiritual qualities of Holy Land goods increased doctors' sense of their healing properties. Similarly, the ability of alum to corrode and cleanse flesh was observed in clinical practice, and understood through its Sodomite backstory.

The Miners' Sickness

Alum was both cure and cause of disease in the late medieval period. The Swiss physician, theologian, and alchemist Theophrastus von Hohenheim (1453–1541), known as Paracelsus, described the impact of alum on those who worked in the mines in his posthumously published treatise *On the Miners' Sickness* (1567). The text is regarded as a foundational work of occupational medicine, and draws on the same translated traditions which provided the basis for dietary and surgical practice. Based on personal observation of mining conditions, Paracelsus comments on the lack of attention to these issues in ancient texts, implying that the concerns which he documents have been present for centuries. Of alum mines, Paracelsus writes that 'those who work . . . in alum and sulphur ore . . . succumb to the lung disease, to consumption of the body and to stomach ulcers'.[113] He identifies the alum and acid in the mines as the cause of asthma, or 'hoarseness of the lung'.[114] The miners coughed and wasted as they dug for alum rock. In Genoese-run mines in Phokaia, enslaved labour was enlisted in these unsafe practices.

If the miners' sickness was detected, then Paracelsus recommended a cure: alum. Basing his advice on the Greek concept of the *pharmakon* – a word which means both cure and poison – Paracelsus writes that: the 'physic is in mercury, sulphur and salt, and our poison is also in these three things'. He recommends that miners suffering from alum-induced sickness should take salt boiled from alum, which should be used instead of medicinal spice.[115] This concept of the *pharmakon* can be seen at work in the use of alum in medicine more broadly. The substance seen as the cause of spiritual infection was seen as the cure for physical infections. The surgeon John Arderne used the ulcer-inducing mineral to treat ulcers in the anuses of the elite.

Alongside miners, goldsmiths, minters, and smelters, the other category of workers identified by Paracelsus as suffering from 'the mineral diseases' were the alchemists.[116] Himself a practitioner of the art, the impact of mercurial smoke and acidic vapours on the lungs of alchemists would have been known first-hand to Paracelsus. There are literary figures of which this diagnosis can be made. In Chaucer's prologue to 'The Canon's Yeoman's Tale', the Yeoman's complexion is described as being discoloured through alchemical practice which has, he claims, left him unable to blush: 'for fumes diverse | Of metals, which you have heard me rehearse, | Consumed and wasted have my *reednesse*' (VIII. 1098–100). As a sufferer of the miner's sickness, the Yeoman receives no treatment, alum-based or otherwise. Instead the Yeoman becomes a compulsive raconteur, substituting verbal articulacy for the loss of nonverbal expression caused by mineral smoke. He lists the strange terms of his craft – his alum-based 'gibberish' making him a compelling narrator. The suffering of alchemists survives in medieval texts which centre these figures as authors and subjects. By contrast, the suffering of the alum miners survives in the posthumously published work of an external observer of their labour – their experience is the unremembered context for an unacknowledged object.

Alum is the invisible witness of ephemeral historical subjects: the imagined Sodomites and unrecorded miners whose bodies were disfigured and destroyed in the process of making the glassy base of medieval cultural production.

'Aluminated' Manuscripts

Alum was involved in the core acts of creation of the medieval book: used in glues for bookbinding, in the rulings for text boxes, in the preparation of the parchment to receive texts and images, and in the inks which were used to paint the illuminations and letters onto the page. These recipes are recorded in dedicated dyers' manuals, but are also found in manuscripts which compile practical texts alongside other varied genres. One late fifteenth- or early sixteenth-century notebook, signed by Robert Reynes of Acle in Norfolk, contains recipes for ink, paint, and book glue alongside charms, astrology, memoranda, medical recipes, and miscellaneous

Christian texts and verses.[117] These manuscripts witness a shared vocabulary and imaginary between these diverse crafts, juxtaposing the making of texts with the making of gold, with the mineral alum running seamlessly between these blurred disciplines. In addition, the manuscripts in which ink recipes are found assert the continued relevance of Arabic scientific traditions. For example, one fifteenth-century manuscript contains recipes 'for to *makyn vernysch*' and pigments for bookmaking alongside translations of Hippocrates and Ibn Sīnā, alchemical and astronomical texts, charms, cosmetic recipes, and herbals.[118] These manuscripts move between interrelated environments: mercantile, medical, scribal, occult. These books and the texts which they contain are the products of a unified imagination, industrial-poetic.

The use of alum to make inks is recorded in the works of the Trinity Encyclopaedist: 'For to make a colour which *lymenours* call *colour de rose.* Take the shavings of brasilwood that be fine 2. ounces, of fair small powder of *alum de glas* 1. ounce, and of fair powder of chalk half an ounce.'[119] The recipe code-switches between Middle English and French, gesturing to the multilingual workshops of the lymnors – the illuminators' guild. Medieval manuscripts were the products of multilingual environments both in their composition – which often involved acts of translation – and in the spaces in which the physical materials were made. The Trinity Encyclopaedist's manual evokes the scene of a circle of craftspeople working with imported items, many of whom were themselves immigrants, such as the Belgian 'Copyn *de Brugges*', named towards the conclusion of the collection.[120] The transnational groups who were employed to work with alum belonged to the international networks which brought the mineral to England – there was a direct path from the trading routes into the workshop.

As with dyes and medicines, alum was mixed with everyday local objects in the process of ink-making. For example, the Trinity Encyclopaedist gives instructions 'For to make *tornesole.* Take the black elderberries or else *blackberies* that grow on hedges, and stamp them in a mortar and wring out the juice into a fair vessell, then take the *alum glas* and dissolve it in clean water over the fire.'[121] 'Turnesole' is the term for a dye extracted from a natural flower. Alum glass is mixed with fruit picked from hedges, the archetypal image of the English countryside '*resolved*' with the imported mineral over the hearth. These purplish and pink inks recall the hues used, for example, in the previously discussed illustration of Sodom burning [Figure 5.2]. The mineral salts which were imagined to have been dredged from the Dead Sea were now being used to help colour Lot's daughter's fetching pink turban.

Alum was also used in the construction of the text blocks which were the first stage of preparing the page to receive words, and in text ink itself.[122] Although such rulings were often made using lead pencil, one smaller compilation of ink recipes recommends:

> To make fine resin to write withal or to rule thus. Take *brasell* and *schaf* [shave] it small, and put it in an earthen *potte*, and take thy *pisse* and put thereto, and let it stand all the night, and at morning take a little *alome glasse* . . . and let it seethe.[123]

The book-maker pisses into a clay pot before boiling it with alum – that is the fluid in which language will receive its material form. Present in page rulings and resin used for writing, alum was integral to the formation of the medieval book.

The London mercer John Colyns (d. c. 1542) copied out a series of fifteenth-century poems, medical prescriptions, astrological works, and regulations against foreign merchants' activities alongside recipes for dyes, pigments, and book production. John Colyns' book operates in what seems now to be a miscellany mode, but the varied trades and genres which are recorded within these pages are not distinct from one another. The book moves between interrelated environments – mercantile, medical, scribal, occult – and in so doing witnesses the movement of people and objects across intellectual and professional boundaries. Just as one manuscript might be needed in multiple workshops, so alum slips from the alchemist's den to the scriptorium and back. Colyns' book includes a recipe which recommends alum as a fixative in preparing the manuscript sheet:

> if thou wilt make *staunche greyne* to amend thy parchment and make it to receive *inke*. Take 2 parts of *rosyn* and one of *alom* and *grynde* them in a dry brass mortar to powder . . . and when thou wilt, *sawe* it *thynne* on thy *boke* and *rubbe* it over with thy *hande*. And write then.[124]

Alum is ground, dried, and shaken over the parchment through a sieve – not melted into a liquid, or stirred into egg-white, as seen elsewhere in the process of textual production. The page is rubbed by hand – in a physical, individualised act of making.

One fifteenth-century treatise on ink-making records that alum was used to enable other objects to receive texts, beyond books: 'Item to write on a *swerd* or a *knyf*. Take powder of *alomglas* and *sal gemme* and temper it up with olde urine.'[125] As a fixative, alum became invisible in the process of being dissolved and mixed, but remained essential to the generation of recorded language. Melted and mixed away, the traces of alum cling to the words, images, and apparatus of the medieval book.

No wonder then that some medieval compilers began to think of their craft not as 'illumination' but 'alumination'. One collection advises: 'To make *lettres* of *golde* on *alomnyng* do thus: First form thy letters with thy *cyse* [dilute glue] and let them dry all that day, and look thou touch them not with thy hands for if thou do they will take no *golde*.'[126] The process which follows does not contain alum. The scribe has slipped between words: '*lymnyng*' has become '*alomnyng*' – an error which is encouraged by both the similarity of sounds and the association between alum and the craft described. The slip is repeated. In another collection – the same manuscript in which squirrels' tails were recommended as glazing brushes – a recipe reads: 'To dry *brasil water* when it is *cruddid* [crusted] to be substantial for *alumpnars* or *steynars*'.[127] The recipe describes the preparation of brasilwood pigment, for use in illumination or cloth-dying. Instead of the 'lymnors' – the illuminators' guild – the group of workers has been named as the '*alumpnars*'. The craft becomes named as the practice of those who work with alum: the bookmakers and the painters are 'alumners'. Gilded manuscripts are defined through the presence of light-bringing salt. The mutable mineral becomes a descriptor for the making of medieval books. Without alum, the words would not have stayed fixed to the page.

When precious silk threads were woven into lettering, the fabric became the object of devotion: the textile glimmered, the material and the text contemplated together. By contrast, when alum was melted, shaken, and painted onto medieval pages, it was taken for granted more than it was worshipped. Alum has a long-standing use in the production of invisible inks around the world and across time: by 980 CE, secret messages were being written in alum in China, where there were also alum mines. In the sixteenth-century, those accused of heresy during the Inquisition, Elizabethan spies, and forbidden lovers passed each other notes in alum.[128] The medieval story of alum itself has been written in invisible ink: held up to the light, it becomes visible again.

Conclusion: Restoring a Melted Rock to View

Chaucer's dream vision *The House of Fame* builds towards an image which crystallises the significance of alum as a cultural substance. The dream begins with the narrator, self-referentially named 'Geoffrey', walking around a temple made of glass, in the middle of a Libyan desert. From this arid, glittering shrine, Geoffrey is picked up by an eagle, who carries him through the skies and across the oceans until, in the third book of the poem, he is dropped off on a marvellously bright rock. He recounts how 'up I *clomb*' – climbed – 'with *alle payne*' – in pain, persevering even 'though to *clymbe* it grieved me'. He desires to see 'what *maner stoon this roche was.* | For it was like *alum de glas*'. Alum glass and this glittering rock are alike, except that the stone shines 'full more clear'.[129] The bright, transparent rock is inscribed with famous names: 'but I could scarcely know | Any letters to read | Their names by; for, *out of drede*' – without doubt – 'they were almost *ofthowed*' – thawed off, until 'of the letters *oon* or two | Was *molte* away of every name'.[130] The iced letters melt away, as alum glass is melted in the processes of ink-making and alchemical experimentation. The unfixity of alum becomes the unfixity of the material text itself, its potential to alter in transmission, through damage and the unreliability of reception.

In the absence of critical awareness of the significance of alum in medieval culture, economy, and imagination, literary references to alum have been easy for scholars to overlook. Kathy Cawsey has argued for a correction of critical editions of this text such that this line would read '*lyk alymed glas*'. For Cawsey, changing 'alum de glas' to 'alymed glas' would bring out what she assumes is the intended primary image: the engraved rock standing on the shore like a large stained (or 'illuminated') glass window. This modern editorial change, curiously, would replicate the medieval scribal slippages found in dyers' manuals, in which 'to alum' was used as a synonym for 'to illuminate'.[131] For Cawsey, seeing Chaucer's rock as a stained-glass window would emphasise the textuality of the rock, as a stand-in for the fragility of manuscripts, with their breakable pages. Although I agree that Chaucer's image invites the reader to reflect on the fragility of material texts, 'alum de glas' does not need to be altered for that reading to stand. The inscribed alum rock is drawn from observation of the craft of medieval book production. As seen in the Trinity Encyclopaedist's work and elsewhere, '*alum de glas*' was a technical vocabulary used in professional environments. Chaucer's engraved rock is constructed from the materials and the language used by illuminators. Unlike stained glass, alum was often seen melting in medieval England – in the workshops of alchemists, surgeons, stainers, and scribes.

The scribes who wrote 'aluming' for 'lymning' or 'alumpnors' for 'lymnors' did change 'oon or two' letters in each word. Language is always liable to change: in speech and in material documents, words bend to writers' habits, divert into new idioms. But medieval manuscripts – precious, rare, and so precarious at each complex stage of their production – kept this frailty of language at the foreground of authors' minds. Medieval writers knew their books would be miscopied, and might not last. When he looks at the gleaming, engraved, and obviously transient rock, Geoffrey thinks first of 'alum de glas': the material at the base of manuscripts, on which words at first seem fixed, but are likely to slip. In fact, as Geoffrey looks closer, he sees that the rock is made from ice. But the comparison with alum lingers as Geoffrey gazes on the vanishing letters.

In *Cleanness*, the collapse of Sodom and Gomorrah is described as the tearing of a manuscript. The walls burst 'as loose leaves of the book that *lepes* in two'.[132] The verb 'lepe' can mean fall apart, crack, smash – but when describing the action of liquid it means 'gush'; describing waves, it means 'surge', and when light is the subject, it means 'to shine'. As the cities break apart, their fragments become ashes, become water, become minerals – become the basis for illumination. The metaphor undercuts the official narrative of triumph over sin. The destruction of the cities becomes an image of the disappearance of knowledge, language, and imagination. Presenting the sunken communities as a torn book, the *Pearl*-poet leads the reader to mourn their absence. In this image, alum becomes the last trace of the lost book of Sodom: a salty fragment of a shredded page. There is a precedent for finding books near the site of Sodom. Between 1947 and 1956, a number of biblical, apocryphal, and sectarian manuscripts dated from the third century BCE to the first century CE were discovered in the caves near Khirbet Qumran, on the shores of the Dead Sea. Today the Dead Sea Scrolls are kept in the Shrine of the Book at the Israel Museum, in Jerusalem: the excavated text in the museum, the museum as a nation-making shrine. Meanwhile the Sodomite minerals eroding into the waters left behind them a polluted and paradoxical transnational inheritance.

The theorist Zygmunt Bauman has described the present condition of late modernity as a state of fragility and constant change: a state of liquidity, compared to the 'heaviness' which characterised modernity, during the establishment of colonial settlements and industrial practices.[133] The medieval representations of alum are scenes of the fragility and constant change which came before those conditions of modernity became fixed: scenes of the fluid premodern. These are transformative ashes, fragmentary reminders of loss. Alum anticipates present-day discourses and experiences of melting and dissolution, pollution and cultural instability. Viewed like ice in the glassy rock of Chaucer's dream, alum was a dynamically articulate, unstable substance.

Like oil today, alum was fundamental to medieval industry, imported through politically charged networks, making huge fortunes for individuals and states. Like oil today, alum was both essential and cursed: tainted with the understanding of its disreputable origins and, in the case of alchemy, its disreputable uses. The slipperiness of alum is representative of medieval attitudes towards the material, and especially towards the material imports of the Holy Land. Counterintuitive and paradoxical, alum melts away beneath language even as labels are graven into its side. Inscribed in alum-made stains on alum-powdered pages, Maria Prophetissa's instruments and theories are mostly unknown to modern readers, whose bain-marie now sits inexplicably named in the cupboard. Fundamental to the making of manuscripts, remedies, and dyes, this imported mineral directs us to acknowledge the translated texts which lay at the foundations of medieval literature and science.

The encounter with alum left medieval English culture full of Sodomite gibberish. That is: fluid materials and multilingual books. In use and imagination, alum was transmutational, suspect, sacred, and marketable. Seen through the shifting lens of the mineral alum, the alchemy of medieval trade becomes apparent. Medieval Syriana was both element and product of this economic process: circulating in multiple realities, transforming and being transformed.

CHAPTER 6

Coda: The English Market as the Temple of Jerusalem

John shook. Robert Sturmy had gone.

Desire has been seen as the principle underlying the modern capitalist economy.[1] The narratives of medieval Syriana articulate an alternative, ambivalent relationship between religion and money, floating on the desires which came before the cultural, economic, and political shifts of the Reformation and the Industrial Revolution.[2]

The last trace of Sturmy's cargo of Syriana is written in coins, the cargo itemised as a demand for golden compensation.[3] Sturmy's ships also contained '*coyne* and plate, that is to say nobles, salves and *dokettes* and other coin of *dyvers* countries received at Pisa, Naples and Rhodes and other places in their voyage to the sum of ... £1,200'.[4] Nobles minted in the Tower of London or Calais sit beside ducats and the illegible currencies of 'diverse countries'. These unlabelled '*other coyne*' could signal the presence on Sturmy's ship of dinars, dirhams, and ashrafis, the primary Mamlūk currencies, in circulation in the contact zones between Syria and England.[5] In the medieval period there was no notion of 'legal tender', with coins circulating with few restrictions across territories: there would have been nothing to prohibit the absorption of these coins into English markets except symbolic attachment – which could have seen them treasured instead of exchanged.[6] The 'salve', the last named coin on Sturmy's ship, bore the image of the Annunciation.[7] The imprinting of words and images on coins drew language and iconography into the marketplace: symbolic goods in circulation.[8]

The use of Christian iconography on coins meant that religious objects marked with these same stamps were at risk of marketisation – as the religious objects throughout this book have been riskily associated with the marketplace.[9] The illuminations of crusading kings on vellum sheets, the gold-haloed likenesses of Christ became disconcertingly laced with the memory of coins, contaminating these spiritual signs with financial associations. There was a dangerous potential for devotion to the coins on which these devotional images were printed, implying worship of the market itself. As Marc Shell has commented, the communion wafer was 'expressly manufactured like coin: it was pressed between wafer irons and impressed with insignia like those of coins'.[10] The use of communion tokens – imprinted disks used as tickets for Mass ceremonies – ran in parallel with the increasing use of bills of exchange, alongside records of the sale and purchase of debts.[11] These two forms of printed or inscribed tokens circulated simultaneously, both exchanged for disks which could bear the name or image of Jesus. The stamp which should have acted as the incontrovertible holy marker of authentication became dangerously unstable. The wafer and the coin, which should have been distant, became proximate.

The items on Sturmy's ships were articulate currency. The medieval trade in Holy Land products caused the material to become intertwined with the spiritual, as relic-like objects became inseparable from the marketplace in which they originated – and vice versa, as the medieval market subsumed and carried within it the translation of relics. In fact, insofar as the market for imported elite goods directly created the need for pocketable, high-value tokens of exchange, it can be said that medieval Syriana summoned these objects – coins – into being. The increased circulation of money in the Latin West in the late medieval period has been directly linked to the 'growth of luxury'.[12] As Esther Leslie writes, 'The commodity must have its crystal equivalent, its mineral twin, in order to keep flowing in the sea of consumption.'[13] The description illuminates the relationship between Holy Land commodities and medieval coins. The commodity and the coin were twinned, symbiotic and often synonymous. The monetary function of these items is made explicit in records of their use, for example as settlements for private financial debts: as in Elizabeth de Burgh's bequests of camacas and silk vestments to her creditors.[14] Pepper and fabric were routinely used as non-metallic coins by Genoese merchants.[15]

The spiritual value of Holy Land goods collided not only with their marketplace reality but also with the spiritual values of the economy: the supernatural transformation of objects into gold. Marx wrote of the creation of the commodity that: 'Everything becomes saleable and buyable. . . . Not even are the bones of saints . . . able to withstand this alchemy.'[16] The association between alchemy and the economy was already present in the Middle Ages.[17] In 'The Canon's Yeoman's Tale', an unnamed and disreputable figure reflects that:

> Us must put our good in *aventure*.
> A merchant, *pardee*, may not always endure . . .
> Sometimes his good is drowned in the *see*,
> And *somtyme* it comes safely into the land. (VIII. 946–50)

The 'aventure' of medieval English alchemists and merchants is comparable in a number of aspects: unpredictable, promising huge quantities of gold, reliant on transnational networks. Sturmy's lost cargo hovers on the edge of this image: the drowned Bristol merchant did not come safely into land and his precious boatload did not reach its intended shores. There is a sense of an international network of traders and alchemists: the Canon of Chaucer's tale demands a high price of £40 for his trickery: 'for save I and a friar, | In *Engelond* there can no man it make' (VIII. 1355–6). The decision to gamble in the marketplace lay at the heart of both transnational trade and transmutational practice.

When discussing the sale of relics, Marx does so to demonstrate the expansive reach of the market, its capacity to touch even holy goods. Marx treats relics as an outlier: the expectation is that the God-given value of such things should overwhelm the market-given value of commodities. But instead of saints' bones being an exception – 'not even' able to withstand commodification – the significance of Syriana in medieval trade was such that it may be said that relics were at the foundation of medieval markets.[18] The distinction between the commodity and the relic was impossible to uphold – both were objects which hovered between material and spiritual values. Jacques Derrida emphasised the occult aspect of Marx's theory in his characterisation of commodification as the 'transmutation into a sensuously supersensible thing'.[19] That is: the typical commodity is above the senses and yet at the same time is experienced through the senses – the body wants it because the imagination has made it desirable.

The Traders in the Temple

One of the dominant medieval images of monetary exchange took place in the biblical Temple of Jerusalem: 'And Jesus went into the Temple of God, and cast out all them that sold and bought in the temple, and overthrew the tables of the money changers . . . And he saith to them: It is written, my house shall be called the house of prayer, but you have made it a den of thieves.'[20] The circulation of images of Christ's expulsion of the traders

Figure 6.1 Jesus whips a trader. Source: Bodleian Library, Oxford. MS. Douce, fol. 4. Printed with permission of Bodleian Libraries, University of Oxford. Photo: © Bodleian Libraries, University of Oxford. Image permission granted under Creative Commons 4.0 International Public License (CC BY-NC 4.0).

from the Temple can be seen as a vivid endeavour to maintain the binary of sinful (Jewish) material and holy (Christian) spiritual values, in a world where that binary was constantly collapsing.

Medieval renditions of this episode, the so-called Purification of the Temple, frequently heightened the violence of the text. One mid fifteenth-century manuscript of the *Speculum Humanae Salvationis*, of uncertain Flemish origin, places a whip in Christ's hand, as if pre-emptively turning the instrument of the Passion against his future assailants [Figure 6.1]. The whip motif also occurs in a decorated initial from the fourteenth-century 'Bohun Psalter', produced in the South-East of England, the illuminator's gilding gleaming on both Christ's halo and the rejected tables of gold behind him.[21] The juxtaposition between halo and coins both hints at and attempts to assuage Christian anxiety. These coins are blank disks, stampless empty signifiers, while the halo contains the human incarnation of God, Christ's frowning face providing bodily inscription.

The scene receives literary retelling in Langland's fourteenth-century alliterative poem *Piers Plowman*, a text which invites economic interpretation: in this work, Jesus is represented by an agricultural labourer, Piers.[22]

Passus 16 opens with a discussion of charity, swiftly moving on to Jesus' rejection of his Jewish critics:

> then are you *cherles*, said Jesus ... for I have saved yourselves ... And *mysseide* the *Jewes* manfully, and menaced them to beat and *knokked* on them with a cord, and cast down their stalls that in the church *chaffarden* or *chaungeden* any money and said it in sight of them all, so that all heard: I shall overturn this temple.[23]

Jesus' manly slander of the Jews is strengthened by his self-proclaimed physical violence. Jesus is a one-man mob, vanquishing the traders through brutal force. The language here is revealing – the activities of the traders are described as both 'chaffare' (trade) and 'chaunge' (exchange). The verb 'chaungen' was used to describe both financial exchange and alchemical process.[24] The actions of the traders in the Temple were transmutational.

In the Middle Ages, Christ's expulsion of the traders was repeatedly set in causal relation to the crucifixion. That is: the Passion was represented as the revenge of the envious money changers, with the crucifixion seen as a financial transaction. In Langland's words, Jesus rebukes the Jews: 'I am *solde* through *sum* of *yow*.'[25] The expulsion of the traders was a crucial image for medieval Christians, as the origin point of Christ's suffering. The 'sale' of Jesus by Judas tarred not only all Jewish merchants but all Jewish people in medieval Christian imaginations, overlaying humanity with presupposed financial incentive, such that subjectivity itself was hidden beneath the cloud of marketisation. The presence of Jewish traders in the Temple was a Christian nightmare of their own creation – but it was also a reality, with Syrian and Mediterranean produce traded via Jews and Muslims in wide circulation. English merchants continued to risk their property and their lives in the hope of gaining access to the gold-making centres of Jerusalem. After his death, Sturmy's widow, Ellen Talbot, continued to operate as a 'sole merchant', taking on her own business.[26]

Replicas of the Holy Sepulchre and other sacred Jerusalem sites were constructed across medieval Europe – England was no exception. The marketplace strewn with spices, silks, jewels, and sweet wines can be seen as another such replica, in which the Temple of Jerusalem stood again as the site of exchange, and insofar as the traders had left the Holy Land, it was to come to sell their wares in Europe.

Conclusion: Christopher Columbus in Chios

In 1474, Christopher Columbus came to Chios. As a Genoese settlement, Chios was an obvious location for him to travel to: born into a family of Genoese cloth merchants, Columbus' heritage was in the world of textiles and mineral extraction and exchange.[1] Columbus likely stayed through the autumn of 1474 through the winter of 1475. He is said to have stayed with his friend Andrea Banca Giousiniani, in the village of Pyrgi, which is one of the 'mastic villages'. Pyrgi is an inland community, said to have been founded by medieval residents who wanted to escape the frequent pirate raids on the coasts and harbours of the island. The streets are winding, interlocking – creating the seclusion of a fortress without the stability of castle walls. The ruins of premodern walls are unrepaired in places, adjoining lived-in houses – broken turrets linked to modern homes. In addition to the original urban design, the residents have preserved a distinctive style of decoration, called *xysta*: a type of sgraffito decoration which covers the outsides of houses, shops, and churches. The whitewashed plaster is scraped from the walls within the lines of stencilled designs: vases, animals, geometrical shapes with the effect of an optical illusion, spiralling. The walls are smoothed and textured in turn, apartments with balconies overlooking the streets like a series of inhabited ceramic vessels.

Today the house in which Columbus stayed as a guest is marked with a plaque [Figure C.1]. The portrait is dated 1857, showing a stylised figure in robes standing on a low plinth between sloping houses. The frame of the plaque recalls the structure of the shrines which stand on the streets: a pointed top like a house, and curtain-like borders. Below this scene are animals like the leopards of medieval bestiaries looking out on each side of a cantering horse. Below that, an oval wreathed with figurative curls, and three bodiless angels' heads arranged in a circle around a Cross, the edges of their wings touching. The two lower angels stretch out their hands above – behind – their heads to grasp the base of the Cross. The image memorialises Columbus' voyage as sacred travel: the triumph of Christendom.

Figure C.1 Columbus' house, Pyrgi, Chios. Source: author's own photograph.

At this house, the *xysta* designs are less brightly renovated than those on the house next door: the grooves in the plaster are deep but the contrast between light and dark is between sandy-brown and off-white, not black and white. Perhaps this crumbling look is the result of a desire to preserve a sense of authenticity – keeping the paleness of a historic palette, not overlaying it with contemporary craft. On the upper level of the house the wooden shutters are splintered. Despite the plaque, the tourist industry which surrounds the house is not a shrine to Columbus – there are no postcards of the house or merchandise with his name on in the racks of brightly coloured maps of Chios and miniature *xysta* tiles for sale. Pyrgi is a UNESCO heritage site because of its architecture and ornamentation – it is not reliant on colonial nostalgia. However, there is a strong local narrative around Columbus' time in the village – I am told that Columbus came to Chios 'to find maps for his voyage to America' and that the sailors on his voyage came from the island. These are not verifiable histories – these are the mythologies of the premodern.

When Columbus departed from Granada in May 1492 – itself newly conquered by the Christian rulers Ferdinand and Isabella – he wrote: 'In the name of our Lord Jesus Christ . . . So it was that, after having expelled the Jews from your kingdoms and domains . . . your highnesses . . . bestowed great favours on me', calling him the Lord High Admiral of the Ocean Sea.[2] In October 1492, when Columbus reached his first territorial landing point, Guanahani, which he renamed San Salvador, he wrote to Ferdinand and Isabella that he had found spices, cotton, 'and mastic, hitherto found only in Greece, in the island of Chios' – along with 'slaves, as many of these idolators as their Highnesses shall command to be shipped'.[3] Columbus' reaction to this new environment recalls the sights he had witnessed in Chios: the mastic groves, weeping moneymaking gum, and the slave markets. Freedman comments that Columbus had probably 'mistaken the gumbo-lindo tree' for mastic.[4] Accurately viewed or not, the commodities and cultures of the medieval Mediterranean trading zones shaped the desires and actions of European traders in the New World settlements. The jewels and spices, textile fibres and resins which were encountered in Chios as signs of European dependence on global networks are here altered as they become integrated into a new project of territorial expansion. Valerie Flint has shown that Columbus was not exceptional but representative of the imaginative scope of the culture in which he lived.[5] Likewise, Sturmy's desires can be assumed to have derived from the recollected narratives of the objects on his ships – which do not tell the same narratives as those on the *Santa Maria*. In the fifteenth century, the English were still voyeurs on these shifting voyages, marginal in Europe as it was beginning to re-expand: for that reason, 1492 has not been the cut-off for this study. The arrival of Columbus' ship had widespread consequences, but these global shifts were not immediately registered in England.[6]

Ship in a Vitrine

At the Maritime Museum in Chios Town, there is a model of Columbus' ship, the *Santa Maria*, on display within a glass vitrine [Figure C.2]. The hand-stitched sails are pulled tight above miniature boards – a hatch is left ajar on the deck, as if a sailor is about to come through the trapdoor. The label describes how Columbus received 'information concerning the unknown sea which extended beyond Gibraltar from Chian sailors mainly from charts' and comments that today 'several residents of Pyrgi have the name Columbus as a surname'. The label includes a reproduction of Columbus' signature, *Xristoferens*, and ends: 'in any case, Christopher Columbus was a courageous, pioneer explorer'. Labelled in this way, the dinky model ship – which could

Figure C.2 The *Santa Maria* in a vitrine, Maritime Museum, Chios Town. Source: author's own photograph.

almost be a child's toy, a ship in a glass bottle – becomes the vessel of history, a triumphalist account of European colonialism.

Sturmy came to Chios in 1458, fifteen years before Columbus visited the island. In 1497, five years after Columbus set sail in the *Santa Maria*, the Genoese-born John Cabot left Bristol for North America, bringing the transatlantic routes to England.[7] Sturmy's failed voyage has no enduring consequences from which his intentions can be retrospectively constructed. If he had returned to Bristol, Sturmy might have become a Columbus or a Cabot, using the wealth of his newfound alum access to fund transatlantic travel – but he never came back, so he never went onwards. Sturmy's timely death saved him from becoming a statue, a lightning rod for nationalist adulation. His redirected ships are too ambivalent to be placed into a glass case; a triumphalist label would be an overt speculative fantasy.

Writing Sturmy's voyage back into a narrative of medieval English culture, I do not want to reconstruct his ships within a vitrine. These remnants tenderly remember the premodern failures which kept England marginal for a few decades longer, holding a breath for an alternative history of this archipelago, the British Isles before the British Empire. I want to leave his biography in the condition of debris: submerged and useless fragments which cannot be pieced together in the form of a flag or a monument.

British-Guyanese artist Hew Locke employs a sculptural mode of reconstruction which resonates with Rakowitz's practice: these are ostentatious forgeries which address partially remembered colonial histories, through materials and appearances which evoke the ongoing realities of international trade and travel. In Locke's 2016 installation *The Wine Dark Sea*, vessels hang from the air in a gallery.[8] The title is taken from Homer's epithet for the Aegean Sea. Sailing through the air – a skiff, a cargo ship, a refugee boat, a galleon, a model of Sir Francis Drake's flagship – these ships are made of wood, papier mâche, and found materials, adorned with plaques, plastic beads, model masks, and miniature sacks. The procession can be seen as funeral: ghost ships. Boat BB in the series wears a white veil embroidered with medieval illuminations, including the dance macabre [Figure C.3]. The

Figure C.3 Hew Locke, Boat BB, *The Wine Dark Sea*. Source: Photography by Charles Littlewood. Printed with permission of DACS/Artimage.

artwork mourns these vessels ambivalently, unevenly, preserving disparate experiences of travel in close proximity. These gaudy replicas, suspended from the ceiling, refuse to occupy a stable position. The aerial procession sets deconstructed colonial monuments alongside memorials to migrants' journeys, refashioned in shared materials of cardboard, plastic beads, and netting hanging from the prow. A trading vessel holds a tiny shipment, like a souvenir. Locke's juxtapositions sustain the contradictions in the history of Mediterranean crossings. Likewise there is not a stable answer to what Sturmy's ships meant: stolen, their significance did not reach a resolution. Instead of aiming for closure, I briefly visualise the *Katherine Sturmy* and the *Marie* joining Locke's aerial procession: not in a vitrine but hanging between histories, inauthentic and aspirational, remade from the same bright tin as Rakowitz's Lamassu.

Epilogue: The Verdict of the Trials of the Genoese

When John got home, he took out his frustration and grief on the nearest scapegoats, the Genoese immigrants of England, calling on the highest authority, the King, to witness his revenge.

Sturmy's voyage came at a tipping point in the history of migration and nationhood, both in terms of the advent of European colonialism, and in terms of specifically English legislation around national minorities. The Genoese who happened to be in Southampton and London in 1458 were caught in the crossfire of these geopolitical events.

Recollecting the Genoese on Trial

In August 1458, the Genoese residents in England were put on trial for the value of Sturmy's lost goods. The trial transcripts do not name individual defendants – they are grouped anonymously as 'Januenses': the Genoese. But the Genoese residents in England around the time of the trial can be found in the fiscal records. In 1440, the English Parliament introduced a tax, called the 'alien subsidy', to be paid by all non-native-born residents of England over the age of twelve. Householders were charged 16 pence each, per year, while non-householders were charged 6 pence. These 'alien subsidy' records document the immigrant population of medieval England – payments were listed alongside names, nationality, occupations, and place of residence. In the decade 1450–1460, of the 150 Genoese residents whose names are preserved in the 'alien subsidy' records, 108 are listed as non-householders, with 42 householders. Among these aliens who paid their taxes between 1456 and 1459 must be the Genoese who were locked in the Fleet, so here are some of their names: Rafaell de Aurea, Lewis Baptiste, Baltezardus de Barde, Kirigo Bronyon, Gentil de Camilla, Edward Catan, Gregory de Frank, Francus Furnariis, Siprianus Furnell, George de Gene, Jeronimus Ilome, Lancelettus de Lago, Augustino de

Lario, Cosine de Negre, Angelus Penel, Franciscus Salvage, Everard Salvyot, Anthony Senturian, Napoleone Spynell, Raphaell Spynell.[1] These men were mostly merchants, attorneys, brokers, and clerks. They lived in London, Southampton, or Kent – apart from a man named as John Michell, who lived in Lincoln. Some of the men in this list could have left before Sturmy's ship was sunk, and others might have been locked up who, for whatever reason, did not pay the subsidy during those years. But these names record the existence of a community, grouped in several centres around England, near the ports and streets where these men had moved to work. This was the community which was dispossessed when John Heyton brought his case before the King.

The First Response of the Genoese

The Genoese submitted their first defence on 22 August 1458: 'First we say that the pirate who captured the ships of the English is not Genoese, nor is he a subject of Genoa, but rather a notorious pirate, born in Greece on a certain island called Mitilini Vellenio over which the Genoese government has no authority.' When the Genoese were asked 'if any Genoese were in the ship with the said pirate at the same time he captured the English, they said that they did not know'.[2] In this initial plea, the defendants accept the logic of the case – agreeing that if Gatillusio were shown to be Genoese, then as Genoese citizens, they would be liable for damages. They attempt to distance themselves from guilt on the basis that Gattilusio belonged to a different national group.

Until the fifteenth century, immigrants to England were typically not required to produce or keep identification papers.[3] The 'alien subsidy' tax reflected a growing move to legislate on the basis of an imaginative discourse of national identity.[4] The tax included people from the dependent territories in Ireland, the Channel Islands, Normandy, and Gascony, but excluded those from Wales. Although the 1440 tax was a new policy, the 'fiscal alien' had been a category since the fourteenth century. As seen in earlier discussions of sumptuary laws, legislation was repeatedly introduced against 'alien merchants', distinguishing 'aliens' involved in overseas trade from English merchants who worked in the same field, with 'aliens' paying higher duties on commodities.[5] The 'resident alien' was a category which recurs in parliamentary records as a subject of debate, created in a context of international conflict and territorial dispute: the lives of long-term migrant inhabitants were legislated in consequence of events abroad.

While the premodern discourse of 'nation' is not the same as its later incarnation in the nation-state, the vocabulary and legislative system of the modern nation had already started to develop in these laws.[6] Once it had been introduced, the 'alien' was an enduring legal category. The 1905 Aliens Act was the first act of Parliament to introduce official controls over immigration numbers; this was the first act to give the Home Secretary responsibility for restricting entry to 'undesirable immigrants' – at that time, coded Jewish.[7]

Medieval immigrants could stop being 'aliens' if they could afford to go through the bureaucracy. In 1377, at a moment of particular crisis during the Hundred Years' War, all French residents were threatened with expulsion – excepting those who were willing to swear their allegiance to the English King.[8] The chance to swear an oath of fealty came at a price – a 'letter of protection' could be purchased for £2 or – even better – a 'letter of denization' was available for purchase for £50.[9] A 'letter of denization' officially made the formerly 'alien' subject legally identical to a person born in England. This event created the formal category of the 'denizen' – a term for a non-native resident who had gone through a legal and administrative process of redefining themselves as a loyal subject of the English Crown. Today, in an echo of these medieval conditions, adults applying for indefinite leave to remain in the UK have to pay a fee of £3,029. Those applying for British citizenship have a legal requirement to swear an oath of allegiance to the King. From its inception, the immigration system in England deployed a discourse of national security as a means of securing profit from non-native residents. Anyone in possession of a letter of denization was exempt from the 'alien subsidy' tax – but since the tax of 6d or 16d was much less than the cost of denization, the real benefits of becoming a denizen were social and legal: the price of belonging.

The term 'denizen' comes from the Anglo-French 'deinz-ein' – 'denz' meaning 'inside'. The term 'denizen' could refer to a legal inhabitant of a city or borough in addition to describing those who had formalised their residence in England. Some people born in England became 'denizens' when they moved towns and secured residence in their new locale. The state of 'being-inside' requires its inverse, the 'alien': those non-denizen subjects who were resident in England were outsiders, not able to live 'inside'. The category of the 'denizen' overlapped with the category of the 'citisein', which referred to a freeman or established inhabitant of a country, town, or region. The citizen was supposed to perform virtue and nobility: qualities which would make them just recipients of their freedom. A person born within England could find themselves seeking 'citizenship' if they moved to a new town – requiring a residency permit to formalise the right to live outside the city of their birth. In other words, the English could lose their 'citisein' status within England if they moved a few miles from their home town.[10] The category of the 'citisein' remains relevant for understanding medieval English concepts of migration, which was understood to operate on a regional scale, and in relation to movement between rural and urban spaces, not exclusively on a national scale. But the formal process through which a person born outside of England would be given the same rights as an English-born subject – the beginning of the modern-day process of 'naturalisation' – was not described in terms of citizenship, but 'denization'.

Targeted as a group, the majority of these Genoese residents could be assumed to be non-denizen – that is, 'alien' – residents, but the question of their legal status is not raised in the trial documents. Their nationhood is given as Genoese. When the Genoese residents submitted their plea that they were innocent because the pirate was not Genoese but Greek, they effectively submitted to the legal framework of their prosecutors, which categorised them as precarious, alien subjects in their host nation. It did not work.

The Medieval Right to Remain

On 23 August 1458, the Genoese were informed – in response to their plea of innocence – that they needed collectively to find £40,000 sureties to guarantee their right to remain in England, otherwise they would be committed to prison. The targeted community included wealthy merchants – but none so wealthy as to have liquid assets to the value of nearly £26 million in today's money.[11] Unable to find the money at short notice, an unspecified number of the Genoese were committed to Fleet prison, while others were put under house arrest or under the custody of the London sheriffs. All their ships and goods were sequestered.

These Genoese residents were imprisoned as an identifiable, non-English group residing within England. Zygmunt Bauman writes that the legislation of citizenship is a defining feature of modernity.[12] These premodern trials prefigure modernity in that sense: the legal dispute relies on the recognition that national identity is a category with legal, fiscal, and administrative implications. These trials expose the reality that the legal system in medieval England was able to deploy a discourse of identity in order to incarcerate a group of non-native inhabitants, on the basis of a logic of collective national punishment for crimes perpetrated overseas.

This carceral approach to an internal minority group in England is morbidly familiar, even though the premodern world had not yet become fixed within the lines of present-day carceral borders. Those Genoese imprisoned within the Fleet – and in their homes in Southampton, Kent, and London – are now received as distant echoes of those currently imprisoned in detention centres, or in limbo within private residences. When the 2014 Immigration Act formalised the government's hostile immigration policy, citizenship was removed from a generation of British people who had arrived in or after 1948 who did not possess formal documentation.[13] In the fifteenth century, the new requirement to purchase letters of denization to avoid being a fiscal and legal 'alien' was the beginning of a codified and commercialised immigration process which polices access to British nationality on the basis of access to material wealth, and which treats immigrants differently depending on their place of origin. Deploying a discourse of national security, the medieval Crown constructed a bureaucratic apparatus of taxes and administrative documentation which distinguished those who were temporary residents from those who had secured the right to remain, underpinned by a profit motive. Since Genoa and England were in competition across the Mediterranean, these Genoese civilians were made precarious.

When the Genoese were charged to find £40,000 – more than twice the value of Sturmy's ships – the transactional nature of the nascent immigration system was made clear. The idea of the nation was invoked in order to locate a debtor. In the trials of the Genoese, the discourse of 'security' is not mentioned – these Genoese were not seen as dangerous, and not presented as disloyal subjects – but a sum needed to be paid, and these immigrants were the closest people who could be charged to pay it.

The Second Response of the Genoese

On 7 November 1458,

> some of the Genoese being held in Fleet prison were called into the presence of the lords and were interrogated . . . and they themselves . . . attempted to excuse themselves and all the Genoese from the said crime perpetrated, alleging that the complaint put forward by the said Heytone and the others concerned the entire body of Genoa, for which they as individuals did not have authority to answer nor ought to be compelled to do so.[14]

They were assigned a date to respond in writing – 9 November – which was then postponed until 13 November 1458. They had already been held in prison for over two months.

On 14 November the Genoese presented a second written declaration. The letter begins with an address to 'your *goode lordshippes* and *grete wisdomys*' and introduces the defendants as 'the merchants of *Jeanne beyng here* within this full noble realm of England in *dyvers prisons*'.[15] The Genoese describe themselves as *beyng here*. In their language, they do not claim to be denizens – the legal status of those within the group likely varied, with at least some being 'aliens', and with some householders within a group comprised mostly of non-householders. But the statement makes it clear that all the defendants were settled residents. The experience of being a 'denizen' is associatively brought into the plea – they remind the court that they belong 'here'. Their language echoes across time with the Yiddish term *doykayt*, 'being-here': the word which was adopted by the Jewish Bund in the nineteenth century to articulate their political commitment to diasporic identity, a rooted existence in Eastern Europe, and which continues to be used today in diasporic communities.[16] The state of being-here is a state of belonging which is predicated upon the recollection of elsewhere, while asserting the realities of remaining in the land of arrival.

The Genoese gave a new plea, arguing that 'in the *bille of compleynt* put by Robert Sturmy and John Heytone against the Duke and the whole *body of Jeanne*' there was given 'no matter *especialle* of any offence' which was given as perpetrated 'by the said *merchauntez* of *Jeanne beyng hereyng* within this said realm'. The merchants give Sturmy and Heyton as joint prosecutors – proving, if the court cared to listen, their detachment from the events at sea, when Sturmy had been killed. In this letter, they argue that the matter of the case is directed against the Duke and the 'body of Genoa', over which they as 'merchants of Genoa *beyng here* as yet have no *auctorite ne power*' – and 'dare not, can nor may in no manner of wise take upon them to answer to the matter contained in the said bill'. They state that they trust that an ambassador will be sent from the Duke of Genoa to the King 'in all *godely* haste' who will have – unlike them – the authority to respond to the bill.[17] They repeat that 'moreover the said merchants of Genoea *beyne here* within this said realm . . . were not thereto assenting, willing, nor *knowyng*' of the offence which is 'supposed to be done'.[18] The second letter is both more assertive in its rhetoric – with repeated negatives and groups of three – and more deferential to the 'wisdom' of the court. It is presented in a collective voice, even though the imprisoned Genoese were locked up in different circumstances.

Writing from inside their prisons, the Genoese 'pray to have thereof hearing', expecting 'a reasonable day to answer to the same'. They pray that 'by God's grace' their reply shall be such that 'of reason your *grete wysdomys* shall think it sufficiently answered'. The letter ends with 'the said *merchauntez* of Genoa *beyng here*, praying to be *enlarged* out of prison and their *goodes* and merchandises to be discharged'. They hope that 'your *grete wysdomys*' will give 'the said merchants of Genoa *beyng here*' a 'reasonable trial and examination', and if they are asked to find sureties, that this time they will be asked for 'reasonable sums'. And lastly they pray that 'the said Robert and John' will likewise find the surety to 'restore the said merchants of Genoa *being here* of the damages that they have sustained in this kingdom', if their innocence 'be proved according to the law'.[19]

Trusting in God and the English law, the grievance of the Genoese against their treatment lingers in the subtext of last sentence – they trust that they will receive restoration for the harm which has been done to them. The repetition becomes reproachful – '*beyng here*', they have been charged with a debt from a theft made faraway.

English Hospitality

In addition to the different rights held by 'alien' and 'denizen' residents, there was a clear hierarchy between immigrant householders and non-householders, with fiscal and legal implications.[20] Rees Jones writes that 'the evidence suggests that most urban immigrants were of lower status and were highly transient'.[21] These transient migrants received a lower taxation charge, but were accordingly more precarious. For 'merchant strangers' there were hosting laws – these legislated visitors were permitted to stay in England only in the homes of freemen 'hostelers'. These workers were dependent on the personal hospitality of official citizens – instead of the structures of a state, these designated domestic interiors were the sites in which migration was controlled, with residence conditionally offered on interpersonal acceptance. The notion that an immigrant is a 'guest' in the 'home' of the host nation remains a pressing theme today.[22] These medieval hosting laws literalised that metaphoric state. The right to become a householder was controlled.

Those born in England but without a stable home were also regulated, with repeated laws introduced during the fourteenth century against the 'vagrant', the '*wastour*', and the 'vagabond'. Those found not working in a town which was not the town of their birth would be sent back. These migrant subjects were associatively proximate to these English 'wanderers' – guests in temporary hostels, kept close to the harbours from which they had arrived. In the late medieval period, non-denizens and vagabonds were codified as two differently disenfranchised groups *beyng here* with nowhere to go.

On 15 November 1458, Heyton and his associates sent a bill to the court, replying to the Genoese. Heyton's letter refers back to the first defence of the Genoese, which argued that the pirates were not Genoese, but Greek. Heyton comments acidically that after all these testimonials, the Genoese 'have put before your *lordshippes* a bill' which is 'insufficient, *contrarius* and repugnant and discordant unto their said first answer, intending . . . only *fraude*, *subtilee* and delay against the said merchants *Englisshe*'.[23] Finding their measured and humble rhetoric met with vitriol, the Genoese '*beyng here*' again submitted a plea to be let out of prison. In response Heyton provided a new witness, who swore before the court that Gattilusio and his crew were Genoese.

The lords deliberated, and stated that Heyton should submit a list of the goods which have been lost and their value, by 27 November. That list is the catalogue of lost goods which has structured this book – summoned into being by a dispute over the culpability of an imprisoned group of unnamed migrants. On 27 November, Heyton submitted his valuation of the ships – then that is the end of this transcript of the trials.

Michael Rakowitz describes the works in the paired series *The invisible enemy should not exist* (2007–) and *May the obdurate foe not be in good health* (2011–) as (g)hosts. These Iraqi and Syrian artefacts are recreated in ephemeral packaging, haunting the spaces in which they are displayed. These (g)hosts transform their supposed hosts into guests, taking control over the space into which they have been introduced. Their bright and breakable surfaces are inhabited temporarily by the summoned presence of lost objects, which are remembered but not exactly reconstituted in these new forms. The tin-can Lamassu found itself in Trafalgar Square – on a plinth which was always intended to be a temporary site of residence, a brief apparition in the public sphere. Looking towards Nelson's column, the Lamassu's fictive gaze directed attention to the lions at the base, which are not guardian deities but sculptures, and like the Lamassu, they have not always been here. The brass lions arrived later than all the objects and subjects in this book, which were themselves arrivals. Rakowitz's recreated artefacts speak to the foundational instability of premodern English culture, arriving in Westminster in order to revive the ghosts of these mobile subjects, those who have always inhabited the condition of *beyng here*. The hostile host makes their guest into a ghost, but the guest can still become a (g)host, haunting and resisting, asserting their presence as another form of being. The body is here but identity is dematerialised, floating across multiple spaces and times, refusing to stay fixed as the self reaches out back and across recollected journeys.

Citizens of the Air and Other (G)hostly Populations

The medieval terms 'denizen' and 'citizen' were also used to describe the population of heaven: those with eternal right to remain in the transcendent City of Jerusalem. A saint was the archetypal '*hevynly citysein*', having gained access through martyrdom.[24] In that sense the 'citizen' as a category was opposed not to the 'immigrant' or the 'alien' but the 'pilgrim'. The citizens of heaven had once been itinerant travellers on earth. As the legal and administrative system of 'denization' developed, that language became part of the late medieval discourse of salvation. In order to reach heaven, a good Christian still needed to purchase indulgences – in the same way that even a model immigrant needed to purchase a letter of protection. Being understood not as a nation but as a city built around a shrine, the architecture and structure of heaven provided a model for Christian societies on earth, walled cities with cathedrals at their centre. Gaining citizenship to these earthly communities was just a stage on the pilgrimage towards the final destination.

In Chaucer's dream vision the *House of Fame*, as the dreamer is pulled through the air by an eagle, the bird speaks, inviting Geoffrey to 'behold this large space, | This air' and see how 'in this region, for certain, | Dwelleth many a *citezeyn*' (ll. 877–81). When Geoffrey finally looks down, he sees the '*ayerissh* [airy] beasts', which are natural phenomena: 'clouds, mists, and tempests, | Snows, hails, rains, winds' (ll. 965–7). The category of citizenship could describe a person with residency rights in a new town on earth. But the ideal citizens were the saints in heaven. In between, the clouds and winds were the citizens of the air.

These medieval images of citizens construct an idealised state of belonging which is immaterial – atmospheric. Instead of defining citizenship as an identity-based category which is fixed through legal frameworks and linked to land-based territories, these airy citizens inhabit vapours and aether. These beings are here – but where, exactly, is hard to say. They are 'denizens', and so they are inside – but inside what? The boundaries of the air, unfixed and changeable, are shaped by the borderless states of its 'citizens', the mists and winds which are born and travel through the skies, this 'large space'. The medieval concept of the universe envisioned the earth set within a series of celestial spheres which would chime as they turned. The citizens of the air revolved around the earth and seas, whose inhabitants were also on the move.

The Verdict

On 25 July 1459, the still-imprisoned Genoese were charged to pay £6,000 damages.[25] The delayed verdict is recorded in the Calendar of the Patent Rolls: dated July 25, Coventry, the note gives a commission to 'John Stourton of Stourton, knight', along with Richard Chock, William Canynges, William Coder, Philip Mede, and – appearing last in the list – the prosecutor John Heyton. These men were to 'receive from the treasurer of England' the stated sum, which they were responsible for distributing among

> the king's lieges of Bristol and other cities and towns of the realm according to their losses at the time when certain ships of Robert Sturmy and John *Eyton*, laden with goods of the said lieges, were taken and spoiled near the island of Malta by certain of Genoa; which sum the king granted to them by advice of the council.[26]

The trials had finally ended in compromise and financial loss for both sides. The first defence of the Genoese – that Gattilusio was Greek – had been thrown out. But the sum awarded is an ambiguous response to the case. Heyton had sought £20,000 – he received far less than the money sunk in the enterprise, suggesting that the court did not judge the Genoese residents to be fully liable. £6,000 is not the 'reasonable' sum which the Genoese had petitioned for, at over £3.8 million in modern currency. It was likely calculated on the basis of the original sum which these individuals had invested in the voyage, not the value of the lost goods or ships. The King and council put an end to the matter. Imprisoned for eleven months, the Genoese *beyng here* were finally free to return to their lives. The river Fleet beside the prison – which today is a subterranean waterway running through the London sewers – flowed out into the Thames, and from there into the sea.

Above them, the winds, rains, and other citizens of the air blew on the sails of the boats still arriving at the harbour.

Notes

Prologue: Robert Sturmy's Last Voyage

1. Stuart Jenks, ed., *Robert Sturmy's Commercial Expedition to the Mediterranean (1457/8): With Editions of the Trial of the Genoese before King and Council and of Other Sources* (Bristol: Bristol Record Society, 2006), p. 7.
2. <www.nationalarchives.gov.uk/currency-converter/#currency-result> [accessed 8 September 2021].
3. Jenks, *Robert Sturmy's Commercial Expedition*, p. 82. Throughout, italics in quotations such as this indicate the Middle English where other text is modernised.
4. My translation, based on the Latin text printed in Jenks, *Robert Sturmy's Commercial Expedition*, p. 54. Note that all translations in the book are by the author unless otherwise indicated.
5. Carlo Ginsburg, 'Minutiae, Close-up, Microanalysis', *Critical Inquiry* 34:1 (2007), 174–189 (p. 181).
6. Michael Wintroub, *The Voyage of Thought: Navigating Knowledge across the Sixteenth-Century World* (Cambridge: Cambridge University Press, 2017). See also John-Paul Ghobrial, ed., *Global History and Microhistory* (Oxford: Oxford University Press, 2019).
7. Jenks, *Robert Sturmy's Commercial Expedition*, p. 50.
8. *ibid.*, p. 82.
9. C.L. Kingsford, ed., *Chronicles of London* (Oxford: Clarendon Press, 1905), p. 169.
10. Bart Lambert and W.M. Ormrod, 'The State and the Immigrant: Negotiating Nationalities in Later Medieval England', in *Migrants in Medieval England, c. 500–1500*, ed. W.M. Ormrod, Joanna Story, and Elizabeth Tyler (Oxford: Oxford University Press, 2020), pp. 298–325 (p. 299).
11. Karma Lochrie, ed., *Imagining a Medieval English Nation* (Minneapolis, MN: University of Minnesota Press, 2004).
12. Jenks, *Robert Sturmy's Commercial Expedition*, p. 72.
13. Elizabeth Lambourn, *Abraham's Luggage: A Social Life of Things in the Medieval Indian Ocean World* (Cambridge: Cambridge University Press, 2018).

14. Paul Gilroy, *The Black Atlantic: Modernity and Double Consciousness* (Cambridge, MA: Harvard University Press, 1995), p. 17.
15. Cord J. Whitaker, *Black Metaphors: How Modern Racism Emerged from Medieval Race-Thinking* (Philadelphia, PA: University of Pennsylvania Press, 2019), p. 18.
16. See Robert Bartlett, *The Making of Europe: Conquest, Colonization and Cultural Change, 950–1350* (London: Allen Lane, 1993).
17. Carole Hillenbrand, ed., *Syria in Crusader Times: Conflict and Coexistence* (Edinburgh: Edinburgh University Press, 2020); 'Outremer, n.', *OED* [accessed 26 October 2021].
18. J.H. Pryor, 'Symposium – the Crusading Kingdom of Jerusalem – the First European Colonial Society?', in *The Horns of Hattin. Proceedings of the Second Conference of the Society for the Study of the Crusades and the Latin East*, ed. Benjamin Z. Kedar (Jerusalem: Yad Izhak BenZvi / Israel Exploration Society & Variorum, 1992), pp. 341–66.
19. See Judith Bronstein, Gil Fishhof, and Vardit Shotten-Hallel, eds., *Settlement and Crusade in the Thirteenth Century: Multidisciplinary Studies of the Latin East* (London: Routledge, 2021).
20. Janet Abu-Lughod, *Before European Hegemony: The World System, A.D. 1250–1350* (New York: Oxford University Press, 1989); Eliyahu Ashtor, *Levant Trade in the Later Middle Ages* (Princeton, NJ: Princeton University Press, 1983).
21. Evan Jones, 'Preface', in Jenks, *Robert Sturmy's Commercial Expedition*, pp. xi–xiii (p. xii).
22. David Abulafia, *The Great Sea: A Human History of the Mediterranean* (Oxford: Oxford University Press, 2011), p. 397.
23. Notable critical works on medieval trade and travel include: David Wallace, *Premodern Places: Calais to Surinam, Chaucer to Aphra Behn* (Oxford: Blackwell, 2004) and David Wallace, ed., *Europe: A Literary History, 1348–1418*, 2 vols. (Oxford: Oxford University Press, 2016); Alfred Hiatt, 'Mapping the Ends of Empire', in *Postcolonial Approaches to the European Middle Ages: Translating Cultures*, ed. Deanne Williams and Ananya Kabir (Cambridge: Cambridge University Press, 2005), pp. 48–76 (pp. 61–4); Michael Murrin, *Trade and Romance* (Chicago, IL and London: University of Chicago Press, 2014); Shayne Legassie, *The Medieval Invention of Travel* (Chicago, IL and London: University of Chicago Press, 2017); Anthony Bale and Sebastian Sobecki, eds., *Medieval English Travel: A Critical Anthology* (Oxford: Oxford University Press, 2019).
24. Douglas Hunter, *The Race to the New World: Christopher Columbus, John Cabot, and a Lost History of Discovery* (New York: Palgrave Macmillan, 2011).
25. Jean Vanes, *Documents Illustrating the Overseas Trade of Bristol in the Sixteenth Century* (Bristol: Bristol Record Society, 1979); David Richardson, *Bristol,*

Africa and the Eighteenth-Century Slave Trade to America (Bristol: Bristol Record Society, 1987).

26. See the AHRC-funded research project 'Reconstructing Sloane', <https://reconstructingsloane.org/about> [accessed 9 November 2021].
27. Matthew X. Vernon, *The Black Middle Ages: Race and the Construction of the Middle Ages* (Basingstoke: Palgrave Macmillan, 2018), p. 160.
28. Édouard Glissant, *Poetics of Relation*, trans. by Betsy Wing (Ann Arbor, MI: University of Michigan Press, 1997), p. 144.
29. E.M. Carus Wilson, 'The Overseas Trade of Bristol', in *Studies in English Trade in the Fifteenth Century*, ed. M.M. Poston and Eileen Power (London: Routledge, 1933; repr. 2015), pp. 183–245 (pp. 225–7).
30. Corpus Christi College, Cambridge MS 210, fol. 135r.
31. *ibid.*, fol. 136r.
32. Jenks, *Robert Sturmy's Commercial Expedition*, p. 23.
33. *ibid.*, pp. 99–100.
34. *ibid.*, p. 10.
35. Abulafia, *The Great Sea*, pp. 291–7.
36. Hannah Barker, *That Most Precious Merchandise: The Mediterranean Trade in Black Sea Slaves, 1260–1500* (Philadelphia, PA: University of Pennsylvania Press, 2019), p. 157.
37. Jan Hinrich Hagedron, *Domestic Slavery in Syria and Egypt, 1200–1500* (Bonn: Bonn University Press, 2020).
38. Thomas Johnes, trans., *A Mission to the Medieval Middle East: Travels of Bertrandon De La Brocquière* (London: I.B. Tauris, 2019), p. 226.
39. Barker, *That Most Precious Merchandise*, p. 169.
40. Abulafia, *The Great Sea*, pp. 291–7, 358.
41. Christopher Wright, *The Gattilusio Lordships and the Aegean World, 1355–1462* (Leiden: Brill, 2014), pp. 237–8.
42. Jenks, *Robert Sturmy's Commercial Expedition*, p. 15.

Introduction: *De Sire*, the Origins of English Desire

1. Jenks, *Robert Sturmy's Commercial Expedition*, p. 81.
2. Anthony Bale, '"*ut legi*": Sir John Mandeville's Audience and Three Late-Medieval English Travellers to Italy and Jerusalem', *SAC* 38 (2016), 201–37 (p. 233).
3. E.M. Carus Wilson, 'The Merchant Adventurers of Bristol in the Fifteenth Century', *Transactions of the Royal Historical Society* 11 (1928), 61–82 (p. 73).
4. See also William Brewyn's 1477 guidebook, containing an itinerary of the Holy Land: Canterbury, Add. MS 68, fol. 4r.

5. Elizabeth Edwards, 'Money and Literature', in *Money and Coinage in the Middle Ages*, ed. Rory Naismith (Leiden: Brill, 2019), pp. 264–86 (p. 278).
6. William Wey, *The Itineraries of William Wey, Fellow of Eton College. To Jerusalem, A.D. 1458 and A.D. 1462; and to Saint James of Compostella, A.D. 1456. From the Original Manuscript in the Bodleian Library*, ed. B. Bandinel (London: J.B. Nichols for the Roxburghe Club, 1857), p. 2.
7. 'drachm, n.', *OED*.
8. John Trevisa, *On the Properties of Things: John Trevisa's Translation of Bartholomaeus Anglicus De Proprietatibus Rerum: A Critical Text*, 2 vols. (Oxford: Clarendon Press, 1975), p. 809.
9. P.D.A. Harvey, *Medieval Maps of the Holy Land* (London: British Library, 2012).
10. Alessandro Scafi, 'Coping with Muslim Jerusalem between the Middle Ages and the Renaissance: Islam and the Holy City on Christian World Maps', in *Between Jerusalem and Europe: Essays in Honour of Bianca Kühnel*, ed. Renana Bartal and Hanna Vorholt (Leiden and Boston, MA, 2015), pp. 257–79 (p. 264).
11. See Sebastian Sobecki, *The Sea and Medieval English Literature* (Woodbridge: Brewer, 2008).
12. Daniel Connolly, *The Maps of Matthew Paris: Medieval Journeys through Space, Time and Liturgy* (Woodbridge: Boydell, 2009).
13. Nicola Ziadeh, *Urban Life in Syria under the Early Mamluks* (Beirut: The American Press, 1953), pp. 27–33.
14. Andrew C. Smith, 'Mamluk Jerusalem: Architecturally Challenging Narratives', *LUX: A Journal of Transdisciplinary Writing and Research from Claremont Graduate University* 3:1 (2013), article 16: <https://scholarship.claremont.edu/lux/vol3/iss1/16> [accessed 10 September 2021].
15. Michael Hamilton Burgoyne, *Mamluk Jerusalem: An Architectural Study* (London: World of Islam Festival Trust, 1987), p. 33.
16. Richard Torkington, *Ye Oldest Diarie of Englysshe Travell: Being the Hitherto Unpublished Narrative of the Pilgrimage of Sir Richard Torkington to Jerusalem in 1517*, ed. W.J. Loftie (Milton Keynes: Lightning Source UK Ltd., 2017), p. 23.
17. *ibid.*, p. 38.
18. For studies of the relations between the Ottoman Empire and Renaissance England, see: Nabil Matar, *Turks, Moors and Englishmen in the Age of Discovery* (New York: Columbia University Press, 1999); Palmira Brummett, *Mapping the Ottomans: Sovereignty, Territory, and Identity in the Early Modern Mediterranean* (New York: Cambridge University Press, 2015); Alexander Bavilacqua, *The Republic of Arabic Letters: Islam and the European Enlightenment* (Cambridge, MA: Belknap Press, 2018).

19. Geoffrey Chaucer, *The Riverside Chaucer*, ed. Larry D. Benson, 3rd ed. (Oxford: Oxford University Press, 2008), p. 28, l. 329. All further references to Chaucer's works are to this edition; further references to *The Canterbury Tales* will be cited by fragment within the text.
20. David Wallace, *Chaucerian Polity: Absolutist Lineages and Associational Forms in England and Italy* (Stanford, CA: Stanford University Press, 1997), p. 187.
21. David Wallace throughout his discussion refers to the merchants in 'The Man of Law's Tale' as Muslim: *Chaucerian Polity*, p. 185. Carol Heffernan states the merchants were 'probably Venetian Christians living in Syria': *The Orient in Chaucer and Medieval Romance* (Woodbridge: Brewer, 2003), p. 42.
22. Paul Gilroy, *Postcolonial Melancholia* (New York: Columbia University Press, 2004), pp. 81–94.
23. *ibid.*, p. 110.
24. *ibid.*, p. 130.
25. Aziz Atiya, *The Crusade in the Later Middle Ages* (London: Methuen, 1938).
26. Geraldine Heng, *Empire of Magic: Medieval Romance and the Politics of Cultural Fantasy* (New York: Columbia University Press, 2003); Nicola McDonald, ed., *Pulp Fictions of Medieval England: Essays in Popular Romance* (Manchester: Manchester University Press, 2004); Lee Manion, *Narrating the Crusades* (Cambridge and New York: Cambridge University Press, 2014); Robert Rouse, 'Romance and Crusade in Late Medieval England', in *The Cambridge Companion to the Literature of the Crusades*, ed. Anthony Bale (Cambridge: Cambridge University Press, 2019), pp. 217–31 (p. 217); Suzanne Yeager, *Jerusalem in Medieval Narrative* (Cambridge: Cambridge University Press, 2008).
27. Lauren Berlant, *Cruel Optimism* (Durham, NC: Duke University Press, 2011) p. 24.
28. Eitan Bar-Yosef, 'The Last Crusade? British Propaganda and the Palestine Campaign, 1917–18', *Journal of Contemporary History* 36:1 (Jan. 2001), 87–109 (p. 87).
29. Nicholas Paul and Suzanne Yeager, 'Introduction: Crusading and the Work of Memory, Past and Present', in *Remembering the Crusades: Myth, Image and Identity*, ed. Nicholas Paul and Suzanne Yeager (Baltimore, MD: Johns Hopkins Press, 2012), pp. 1–25.
30. Select notable publications include: Jeffrey Jerome Cohen, ed., *The Postcolonial Middle Ages* (New York and Houndmills: Palgrave, 2001); Patricia Clare Ingham and Michelle R. Warren, eds., *Postcolonial Moves: Medieval through Modern* (New York: Palgrave Macmillan, 2003); John Ganim, *Medievalism and Orientalism* (Basingstoke: Macmillan, 2005); Sarah Salih, *Imagining the Pagan in Late Medieval England* (Cambridge: Brewer, 2019).

31. *The Invisible Enemy Should Not Exist (Lamassu of Nineveh)*, 2018, 10,500 Iraqi date syrup cans, metal frame. Commissioned for Trafalgar Square's Fourth Plinth, London; *The Invisible Enemy Should Not Exist*, 2007–ongoing, drawings, Arabic newspaper and food packaging cardboard sculptures, museum labels, sound.
32. *RETURN*, 2004–ongoing, Jamaica Centre for Arts and Learning, Queens (2004), Longwood Art Centre, Bronx (2005), Storefront at 529 Atlantic Avenue, Brooklyn, produced by Creative Time (2006).
33. *May the obdurate foe not be in good health*, Arabic newspapers, food packaging, cardboard, museum labels, 2011–ongoing, <www.michaelrakowitz.com/may-the-obdurate-foe-not-be-in-good-health> [accessed 13 October 2021].
34. Alexander Nagel and Christopher Wood, *Anachronic Renaissance* (New York: Zone Books, 2010), p. 18.
35. David Jacoby, 'Oriental Silks at the Time of the Mongols: Patterns of Trade and Distribution in the West', in *Oriental Silks in Medieval Europe*, ed. Juliane von Fircks and Regula Schorta (Riggisberg: Abegg-Stiftung, 2016), pp. 92–123 (p. 113).
36. See Jonathan Hsy, *Trading Tongues: Merchants, Multilingualism, and Medieval Literature* (Columbus, OH: Ohio State Press, 2013).
37. Karma Lochrie, 'Provincializing Medieval Europe: Mandeville's Cosmopolitan Utopia', *PMLA* 124:2 (Mar. 2009), 592–9.
38. Kim Phillips, *Before Orientalism: Asian Peoples and Cultures in European Travel Writing, 1245–1510* (Philadelphia, PA: University of Pennsylvania Press, 2014).
39. See Felipe Fernandez-Arresto, *Before Columbus: Exploration and Colonisation from the Mediterranean to the Atlantic, 1229–1492* (Basingstoke: Macmillan Education, 1987), pp. 105–18.
40. R.R. Davies, *The First English Empire: Power and Identities in the British Isles 1093–1343* (Oxford: Oxford University Press, 2000).
41. Nagel and Wood, *Anachronic Renaissance*, p. 60.
42. The Luck of Edenhall, beaker, maker unknown, 14th century, Syria or Egypt, Museum no. C.1 to B-1959, Victoria and Albert Museum, London <https://collections.vam.ac.uk/item/O3311/the-luck-of-edenhall-beaker-and-case-unknown> [accessed 8 September 2021]. Glyn Davies, 'New Light on the Luck of Edenhall', *The Burlington Magazine* 152 (January 2010), 4–7.
43. Maria Georgopoulou, 'Orientalism and Crusader Art: Constructing a New Canon', *Medieval Encounters* 5:3 (1999), 289–321 (p. 320).
44. Esin Atil, *Renaissance of Islam: Art of the Mamluks* (Washington, DC: Smithsonian Institution Press, 1981).
45. Avinoam Shalem, 'Some Speculations on the Original Cases Made to Contain Enamelled Glass Beakers for Export', in *Gilded and Enamelled*

Glass from the Middle East, ed. Rachel Ward (London: British Museum Press, 1998), pp. 64–8.

46. Barbara Boehm and Melanie Holcomb, eds., *Jerusalem, 1000–1400: Every People under Heaven* (New Haven, CT and London: Yale University Press, 2016), pp. 56, 217.
47. See Felipe E. Rojas and Peter E. Thompson, eds., *Queering the Medieval Mediterranean: Transcultural Sea of Sex, Gender, Identity and Culture* (Leiden: Brill, 2021).
48. Patricia Clare Ingham and Michelle R. Warren, 'Introduction: Postcolonial Modernity and the Rest of History', in *Postcolonial Moves*, ed. Ingham and Warren, pp. 1–15 (p. 8). See Susan Schibanoff, 'Worlds Apart: Orientalism, Antifeminism, and Heresy in Chaucer's Man of Law's Tale', in *Chaucer's Cultural Geography*, ed. Katherine Lynch (New York and London: Routledge, 2002), pp. 248–80; Carol F. Hefferman, 'Mercantilism and Faith in the Medieval Eastern Mediterranean: Chaucer's Man of Law's Tale, Boccaccio's Decameron 5.2, and Gower's Tale of Constance', in *The Orient in Chaucer and Medieval Romance*, pp. 23–44; Geraldine Heng, 'Beauty and the East, a Modern Love Story: Women, Children and Imagined Communities in The Man of Law's Tale and its Others', in *Empire of Magic*, pp. 181–237.
49. Suzanne Conklin Akbari, *Idols in the East: European Representations of Islam and the Orient, 1100–1450* (Ithaca, NY and London: Cornell University Press, 2009).
50. Geraldine Heng, *The Invention of Race in the European Middle Ages* (Cambridge: Cambridge University Press, 2018), p. 157. See Shokoofeh Rajabzadeh, 'The Depoliticized Saracen and Muslim Erasure', *Literature Compass*, 16 (2019) <https://doi.org/10.1111/lic3.12548>.
51. Ella Shohat and Robert Stam, *Unthinking Eurocentrism: Multiculturalism and the Media* (London and New York: Routledge, 2014), p. 374.
52. Jessica Goldberg, *Trade and Institutions in the Medieval Mediterranean: The Geniza Merchants and their Business World* (Cambridge: Cambridge University Press, 2012).
53. For instance, Jewish authors appear only in the footnotes of Michelle Karnes' comparative study, *Medieval Marvels and Fictions in the Latin West and Islamic World* (Chicago, IL: University of Chicago Press, 2022).
54. See Nadia Abu El-Haj, *Facts on the Ground: Archaeological Practice and Territorial Self-Fashioning in Israeli Society* (Chicago, IL and London: University of Chicago Press, 2001).
55. Eyal Weizman, *Hollow Land: Israel's Architecture of Occupation* (London: Verso, 2007), p. 40.
56. Shirin Khanmohamadi, *In Light of Another's Word* (Philadelphia, PA: University of Pennsylvania Press, 2014), p. 2.

57. Gilroy, *The Black Atlantic*, p. 211.
58. Arjun Appadurai, 'Introduction: Commodities and the Politics of Value', in *The Social Life of Things: Commodities in Cultural Perspective*, ed. Arjun Appadurai (Cambridge: Cambridge University Press, 1986), pp. 3–63.
59. See Amitav Ghosh, *The Nutmeg's Curse: Parables for a Planet in Crisis* (London: John Murray, 2021); Fiona Candlin and Raiford Guins, eds., *The Object Reader* (Abingdon: Routledge, 2009).
60. See Supiyra Chaudhuri, Josephine McDonagh, Brian H. Murray, and Rajeswari Sunder Rajan, *Commodities and Culture in the Colonial World* (London: Routledge, 2018).
61. 'commoditẹ̄, n. 3(a) Anything of value [. . .] (b) property', *MED*.
62. Annabel Wharton, *Selling Jerusalem: Relics, Replicas, Theme Parks* (Chicago, IL and London: University of Chicago Press, 2006).
63. 'relik, n.', *MED*.
64. Susan Stewart, *On Longing: Narratives of the Miniature, the Gigantic, the Souvenir, the Collection* (Durham, NC and London: Duke University Press, 1993), p. 135.
65. See Scott Oldenburg and Kristin M.S. Bezio, eds., *Religion and the Medieval and Early Modern Global Marketplace* (London: Routledge, 2022).
66. Avinoam Shalem, 'The Otherness in the Focus of Interest: Or, If Only the Other Could Speak', in *Islamic Artefacts in the Mediterranean World: Trade, Gift Exchange and Artistic Transfer*, ed. C.S. Arcangeli and G. Wolf (Venice: Marsilio, 2010), pp. 29–44 (p. 29).
67. *ibid.*, p. 29.
68. Omar Kholeif draws a link between Rakowitz's art and Edouard Glissant's theory in *Michael Rakowitz: Backstroke of the West* (Chicago, IL: Museum of Contemporary Art Chicago and DelMonico Books, 2017), p. 7.
69. Glissant, *Poetics of Relation*, p. 214, n. 5.
70. Jane Hiddleston and Wen-Chin Ouyang, eds., *Multilingual Literature as World Literature* (London: Bloomsbury, 2021).
71. Glissant, *Poetics of Relation*, p. 69.
72. See E.K. Myerson, 'Collection No Longer on Display: Restoring Medieval England's Arabic Books to View', *Wasafiri* 36:4 (Nov. 2021), 88–96.
73. Dmitri Gutas, *Greek Thought, Arab Culture: The Graeco-Arabic Translation Movement in Baghdad and Early 'Abbasid Society (2nd–4th/8th–10th Centuries)* (London and New York: Routledge, 1998); Jim al-Khalili, *The House of Wisdom: How Arabic Science Saved Ancient Knowledge and Gave Us the Renaissance* (London: Penguin, 2010).
74. Charles Burnett, *The Introduction of Arabic Learning into England* (London: British Library, 1998); Charles Burnett, 'Some Comments on the Translating of Works from Arabic into Latin in the Mid-12th Century', *Miscellanea*

Medievalia (1985), 161–71; Charles Burnett, 'The Institutional Context of Arabic-Latin Translations of the Middle Ages: A Reassessment of the School of Toledo', in *Vocabulary of Teaching and Research between Middle Ages and Renaissance*, ed. O. Weijers (Turnhout: Brepols, 1995), pp. 214–35; Charles Burnett, 'The Coherence of the Arabic-Latin Translation Program in Toledo in the 12th Century', *Science in Context* 14:1 (2001), 249–88.

75. Charles Burnett, 'Antioch as a Link between Arabic and Latin Culture in the 12th and 13th Centuries', in *Occident et Proche-Orient: contacts scientifiques au temps des Croisades: Actes du colloique de Louvain-la-Neuve*, ed. B. van den Abeele, A. Tihon and I. Draelants (Turnhout: Brepols, 2000), pp. 1–78 (p. 15).
76. Doris Behrens-Abouseif, *The Book in Mamluk Egypt and Syria (1250–1517): Scribes, Libraries and Market* (Leiden: Brill, 2018).
77. Dorothee Metlitzki, *The Matter of Araby in Medieval England* (New Haven, CT and London: Yale University Press, 1977). The gap in research has been noted: see Christine Chism, 'Arabic in the Medieval World', *PMLA* 124:2 (2009), 624–31; Shazia Jagot, '"Fin" Amors, Arabic Learning and the Islamic World in the Work of Geoffrey Chaucer' (unpublished doctoral thesis, University of Leicester, 2013). Available online: <https://figshare.le.ac.uk/articles/thesis/Fin_amors_Arabic_learning_and_the_Islamic_world_in_the_work_of_Geoffrey_Chaucer/10158581?file=18307655> (accessed 7 August 2025).
78. Kathleen Kennedy, 'Moors and Moorishness in Late Medieval England', *SAC* 42 (2020), 213–52.
79. Shazia Jagot, 'Chaucer and Ibn al-Haytham (Alhacen): *Perspectiva*, Arabic Mathematics, and Acts of Looking', *SAC* 44 (2022), 27–61 (p. 35).
80. Charles Burnett, 'Humanism and Orientalism in the Translations from Arabic to Latin in the Middle Ages', in *Wissen über Grenzen: Arabisches Wissen und lateinisches Mittelalter*, ed. Andreas Speer and Lydia Wegener (Berlin: De Gruyter, 2006), pp. 22–31.
81. See Venetia Bridges, *Medieval Narratives of Alexander the Great: Transnational Texts in England and France* (Cambridge: Brewer, 2018), p. 11.
82. Jenna Mead, 'Reading by Said's Lantern: Orientalism and Chaucer's *Treatise on the Astrolabe*', *Medieval Encounters* 5:3 (1999), 350–7; Jagot, '"Fin" Amors, Arabic Learning and the Islamic World in the Work of Geoffrey Chaucer', pp. 114–18.
83. Chaucer, p. 662, ll. 25–34.
84. Metlitzki, *The Matter of Araby*, p. 32.
85. F.J. Carmody, *Arabic Astronomical and Astrological Sciences in Latin Translation* (Berkeley and Los Angeles, CA: University of California Press, 1956), pp. 40–6.
86. Aberystwyth, National Library of Wales, Peniarth MS 392D, fol. 116r. <www.library.wales/discover/digital-gallery/manuscripts/the-middle-ages/the-

hengwrt-chaucer/#?c=&m=&s=&cv=&xywh=-1224%2C-1%2C5662%2C4815> [accessed 26 August 2021].

87. Graham D. Caie, 'The Significance of Marginal Glosses in the Earliest Manuscripts of the Canterbury Tales', in *Chaucer and Scriptural Tradition*, ed. David Lyle Jeffrey (Ottawa: University of Ottawa Press, 1984), pp. 74–88.
88. London, British Library, Harley MS 1239, fol. 82r. Stephen Partridge, 'Designing the Page', in *The Production of Books in England 1350–1500*, ed. Daniel Wakelin and Alexandra Gillespie (Cambridge: Cambridge University Press, 2011), pp. 79–103 (p. 83).
89. See Sarah Davis-Secord, *Migration in the Medieval Mediterranean* (Leeds: Arc Humanities Press, 2021).
90. https://missingmigrants.iom.int/region/mediterranean (c) 2023 International Organization for Migration.
91. Alfred Hiatt, '"From Hulle to Carthage": Maps, England and the Sea', in *The Sea and Englishness in the Middle Ages: Maritime Narratives, Identity and Culture*, ed. Sebastian Sobecki (Woodbridge: Brewer, 2011), pp. 133–58 (pp. 155–6).
92. Dragan Todorovic, 'The Migrant's Tale', in *Refugee Tales*, ed. David Herd and Anna Pincus (Manchester: Comma Press, 2016), pp. 1–12.
93. See Jonathan Hsy, 'Pilgrimage: Chaucerian Poets of Colour', in *Antiracist Medievalisms: from 'Yellow Peril' to Black Lives Matter* (Amsterdam: ARC Humanities Press, 2021), pp. 115–32.
94. Chaucer, p. 372, ll. 2122–4.
95. See Rita Felski, *The Limits of Critique* (Chicago, IL: University of Chicago Press, 2015); Rita Felski, *Hooked: Art and Attachment* (Chicago, IL: University of Chicago Press, 2020); Saidiya Hartman, 'Venus in Two Acts', *Small Axe* 26 (2008), 1–14.
96. Carolyn Dinshaw, *How Soon Is Now?: Medieval Texts, Amateur Readers, and the Queerness of Time* (Durham, NC: Duke University Press, 2012), p. 37.

Part I The Dispensary

1. Jenks, *Robert Sturmy's Commercial Expedition*, p. 81.
2. London, Wellcome Library MS 405, fol. 22r.
3. *ibid.*, fol. 21v.
4. For the Arabic Hippocrates, see *Kitāb Buqrāṭ Fi'l-akhlāt (Hippocrates: On Humours); And, Kitāb Al-ghidha' Li-Buqrāṭ (Hippocrates: On Nutriment)*, ed. and trans. J.N. Mattock, Arabic Technical and Scientific Texts, 6 (Cambridge: Heffer, 1971).
5. Zohar Amar and Efraim Lev, *Arabian Drugs in Early Medieval Mediterranean Medicine* (Edinburgh: Edinburgh University Press, 2017), pp. 66–8.

6. Sidney Mintz, *Sweetness and Power* (London: Penguin, 1985), p. 97.
7. 'Spens(e) n.2', *MED*.
8. Quoted in Tsugitaka Sato, *Sugar in the Social Life of Medieval Islam* (Leiden: Brill, 2015), p. 143.
9. *Curye on Inglysch: English Culinary Manuscripts of the Fourteenth Century (including the Forme of Cury)*, ed. Constance B. Hieatt and Sharon Butler (New York: Oxford University Press, 1985), p. 79.
10. Translated by Lambourn, in *Abraham's Luggage*, p. 222. See Abu 'Ali al-Husain Ibn 'Abdallah Ibn Sina, *al-Qanun fi-l-Tibb*, English translation from the critical Arabic edition led by Hakim Abdul Hameed, 5 vols. (New Delhi: Jamia Hamdard, 1993–), I, p. 310.
11. London, Wellcome Library, Wellcome MS 405, fols. 38v–39r.
12. *ibid.*, fol. 39v.
13. *ibid.*, fols. 39v–40r.
14. R.J. Charleston, 'Vessel Glass', in *English Medieval Industries: Craftsmen, Techniques, Products*, ed. John Blair and Nigel Ramsey (London: Hambledon, 1991, repr. 2001), pp. 237–64 (p. 244).

1. Sweet Wine / The English Taste for the Blood of the Holy Land

1. Jenks, *Robert Sturmy's Commercial Expedition*, p. 81.
2. <www.nationalarchives.gov.uk/currency-converter/#currency-result> [accessed 18 May 2020].
3. Miri Rubin, *Corpus Christi: The Eucharist in Late Medieval Culture* (Cambridge: Cambridge University Press, 1991), pp. 313–14.
4. André Simon, *The History of the Wine Trade in England* (London: Wyman and Sons, 1906), p. 238.
5. Susan Rose, *The Wine Trade in Medieval Europe 1000–1500* (London: Continuum, 2011), pp. 54–7; Winifred Harwood, 'Commodities: Wine', in *English Inland Trade 1430–1540: Southampton and its Region*, ed. Michael Hicks (Oxford: Oxbow Books, 2015), pp. 115–32 (p. 116).
6. Simon, *History of the Wine Trade*, p. 238.
7. Mary Carruthers, 'Sweetness', *Speculum* 81 (2006), 999–1013; Mary Carruthers, 'Taking the Bitter with the Sweet', in *The Experience of Beauty in the Middle Ages* (Oxford: Oxford University Press, 2013), pp. 80–107.
8. Rose, *The Wine Trade*, p. 83.
9. A.D. Francis, *The Wine Trade* (London: Adam and Charles Black, 1972), p. 15.
10. Rabei G. Khamisy, 'Frankish Viticulture, Wine Presses, and Wine Production in the Levant: New Evidence from Castellum Regis (Miʿilyā)', *Palestine Exploration Quarterly* 153:3 (2021), 191–221 (p. 194).

11. *ibid.*, p. 216.
12. *ibid.*, p. 217.
13. *ibid.*, p. 219.
14. Alwyn Ruddock, *Italian Merchants and Shipping in Southampton, 1270–1600* (Southampton: University College, 1951), p. 84; Rose, *The Wine Trade*, p. 106.
15. Ruddock, *Italian Merchants*, p. 237.
16. *The Libelle of Englyshe Polycye*, in *Medieval English Travel*, ed. Bale and Sobecki (Oxford: Oxford University Press, 2019), p. 320, ll. 344–47.
17. Ruddock, *Italian Merchants*, p. 101.
18. *ibid.*, p. 179.
19. *ibid.*, p. 55.
20. Rose, *The Wine Trade*, pp. 54–7.
21. *ibid.*, p. 124.
22. *The Household Book of Dame Alice de Bryene, of Actor Hall, Suffolk*, ed. Vincent Redstone, trans. M.K. Dale (Ipswich: Suffolk Institute of Archaeology and Natural History, 1931), p. 119.
23. Quoted in Rose, *The Wine Trade*, p. 129.
24. Miranda Threlfall-Holmes, 'Provisioning a Medieval Monastery: Durham Cathedral Priory's Purchases of Imported Goods, 1464–1520' (unpublished doctoral thesis, Durham University, 1997), pp. 18, 22. Available at Durham E-Theses Online: <http://etheses.dur.ac.uk/4963> [accessed 23 June 2021].
25. *ibid.*, pp. 66–9.
26. Caroline Walker Bynum, *Wonderful Blood: Theology and Practice in Late Medieval Northern Germany and Beyond* (Philadelphia, PA: University of Pennsylvania Press, 2007), p. 94; Ann Astell, *Eating Beauty: The Eucharist and the Spiritual Arts of the Middle Ages* (Ithaca, NY and London: Cornell University Press, 2006).
27. See Julian M. Luxford, 'A Fifteenth-Century Version of Matthew Paris's Procession with the Relic of the Holy Blood and Evidence for its Carthusian Context', *Journal of the Warburg and Courtauld Institutes* 72 (2009), 81–101.
28. Nicholas Vincent, *The Holy Blood: King Henry III and the Westminster Blood Relic* (Cambridge: Cambridge University Press, 2001), p. 171.
29. *ibid.*, pp. 82–108.
30. Martina Bagnoli et al., eds., *Treasures of Heaven: Saints, Relics and Devotion in Medieval Europe* (London: British Museum Press, 2011).
31. Cecilia Gaposchkin, *Invisible Weapons: Liturgy and the Making of Crusade Ideology* (Ithaca, NY: Cornell University Press, 2017), pp. 4, 199.
32. Diana Webb, *Medieval European Pilgrimage, c.700–c.1500* (Basingstoke and New York: Palgrave, 2002).

33. Bridget of Sweden, *The Liber Celestis of St Bridget of Sweden*, ed. Roger Ellis, 2 vols. (Oxford: Oxford University Press, 1987), I, p. 479.
34. *The Defective Version of Mandeville's Travels*, ed. M.C. Seymour (Oxford: Oxford University Press, 2002), pp. 3–4.
35. Diarmaid MacCulloch, *A History of Christianity* (London: Penguin, 2010), pp. 405–6, 565.
36. See Bale, '"*ut legi*"'.
37. Wey, *Itineraries*, p. 6.
38. *ibid.*, p. 16.
39. *ibid.*, p. 124.
40. *ibid.*, p. 124. 'Romney' derived from Romania, that is, the Morea in the Peloponnese; 'Malmsey' from Malvasia, the Venetian name for the port of Laconia in Greece. See 'romenei(e), n.'; 'malvesi(e), n.', *MED* [accessed 6 September 2021].
41. Lambourn, *Abraham's Luggage*, p. 229.
42. Wey, *Itineraries*, p. 102.
43. *ibid.*, pp. 5–6.
44. *ibid.*, p. 7.
45. See Mary-Jo Arn, 'The Emendation of Wine: Wine Recipes from Beinecke MS 163 ("The Wagstaff Miscellany")', *The Yale University Library Gazette* 64:3/4 (Apr. 1990), 109–23.
46. Wey, *Itineraries*, p. 7.
47. Margery Kempe, *The Book of Margery Kempe*, ed. Barry Windeatt (Woodbridge: Brewer, 2004), p. 151.
48. *ibid.*, p. 159.
49. See Marion Turner, *The Wife of Bath: A Biography* (Princeton, NJ: Princeton University Press, 2022).
50. Marion Turner, *Chaucer: A European Life* (Oxford: Princeton University Press, 2019), p. 19; Rose, *The Wine Trade*, p. 129.
51. See Leigh Ann Craig, *Wandering Women and Holy Matrons: Women as Pilgrims in the Later Middle Ages* (Leiden and Boston, MA: Brill, 2009); Graciela S. Daichman, *Wayward Nuns in Medieval Literature* (Syracuse, NY: Syracuse University Press, 1986).
52. *The Defective Version*, pp. 26–7.
53. Metlitzki, *The Matter of Araby*, p. 6.
54. Ashtor, *Levant Trade*, p. 40.
55. *The Defective Version*, p. 62.
56. Avinoam Shalem, ed., *Constructing the Image of Muhammed in Europe* (Berlin: De Gruyter, 2013), p. 149.
57. Qur'ān Sura 5:90–91, in *Online Qur'ān Project* (University of Copenhagen, 2007–2021): <https://al-quran.info/#5> [accessed 7 September 2021].

58. Quoted in Stefane Brinkmann, 'Wine in Hadīth: From Intoxication to Sobriety', in *Wine Culture in Iran and Beyond*, ed. Bert G. Fragner, Ralph Kauz, and Florian Schwarz (Vienna: Austrian Academy of Sciences Press, 2014), pp. 71–135 (p. 72).
59. Khanmohamadi, *In Light of Another's Word*, pp. 113–44.
60. *The Defective Version*, pp. 62–3.
61. *ibid.*, p. 62. The episode of Muhammed and the hermit echoes and is recorded in proximity to Mandeville's version of the Prophet's encounter with Bahīrā, a Syrian Christian monk, which does recur in versions of *Sirat-un-Nabi* [the life of the Prophet]. See Ibn Ishaq, *The Life of Mohammed: A Translation of Ishaq's 'Sirat Rasul Allah'*, trans. by Alfred Guillaume (Oxford: Oxford University Press, 1955), pp. 79–81.
62. John Tolan, 'European Accounts of Muhammed's Life', in *The Cambridge Companion to Muhammed*, ed. Jonathan E. Brockopp (Cambridge: Cambridge University Press, 2010), pp. 226–50.
63. *The Defective Version*, p. 63.
64. Quoted and translated in Martin Jacobs, *Reorienting the East: Jewish Travellers to the Medieval Muslim World* (Philadelphia, PA: University of Pennsylvania Press, 2014), p. 177.
65. *ibid.*, p. 178.
66. *ibid.*, p. 175.
67. Robyn Malo, *Relics and Writing in Late Medieval England* (Toronto: University of Toronto Press, 2013), p. 106.
68. London, British Library, Royal MS 14 E III, fol. 7r.
69. Thomas Malory, *Le Morte Darthur*, ed. Stephen H. A. Shepherd (New York and London: W.W. Norton, 2004), p. 583. See Sarah B. Rude, 'Seeing Is Believing and Achieving: Viewing the Eucharist in Malory's "Sankgreal"', *Arthuriana* 28:2 (2018), 3–27; Malo, *Relics and Writing*, pp. 101–24; Rubin, *Corpus Christi*, pp. 139–42.
70. See David Wallace, 'Imperium, Commerce, and National Crusade: The Romance of Malory's *Morte*', in *New Medieval Literatures, 8*, ed. Rita Copeland, David Lawton, and Wendy Scase (Turnhout: Brepols, 2006), pp. 45–65.
71. *The Squire of Low Degree, in Sentimental and Humorous Romances: Floris and Blancheflour, Sir Degrevant, the Squire of Low Degree, the Tournament of Tottenham, and the Feast of Tottenham*, ed. Erik Kooper (Kalamazoo, MI: Medieval Institute Publications, 2006), p. 145, ll. 473–4.
72. See Robert Rouse, 'Romance and Crusade in Late Medieval England', in *The Cambridge Companion to the Literature of the Crusades*, ed. Anthony Bale (Cambridge: Cambridge University Press, 2019), pp. 217–31.
73. *The Squire of Low Degree*, ll. 753–60.

74. *ibid.*, ll. 826–8.
75. *ibid.*, l. 476.
76. *The Cyrurgie of Guy de Chauliac*, ed. M.C. Ogden (London: Oxford University Press, 1971), p. 9.
77. *ibid.*, p. 8.
78. Venice 1498 MS, fols. 217r–246v. See Lynn Thorndike, *A Catalogue of Incipits of Mediaeval Scientific Writings in Latin*, Mediaeval Academy of America Publication No. 29, ed. by Pearl Kibre (London: Medieval Academy of America, 1963), p. 565.
79. *The Cyrurgie*, p. 312.
80. 'aldaro[u]n, n.', *MED*.
81. *The Cyrurgie*, p. 609.
82. London, British Library, Harley MS 1736, fol. 80r.
83. S.J. Lang, 'The "Philomena" of John Bradmore and its Middle English Derivative: A Perspective on Surgery in Late Medieval England' (unpublished doctoral thesis, University of St Andrews, 1998), p. 134, available at <http://hdl.handle.net/10023/4910> [accessed 2 September 2021].
84. *The Cyrurgie*, p. 483.
85. Trevisa, *On the Properties of Things*, p. 1080.
86. *The Cyrurgie*, p. 431.
87. 'The Consideration of Quintessence: An Edition of a Middle English Translation of John of Rupescissa's Liber de consideratione de quintae essentiae omnium rerum', ed. Margaret A. Halverson (unpublished doctoral thesis, Michigan University, 1998), p. 116, available at MSU Libraries Digital Repository, https://d.lib.msu.edu/etd/47644 [accessed 2 September 2021].
88. William R. Newman, *The Summa Perfectionis of Pseudo-Geber: A Critical Edition, Translation and Study* (Leiden and New York: Brill, 1991), p. 408.
89. Leah DeVun, *Prophecy, Alchemy and the End of Time: John of Rupescissa in the Late Middle Ages* (New York: Columbia University Press, 2009), p. 70.
90. *ibid.*, p. 106.
91. *ibid.*, p. 92; see Arnold of Villanova, *The Earliest Printed Book on Wine*, trans. and ed. Henry E. Sigerist (New York: Schuman's, 1943).
92. See Jagot, '"Fin" Amors, Arabic Learning and the Islamic World in the Work of Geoffrey Chaucer', p. 154.
93. For example, see Oxford, Bodleian Library, Canon Misc. 480, fols. 92r–93r; Cambridge, Trinity College, MS 1102, fols. 137–171r, both in Thorndike, *Catalogue*, ed. Kibre, pp. 812, 879. For wine as medicine, see Jennifer Rampling, *The Experimental Fire: Inventing English Alchemy, 1300–1700* (London: University of Chicago Press, 2020), pp. 43, 51–2, 54, 339.

94. Bridget of Sweden, *Liber Celestis*, p. 437.
95. *ibid.*, p. 440.
96. *Cultures of Piety: Medieval English Devotional Literature in Translation*, ed. Anne Clark Bartlett and Thomas H. Bestul (Ithaca, NY: Cornell University Press, 1999), p. 197.
97. Trevisa, *On the Properties of Things*, p. 1071.
98. Finger-ring, gold, engraved, late 15th century, England, Museum no. AF.897, British Museum, London <www.britishmuseum.org/collection/object/H_AF-897> [accessed 8 September 2021].
99. Elizabeth Cleland, 'Small-Scale Devotional Tapestries – Fifteenth and Sixteenth Centuries, Part 2: The "Mystic Grapes" Group', *Studies in the Decorative Arts* 16:2 (2009), 141–64 (p. 151); Anne E. Wardwell, 'The Mystical Grapes, a Devotional Tapestry', *The Bulletin of the Cleveland Museum of Art* 62:1 (Jan., 1975), 17–23; Adolfo Salvatore Cavallo, *Medieval Tapestries in the Metropolitan Museum of Art* (New York: Metropolitan Museum of Art, 1993), pp. 336–8.
100. Quoted in Cleland, 'Small-Scale Devotional Tapestries', p. 159.
101. London, British Library, Additional MS 35166, fol. 24r; London, British Library, Yates Thompson MS 10, fol. 25r; New York, Morgan Library, MS M.917, fol. 129r; Oxford, Bodleian Library, MS Douce 180, fol. 81.
102. Bynum, *Wonderful Blood*, p. 4; Rubin, *Corpus Christi*, p. 313.
103. *The Christ Child Pressing the Wine of the Eucharist*, c. 1500, South Netherlandish, linen warp; wool, silk, and gilt weft yarns (50.5 x 46.4 cm), Metropolitan Museum of Art, Accession Number: 14.40.709a.
104. For Caleb and Joshua's hats, see Debra Higgs Strickland, *Saracens, Demons, and Jews: Making Monsters in Medieval Art* (Oxford: Princeton University Press, 2003), p. 148.
105. *The Defective Version*, p. 9.
106. *Gilte Legende*, ed. Richard Hamer, 2 vols. (Oxford: Oxford University Press, 2006), I, p. 329.
107. William Shakespeare, *The RSC Shakespeare: William Shakespeare: Complete Works*, ed. Jonathan Bate and Eric Rasmussen (London: Macmillan, 2008), *The Tragedy of Richard III*, p. 1324, I.4.135–7.

2. Spices / English Digestion and Indigestion

1. Jenks, *Robert Sturmy's Commercial Expedition*, p. 81.
2. E.W.W. Veale, ed., *The Great Red Book of Bristol* (Bristol: Bristol Record Society, 1938), p. 58.
3. S. Francia, 'The Use of Trade Accounts to Uncover the Importance of Cumin as a Medicinal Plant in Medieval England', in *Critical Approaches*

to the History of Western Herbal Medicine: From Classical Antiquity to the Early Modern Period, ed. S. Francia and A. Stobart (London: Bloomsbury Academic, 2014), pp. 111–30 (pp. 112–13).

4. Ziadeh, *Urban Life*, p. 132; Sato, *Sugar*, pp. 23–5.
5. Ashtor, *Levant Trade*, p. 165.
6. Susan Harvey, *Scenting Salvation: Ancient Christianity and the Olfactory Imagination* (Berkeley and Los Angeles, CA and London: University of California Press, 2006), p. 88.
7. As Amitav Ghosh writes: 'they came because plant products like nutmeg had already travelled in the other direction': *The Nutmeg's Curse*, p. 9. Paul Freedman, *Out of the East: Spices and the Medieval Imagination* (New Haven, CT and London: Yale University Press, 2008).
8. David Jacoby, 'Refugees from Acre in Famagusta around 1300', in *The Harbour of All this Sea and Realm: Crusader to Venetian Famagusta*, ed. Michael J.K. Walsh, Tamás Kiss, and Nicholas Coureas (Budapest: Central European University Press, 2014), pp. 53–68.
9. Richard Kyngeston, *Expeditions to Prussia and the Holy Land made by Henry, Earl of Derby (afterwards King Henry IV) in the years 1390–1 and 1392–3: being the accounts kept by his treasurer during two years*, ed. Lucy Toulmin Smith (London: Camden Society, 1894), p. 299.
10. *ibid.*, pp. 246, 257–8.
11. *ibid.*, p. 228.
12. Ashtor, *Levant Trade*, p. 40.
13. In her account of medieval pet-ownership, Kathleen Walker-Meikle has shown that bird owners bought their birdseed from apothecaries – and that monkeys were fed imported almonds: *Medieval Pets* (Woodbridge: Boydell, 2012), pp. 41–4.
14. Kyngeston, *Expeditions*, p. 229.
15. *ibid.*, p. 163.
16. For example, the 'Touch' tapestry in the *The Lady and the Unicorn* series, late fifteenth/early sixteenth century, France, Cl. 10831–10836, 311–377 cm x 290–473 cm. Musée de Cluny, France.
17. Trevisa, *On the Properties of Things*, p. 1105.
18. Aberdeen, Aberdeen University Library, MS 24, fols. 8v–9r. Available online at: <https://www.abdn.ac.uk/bestiary/ms24/f8v>.
19. London, British Library, Additional MS 11283, fol. 2v.
20. Robert Alter, trans., *The Hebrew Bible: A Translation with Commentary*, 3 vols. (New York: Norton, 2019), III, 4. 8. Further references to the Song of Songs are to Alter's translation.
21. *ibid.*, III, p. 600.
22. Ann Astell, *The Song of Songs in the Middle Ages* (Ithaca, NY: Cornell, 1990).

23. Freedman, *Out of the East*, pp. 89–95; Paul Freedman, 'Health, Wellness and the Allure of Spices in the Middle Ages', *Journal of Ethnopharmacology* 167 (June 2015), 47–53.
24. Mintz, *Sweetness and Power*, p. 28.
25. E. Jones, K.D. Politis, H.F. James, A.J. Hall, R.E. Jones, and J. Hamer, 'The Sugar Industry in the Southern Jordan Valley: An Interim Report on the Pilot Season of Excavations, Geophysical and Geological Surveys at Tawahin as-Sukkar and Khirbat ash-Shaykh 'Isa, in Ghawr as-Safi', *Annual of the Department of Antiquities of Jordan* 46 (2002), 591–614 (pp. 593–4).
26. Ziadeh, *Urban Life*, pp. 134–40.
27. *The Defective Version*, p. 24.
28. *ibid.*, p. 144.
29. Marianne O'Doherty, *The Indies and the Medieval West: Thought, Report, Imagination* (Turnhout: Brepols, 2013), p. 223.
30. Kyngeston, *Expeditions*, pp. 225, 219, 222.
31. Wey, *Itineraries*, p. 5.
32. Harvey, *Scenting Salvation*, p. 120.
33. *The Book of Margery Kempe*, p. 161.
34. See Laura Kalas, *Margery Kempe's Spiritual Medicine: Suffering, Transformation and the Life-Course* (Woodbridge: Boydell and Brewer, 2020).
35. Caroline Walker Bynum, *Christian Materiality: An Essay on Religion in Late Medieval Europe* (Cambridge, MA and London: MIT Press, 2011), p. 18.
36. *The Book of Margery Kempe*, p. 304.
37. Chaucer, p. 701, ll. 1367–72.
38. Ashtor, *Levant Trade*, p. 165.
39. For a discussion of the *Libelle* and mercantile interests, see Sobecki, *The Sea*, pp. 145–52.
40. Freedman, *Out of the East*, p. 160.
41. *The Libelle of Englyshe Polycye*, ll. 344–8.
42. Brian Foster, ed., *The Local Port Book of Southampton for 1435–36* (Southampton: Southampton University Press, 1963), p. 84.
43. *ibid.*, pp. 94, 100, 106, 110.
44. *The Libelle of Englyshe Polycye*, ll. 355–9.
45. *ibid.*, ll. 366–7 and 374.
46. Trevisa, *On the Properties of Things*, pp. 896, 925, 1025.
47. *The Libelle of Englyshe Polycye*, l. 369.
48. Trevisa, *On the Properties of Things*, p. 1090.
49. *ibid.*, p. 1091.
50. Ashtor, *Levant Trade*, p. 207.

51. M.M. Sadek, *The Arabic Materia Medica of Dioscorides* (Quebec: Éditions Du Sphinx, 1983).
52. Trevisa, *On the Properties of Things*, p. 1032.
53. *ibid.*, p. 1091.
54. Charles Perry, trans. and ed., *Scents and Flavors: A Syrian Cookbook* (New York: New York University Press, 2017), p. 159.
55. Sato, *Sugar*, p. 101. See also Ibn al-Baytar's encyclopaedia of drugs: *ibid.*, pp. 92–4; Ibn Butlan, p. 159; Ibn al-Quff, p. 165.
56. Trevisa, *On the Properties of Things*, p. 1031.
57. See 'Sugar as Medicine' in Sato, *Sugar*, pp. 91–113. For a discussion of the use of sugar to treat fevers, see Lambourn, *Abraham's Luggage*, p. 221.
58. Kyngeston, *Expeditions*, pp. 11, 21–2.
59. *ibid.*, p. 19.
60. 'candy, n.1', *OED*.
61. 'penide, n', *OED*.
62. Megan Tiddeman, 'More Sugar and Spice: Revisiting Medieval Italian Influence on the Mercantile Lexis of England', in *The Multilingual Origins of Standard English*, ed. Laura Wright (Berlin: De Gruyter, 2020), pp. 381–410.
63. Glissant, *Poetics of Relation*, p. 69.
64. J.H. Galloway, 'The Mediterranean Sugar Industry', *Geographical Review* 67:2 (Apr. 1977), 177–94 (p. 193).
65. Mintz, *Sweetness and Power*, p. 29.
66. Fernandez-Arresto, *Before Columbus*, p. 118.
67. *Libelle of Englyshe Polycye*, ll. 396–9.
68. *ibid.*, ll. 610–13.
69. *ibid.*, ll. 686–7.
70. *Medieval English Travel*, ed. Bale and Sobecki, p. 303; Brendan Smith, 'Disaster and Opportunity: 1320–1450', in *The Cambridge History of Ireland: 600–1550*, ed. Brendan Smith (Cambridge: Cambridge University Press, 2017), pp. 244–71.
71. *Croxton, The Play of the Sacrament*, in *Medieval Drama: An Anthology*, ed. Greg Walker (Oxford: Blackwell, 2000), p. 215, ll. 17–19.
72. *ibid.*, ll. 9–11.
73. *ibid.*, ll. 15–34.
74. *ibid.*, ll. 61, 63, 66.
75. *ibid.*, ll. 69–79.
76. Goldberg, *Trade*, p. 37.
77. Heng, *The Invention of Race*, p. 113.
78. Compare Silvia Tomasch, 'Postcolonial Chaucer and the Virtual Jew', in *The Postcolonial Middle Ages*, ed. J.J. Cohen (New York: Palgrave Macmillan, 2000), pp. 243–60.

79. Cambridge University Library, T-S 12.435, S.D. Gotein's unpublished edition, available online through the Princeton Geniza Project <https://geniza.princeton.edu/documents/3164>.
80. *Croxton*, ll. 95, 103.
81. *ibid.*, ll. 93–106.
82. *The Household Book of Dame Alice*, pp. 103–4.
83. Ashtor, *Levant Trade*, p. 261.
84. *The Household Book of Dame Alice*, p. 103.
85. *ibid.*, pp. 120, 137.
86. *Curye on Inglysch*, p. 70.
87. For the medicinal properties of sweetness, see Mary Carruthers, 'Sweetness', *Speculum* 81 (2006), 999–1013.
88. Gilroy, *Postcolonial Melancholia*, p. 130.
89. *Croxton*, ll. 171, 205.
90. Anti-Jewish host desecration libels were common. See Bynum, *Christian Materiality*, p. 259.
91. *Croxton*, l. 451.
92. Trevisa, *On the Properties of Things*, p. 438.
93. *Croxton*, l. 580.
94. *ibid.*, 633.
95. *ibid.*, 889.
96. See Ella Shohat, *On the Arab-Jew, Palestine, and Other Displacements* (London: Pluto Press, 2017). See also James Renton and Ben Gidley, eds., *Antisemitism and Islamophobia and Europe: A Shared Story?* (London: Palgrave Macmillan, 2017). See also Michael Rakowitz's project *Dar al-Sulh* [Domain of Conciliation]: the artist, in collaboration with Regine Basha and Ella Shohat, opened an Iraqi-Jewish restaurant in Dubai (1–8 May 2013). The title *Dar al-Sulh* refers to the historical agreement in the Middle East, under which non-Muslims lived with freedom of religion, autonomy, and protection. www.michaelrakowitz.com/dar-al-sulh [accessed 28 February 2020].
97. Kyngeston, *Expeditions*, p. 154.
98. Christina Normore, *A Feast for the Eyes: Art, Performance, and the Late Medieval Banquet* (Chicago, IL and London: University of Chicago Press, 2015), p. 31.
99. Turner, *Chaucer*, p. 434.
100. Kyngeston, *Expeditions*, pp. 163, 230, 233, 287.
101. Normore, *A Feast for the Eyes*, p. 44.
102. *Curye on Inglysch*, pp. 45, 67, 79, 106, 144.
103. *ibid.*, p. 67.
104. See *ibid.*, pp. 45, 68, 88, 102, 144.
105. Perry, *Scents and Flavors*, pp. 145–6.

106. Sato, *Sugar*, p. 165.
107. Maxime Rodinson, trans. by Barbara Inskip, 'Ma'muniyya East and West', *Petits propos culinares* 33 (1989), 15–25.
108. *Curye on Inglysch*, p. 117.
109. Freedman, *Out of the East*, p. 26.
110. Phillips, *Before Orientalism*, p. 100.
111. Mintz, *Sweetness and Power*, p. 88.
112. Francia, 'The Use of Trade', p. 114.
113. *The Feast of Tottenham*, in *Sentimental and Humorous Romances*, ed. Kooper, p. 206, ll. 29, 34–5, 40–2.
114. *Medieval English Political Writings*, ed. James Dean (Kalamazoo, MI: Medieval Institute Publications, 1996), p. 224, ll. 69–72.
115. Turner, *Chaucer*, p. 3.
116. Edward Said, *Orientalism* (London: Penguin, 2003), p. 250.
117. Aijaz Ahmad, *In Theory: Classes, Nations, Literatures* (London: Verso, 2008), p. 181.
118. Caroline Walker Bynum, *Holy Feast and Holy Fast: The Religious Significance of Food to Medieval Women* (Berkeley: University of California Press, 1987).
119. See Iwona Blazwick and Carolyn Christov-Barkargiev, eds., *Michael Rakowitz* (London: Silvana Editoriale, 2019), p. 157.
120. Ella Shohat, 'Culinary Ghosting: A Journey through a Sweet and Sour Iraq', in *Michael Rakowitz: Backstroke of the West*, ed. Kholeif, pp. 44–52 (p. 47).
121. Blazwick and Christov-Barkargiev, *Michael Rakowitz*, p. 152.
122. Kyngeston, *Expeditions*, p. 276.

Part II The Treasury

1. Susan Jenkins, 'The Politics of Public Monuments: Parliamentary Commissions of Monuments for Westminster Abbey in 1798', *Sculpture Journal* 30:1 (2021), 9–29 (p. 12).
2. Richard Jenkyns, *Westminster Abbey* (Cambridge, MA: Harvard University Press, 2005), p. 6.
3. Paul Binski and James G. Clark, 'A House of Kings: 1100–1307', in *Westminster Abbey: A Church in History*, ed. David Cannadine (New Haven, CT and London: Yale University Press, 2019), pp. 45–88 (p. 46).
4. Nagel and Wood, *Anachronic Renaissance*, p. 161.
5. <www.nationalarchives.gov.uk/currency-converter/#currency-result> [accessed 15 August 2025].
6. Binski and Clark, 'A House of Kings', p. 45.
7. For Westminster Abbey consumption see Barbara Harvey, *Living and Dying in England 1100–1450* (Oxford: Oxford University Press, 1993), pp. 44, 58.

8. J.W. Legg, ed., *An Inventory of the Vestry of Westminster Abbey taken in 1388, Communicated to the Society of Antiquaries by J.W. Legg* (Westminster: Nicholls and Sons, 1890), p. 35.
9. *ibid.*, p. 55.
10. See Michael Camille, *Image on the Edge: The Margins of Medieval Art* (London: Reaktion, 1992), p. 130.
11. Legg, *An Inventory*, p. 59.
12. *ibid.*, p. 59.
13. *ibid.*, p. 58.
14. *ibid.*, pp. 26, 28, 31.
15. *ibid.*, p. 45.
16. *ibid.*, p. 37.
17. *ibid.*, p. 44.
18. *ibid.*, p. 32.
19. Fabienne Boursiquot, 'Ethnographic Museums: From Colonial Exposition to Intercultural Dialogue', in *The Postcolonial Museum: The Arts of Memory and the Pressures of History*, ed. Iain Chambers et al. (London: Routledge, 2014), pp. 63–71 (p. 64).

3. Silks and Velvets / The Fabrics of English Identity

1. Jenks, *Robert Sturmy's Commercial Expedition*, p. 81.
2. Alixe Bovey, *Tacuinum Sanitatis: An Early Renaissance Guide to Health* (London: Sam Fogg, 2005), p. 73.
3. 'William Wey's Will', in *Medieval English Travel*, ed. Bale and Sobecki (Oxford: Oxford University Press, 2019), pp. 397–400 (p. 398).
4. *ibid.*, p. 400.
5. On replicas of Jerusalem, see Alfred Hiatt, *Dislocations: Maps, Classical Tradition and Spatial Play in the European Middle Ages* (Toronto: Pontifical Institute of Medieval Studies, 2020), pp. 5–6.
6. Nagel and Wood, *Anachronic Renaissance*, pp. 60–1.
7. Stewart, *On Longing*, p. 151.
8. For Wey's chapel as a reiterative meme of Jerusalem, see Anthony Bale, '"*ut legi*": Sir John Mandeville's Audience of Three Late Medieval English Travellers to Italy and Jerusalem', *SAC* 38 (2016), 201–37.
9. For virtual pilgrimage, see Kathryn M. Rudy, *Virtual Pilgrimages in the Convent: Imagining Jerusalem in the Middle Ages* (Turnhout: Brepols, 2011).
10. David Jacoby, 'Oriental Silks Go West: A Declining Trade in the Later Middle Ages', in *Islamic Artefacts*, ed. Arcangeli and Wolf, pp. 71–88 (p. 76). See also David Jacoby, 'Society, Culture and the Arts in Crusader Acre', in *France and the Holy Land: Frankish Culture at the End of the Crusades*, ed.

Daniel H. Weiss and Lisa Mahoney (Baltimore, MD and London: Johns Hopkins Press, 2004), pp. 97–137.

11. Ziadeh, *Urban Life*, pp. 133–37.
12. Jacoby, 'Oriental Silks Go West', p. 78.
13. Jacoby, 'Oriental Silks at the Time of the Mongols', p. 103; Anna Muthesius, 'Silk in the Medieval World', in *Cambridge History of Western Textiles*, 2 vols. (Cambridge: Cambridge University Press, 2003), I, pp. 325–54.
14. Jacoby, 'Oriental Silks Go West', p. 71.
15. Ibn Battuta visits 'Zaitun' and comments on the satins, velvets, and damask produced there. See Ibn Battuta, *The Travels of Ibn Battuta*, abridged, annotated and trans. by Tim Mackintosh Smith (London: Macmillan Collector's Library, 2016), p. 265. For etymologies, see *OED*: 'tabby, n. and adj.', 'taffeta, n. and adj.', 'camaca, n.', 'satin, n. and adj.' [accessed 6 September 2021]; Donald King, 'Types of Silk Cloth Used in England 1200–1500', in *La seta in Europa secc. XIII–XX*, ed. Simonetta Cavacioschi (Florence: Le Monnier, 1993), pp. 457–64.
16. See Lisa Monnas, *Merchants, Princes and Painters: Silk Fabrics in Italian and Northern Paintings, 1300–1550* (New Haven, CT and London: Yale University Press, 2008), p. 231.
17. Kyngeston, *Expeditions*, p. 280.
18. *ibid.*, p. 284.
19. Threlfall-Holmes, 'Provisioning a Medieval Monastery', p. 69.
20. *Libelle of Englyshe Polycye*, ll. 332–3.
21. Tasha Vorderstrasse, 'Trade and Textiles from Medieval Antioch', *Al-Masāq* 22:2 (2010), 151–71 (p. 159).
22. Jacoby, 'Oriental Silks at the Time of the Mongols', p. 113.
23. J. Dart, *History and Antiquities of the Cathedral Church of Canterbury* (London: J. Cole; J. Hoddle, 1726), p. xvii. See Vorderstrasse, 'Trade and Textiles', p. 169.
24. Jacoby, 'Oriental Silks at the Time of the Mongols', p. 113.
25. *Medieval Drama: An Anthology*, ed. Walker, p. 160, l. 1.
26. *ibid.*, p. 159.
27. See Thomas D. Hanks, '*Emaré*: An Influence on the Man of Law's Tale', *Chaucer Review* 18:2 (Fall 1983), 182–6.
28. *Emaré, in Middle English Breton Lays*, ed. Anne Laskaya and Eve Salisbury (Kalamazoo, MI: Medieval Institute Publications, 1995), p. 153, ll. 13–15, 22–3.
29. For the merchant class audience of *Emaré*, see Elizabeth Scala, 'The Texture of *Emaré*', *Philological Quarterly* 85 (2006), 223–46.
30. *Emaré, in Middle English Breton Lays*, p. 184n.

31. *ibid.*, l. 59. For the historical accuracy of this motif, see Anne Sutton, *The Mercery of London: Trade, Goods, and People, 1130–1578* (Aldershot: Ashgate, 2005), p. 208.
32. *Emaré, in Middle English Breton Lays*, l. 109.
33. See A. Hopkins, 'Veiling the Text: The True Role of the Cloth in Emare', in *Medieval Insular Romance: Translation and Innovation*, ed. Judith Weiss, Jennifer Fellows, and Morgan Dickson (Cambridge: Brewer, 2000), pp. 71–82. Hopkins comments that such symbolic objects are a defining feature of the Breton Lay genre.
34. *Emaré, in Middle English Breton Lays*, ll. 98–101.
35. *ibid.*, ll. 172–4.
36. See Ivan Lindsay, 'The Crusades and the Sack of Constantinople', in *History of Loot and Stolen Art from Antiquity until the Present Day* (London: Unicorn Press, 2014), pp. 42–56.
37. *Emaré, in Middle English Breton Lays*, l. 226.
38. *ibid.*, ll. 242–5.
39. *ibid.*, l. 248.
40. *ibid.*, l. 254.
41. *ibid.*, ll. 343–5.
42. *ibid.*, ll. 345–50.
43. *ibid.*, ll. 376–7.
44. *ibid.*, ll. 396.
45. *ibid.*, ll. 446–7.
46. London, Museum of London, DUK 77 [494]<133> and <208>.
47. *Medieval Finds from Excavations in London, 4. Textiles and Clothing c. 1150–1450*, ed. E. Crowfoot, F. Pritchard, and K. Staniland (Woodbridge: Boydell, 1992), pp. 107–12. I am grateful to Dan Nesbitt at the Museum of London archives for allowing me to access these objects in person.
48. See Avinoam Shalem, *Islam Christianized: Islamic Portable Objects in the Medieval Church Treasuries of the Latin West* (Frankfurt am Main and New York: P. Lang, 1998).
49. London, Museum of London, TB91[55]<1645/15>.
50. *Textiles and Clothing*, ed. Crowfoot, Pritchard, and Staniland, pp. 115–16.
51. Monnas, *Merchants*, pp. 222–5.
52. For the complexities of pseudo-Kufic script in Sicily, see Shalem, *Islam Christianized*, p. 137.
53. Ibn Jubair described the surprise of witnessing peaceful trade between warring crusaders: Ziadeh, *Urban Life*, p. 138.
54. For a discussion of pseudo-Arabic silks in relation to the construction of the 'Moor', see Kathleen Kennedy, 'Moors and Moorishness in Late Medieval England', *SAC* 42 (2020), 213–52.

55. *The Squire of Low Degree*, ll. 741–4.
56. *ibid.*, p. 152, ll. 781–6.
57. Frances A. Underhill, *For Her Good Estate: The Life of Elizabeth de Burgh* (Basingstoke: Macmillan, 1999).
58. Jennifer Ward, ed. and trans., *Elizabeth de Burgh, Lady of Clare (1295–1360): Household and Other Records* (Woodbridge: Boydell, 2014), pp. 143–5. See also Jennifer Ward, 'Elizabeth De Burgh, Lady of Clare, d. 1360', in *Medieval London Widows, 1300–1500*, ed. Caroline Barron and Anne Sutton (London: Hambledon, 1994), pp. 29–45.
59. Ward, *Elizabeth de Burgh*, p. 143.
60. *ibid.*, p. 142.
61. Ward, 'Elizabeth', p. 37.
62. *The Fifty Earliest English Wills in the Court of Probate, London, A.D. 1387–1439, with a Priest's of 1454*, ed. F.J. Furnivall (London: Oxford University Press, 1964), p. 109.
63. *ibid.*, p. 118.
64. See Nicola A. Lowe, 'Women's Devotional Bequests of Textiles in the Late Medieval English Parish Church, c. 1350–1550', *Gender and History* 22:2 (August 2010), 407–29.
65. Ward, *Elizabeth de Burgh*, p. 143.
66. *ibid.*, p. 146.
67. *ibid.*, p. 143.
68. *Fifty Earliest English Wills*, pp. 132–3.
69. 'Sturgeon, N(icholas?) (- between 31 May and 8 June 1454)', in *The Harvard Biographical Dictionary of Music*, ed. Don Michael Randel (Cambridge, MA: Harvard University Press, 2003), p. 884.
70. In another medieval will, Alice West of Hampshire left a red sendal coverlet to her son Thomas, and a tawny silk bed to her daughter Alianore. See *Fifty Earliest English Wills*, pp. 5–6.
71. *The Squire of Low Degree*, ll. 835–8.
72. *ibid.*, l. 842.
73. *ibid.*, ll. 846–8.
74. *ibid.*, ll. 940–2.
75. Chaucer, p. 333, ll. 251–3, 255.
76. Sarah Stanbury has argued that the values of the bedchamber fabrics in the *Book of the Duchess* are derived from their origins in international marketplaces: see 'The Place of the Bedchamber in Chaucer's *Book of the Duchess*', *SAC* 37 (2015), 133–62.
77. Chaucer, p. 693, l. 650.
78. *ibid.*, p. 693, l. 602. See Alessandro Scafi, *Mapping Paradise: A History of Heaven on Earth* (London: British Library, 2006).

79. Chacuer, p. 702, ll. 1420–2.
80. Ranjana Khanna, *Dark Continents: Psychoanalysis and Colonialism* (Durham, NC: Duke University Press, 2003), p. 27.
81. Marina Warner, *Stranger Magic: Charmed States and the Arabian Nights* (Cambridge, MA and London: Harvard University Press, 2012), pp. 410–16.
82. Clothing laws were not particular to European cultures: in Mamlūk society, certain styles and colours of clothing were restricted to elite social groups. See Atil, *Renaissance of Islam*, p. 225; Karl Stowasser, 'Manners and Customs at the Mamluk Court', *Muqarnas* 2 (1984), 13–20.
83. *The Statutes of the Realm: printed by command of his majesty King George the Third, in pursuance of an address of the House of Commons of Great Britain. From original Records and Authentic Manuscripts*, ed. Alexander Luders et al., 11 vols. (London: Dawsons of Pall Mall, 1810; repr. 1965), I: 1101–1377, p. 380.
84. *ibid.*, I, p. 380.
85. *Medieval Dress and Textiles in Britain: A Multilingual Sourcebook*, ed. L. M. Sylvester, M.C. Chambers, and G.R. Owen-Crocker (Woodbridge: Boydell, 2014), p. 206.
86. *ibid.*, p. 212.
87. *Calendar of the Plea and Memoranda Rolls of the City of London, vol. 2, 1364–1381* (London: HMSO, 1929), www.british-history.ac.uk/plea-memoranda-rolls/vol2/pp96-113.
88. Marion Turner, *The Wife of Bath: A Biography* (Princeton, NJ: Princeton University Press, 2023), pp. 4, 65–6.
89. Anne Sutton, 'Two Dozen and More Silkwomen of Fifteenth-Century London', *The Ricardian* 16 (2006), 1–8.
90. See Anne Sutton, 'The Shop-Floor of the London Mercery Trade, c. 1200–c. 1500: The Marginalisation of the Artisan, the Itinerant Mercer and the Shopholder', *Nottingham Medieval Studies* 45 (2001), 12–50.
91. Sutton, *Mercery of London*, p. 1.
92. Barron and Sutton, eds., *Medieval London Widows*, p. 136.
93. *ibid.*, p. 130.
94. *Statutes of the Realm*, II: 1377–1503–4, p. 395.
95. *ibid.*, II, p. 396.
96. *Medieval Dress and Textiles*, pp. 221–4.
97. See N. Harte, 'Silk and Sumptuary Legislation in England', in *La seta in Europa secc. XIII–XX*, ed. Simonetta Cavacioschi (Florence: Le Monnier, 1993), pp. 801–16.
98. See Christopher Dyer, *Standards of Living in the Later Middle Ages: Social Change in England c. 1200–1520* (Cambridge: Cambridge University Press, 1989), p. 88.
99. Harte, 'Silk and Sumptuary Legislation', p. 804.
100. *Medieval Dress and Textiles*, p. 205.

101. *Fifty Earliest English Wills*, pp. 45–6.
102. *Richard Coer de Lyon*, ed. Peter Larkin (Kalamazoo, MI: Medieval Institute Publications, 2015), p. 24, ll. 61–70.
103. *ibid.*, l. 164.
104. See Heng, *Empire of Magic*, pp. 63–113.
105. Malory, *Le Morte Darthur*, pp. 527–8.
106. *ibid.*, p. 503.
107. *Emaré, in Middle English Breton Lays*, ll. 652–3. For sleeves, see Chiara Frugoni, *Books, Banks, Buttons: And Other Inventions from the Middle Ages*, trans. by William McCuaig (New York and Chichester: Columbia University Press, 2005), p. 105.
108. *Emaré, in Middle English Breton Lays*, l. 655.
109. *ibid.*, l. 679.
110. *ibid.*, l. 694.
111. *ibid.*, l. 730.
112. *ibid.*, l. 818.
113. *ibid.*, l. 830.
114. *ibid.*, ll. 835–6.
115. *ibid.*, ll. 950–4.
116. See Nagel and Wood, *Anachronic Renaissance*, p. 18.
117. The Queen's Diamond Jubilee Galleries, Westminster Abbey, London: WAM 12753; WA 0886.2; WA 0837 2; WA 0837 2; WA 2102.
118. Tim Barringer and Tom Flynn, eds., *Colonialism and the Object: Empire, Material Culture and the Museum* (London: Routledge, 1998), p. 11.
119. See Myerson, 'Collection No Longer on Display'.
120. Chasuble, c. 1450–1500, silk and metal thread, Victoria and Albert Museum, London, Museum Number 664–1896; The Clare Chasuble, 1272–1294, silk and metal on blue silk and cotton, Victoria and Albert Museum, London, Museum Number 673–1864.

4. Jewels / English Possession and the Unpossessable

1. Jenks, *Robert Sturmy's Commercial Expedition*, p. 81.
2. My argument both intersects with and deviates from that made in Stephen Greenblatt, *Marvelous Possessions: The Wonder of the New World* (Oxford: Clarendon Press, 1991). Greenblatt argues for 'medieval wonder as a sign of dispossession' in opposition to 'Renaissance wonder as an agent of appropriation', p. 24. I identify medieval wonder as expressing both dispossession and the desire to appropriate.
3. Jeffrey Jerome Cohen, *Stone: An Ecology of the Inhuman* (Minneapolis, MN: University of Minnesota Press, 2015), pp. 232–3.

4. *The Defective Version*, p. 70.
5. See the pearl in the Aberdeen Bestiary: Aberdeen MS 24, fol. 96r <www.abdn.ac.uk/bestiary/ms24/f96r> [accessed 6 September 2021]. The Rochester Bestiary, c. 1230, contains a Latin lapidary and bestiary bound together: London, British Library, Royal MS 12 F XIII.
6. *Pearl*, in *The Poems of the Pearl Manuscript: Pearl, Cleanness, Patience, Sir Gawain and the Green Knight*, ed. Malcolm Andrew and Ronald Waldron, 5th ed. (Liverpool: University of Liverpool Press, 2014), pp. 53–4, ll. 9–10.
7. *ibid.*, l. 59.
8. *ibid.*, l. 116.
9. London, British Library, Cotton MS Nero A X.ii, fols. 41–2, r and v. The quality of these images has been subject to much criticism, and some subsequent defence. See Paul Reichardt, '"Several Illuminations, Coarsely Executed": The Illustrations of the "Pearl" Manuscript', *Studies in Iconography* 18 (1997), 119–42.
10. *Pearl*, ll. 71, 109.
11. *ibid.*, l. 164.
12. *ibid.*, l. 231.
13. *ibid.*, l. 241–2.
14. *ibid.*, ll. 3–7.
15. Helen Barr, *Socioliterary Practice in Late-Medieval England* (Oxford: Oxford University Press, 2002), p. 43. See also Felicity Riddy, 'Jewels in Pearl', in *A Companion to the Gawain-Poet*, ed. Derek Brewer and Jonathan Gibson (Woodbridge: Brewer, 1997), pp. 143–56; Marion Campbell, 'Gold, Silver and Precious Stones', in *English Medieval Industries: Craftsmen, Techniques, Products*, ed. John Blair and Nigel Ramsey (London: Hambledon, 1991, repr. 2001), pp. 107–66; Jill Mann, 'Price and Value in *Sir Gawain and the Green Knight*', in *Life in Words: Essays on Chaucer, the Gawain-poet, and Malory*, ed. Jill Mann and Mark David Rasmussen (Toronto: University of Toronto Press, 2014), pp. 167–86.
16. *Pearl*, ll. 255–9.
17. *ibid.*, ll. 265–7.
18. *ibid.*, l. 735.
19. *ibid.*, ll. 730–2.
20. Ziadeh, *Urban Life*, p. 140.
21. On this subject, see also Robert J. Blanch and Julian N. Wasserman, *From Pearl to Gawain: forme to fynisment* (Gainesville, FL: University Press of Florida, 1995), pp. 141–2; Elizabeth Harper, '*Pearl* in the Context of Fourteenth-Century Gift Economies', *Chaucer Review* 44:4 (2010), 421–39 (p. 426).

22. See J.A. Donkin, *Beyond Price: Pearls and Pearl-Fishing: Origins to the Age of Discoveries* (Philadelphia, PA: American Philosophical Society, 1998), pp. 137–8, 254.
23. David Hinton, *Gold and Gilt, Pots and Pins: Possessions and People in Medieval Britain* (Oxford: Oxford University Press, 2005), p. 221. Hinton also links medieval interest in and supply of gems to the crusades, *ibid.*, pp. 187, 203, 206.
24. Donkin, *Beyond Price*, p. 138. For the Damascus jewel markets, see Ziadeh, *Urban Life*, p. 137.
25. See Marian Campbell, *Medieval Jewellery in Europe 1100–1500* (London: V&A Publishing, 2009), p. 28.
26. For Jewish merchants in the pearl trade, see Donkin, *Beyond Price*, pp. 137–8.
27. Campbell, 'Gold, Silver and Precious Stones', pp. 115, 147; Campbell, *Medieval Jewellery*, p. 24.
28. *Local Port Book of Southampton*, p. 102.
29. Kyngeston, *Expeditions*, p. 287.
30. Legg, *An Inventory*, p. 29.
31. For a broad historical overview, see Diana Scarisbrick, *Rings: Jewelry of Power, Love and Loyalty* (London: Thames & Hudson, 2007).
32. Reliquary ring (the Thame Ring), fourteenth century, amethyst and gold, Ashmolean Museum, Oxford, AN1940.228, <https://collections.ashmolean.org/collection/search/per_page/25/offset/0/sort_by/relevance/object/63737> [accessed 13 September 2021]. See Hinton, *Gold and Gilt, Pots and Pins*: for pseudo-Hebrew, p. 190, and for the Thame ring, p. 244; Campbell, *Medieval Jewellery*, pp. 47, 90.
33. See Martina Bagnoli, 'The Stuff of Heaven: Materials and Craftsmanship in Medieval Reliquaries', in *Treasures of Heaven: Saints, Relics and Devotion in Medieval Europe*, ed. Martina Bagnoli et al. (London: British Museum Press, 2011), pp. 137–47.
34. William Wytelsey's ring, c. 1362–74, gold and sapphire, Victoria and Albert Museum, London, Museum Number M. 191–1975, <https://collections.vam.ac.uk/item/O71727/william-wytleseys-ring-ring-unknown> [accessed 13 September 2021].
35. Jennifer Ward, trans. and ed., *Elizabeth de Burgh, Lady of Clare (1295–1360): Household and Other Records*, general editor Mark Bailey (Woodbridge: Boydell, 2014), pp. 142–7.
36. *Fifty Earliest English Wills*, p. 116.
37. J. Nichols, ed., *A Collection of All the Wills, Now Known to Be Extant, of the Kings and Queens of England . . .* (London: Society of Antiquaries, 1780), p. 155. Discussed in Howard R. Patch, 'Precious Stones in the *House of Fame*', *MLN* 50:5 (1935), 312–17.

38. See Campbell, *Medieval Jewellery*, p. 72.
39. Abbot Suger, *Abbot Suger on the Abbey Church of St-Denis and its Art Treasures*, ed. and trans. Erwin Panofsky, 2nd ed. (Princeton, NJ: Princeton University Press, 1979), p. 106.
40. *Pearl*, l. 922.
41. *ibid.*, l. 840.
42. *ibid.*, ll. 1010–16. See Muriel Whitaker, '"Pearl" and Some Illustrated Apocalypse Manuscripts', *Viator* 12 (Jan. 1981), 183–96.
43. *Pearl*, ll. 1037–40.
44. Exodus 28. 11.
45. *Pearl*, l. 1046.
46. Joan Evans and Mary Serjeantson, eds., *English Medieval Lapidaries* (London: Oxford University Press, 1933), pp. 17–18.
47. *ibid.*, pp. 30–3.
48. *ibid.*, p. 42.
49. *ibid.*, p. 28.
50. *ibid.*, p. 54–5.
51. Chaucer, p. 651, ll. 27–30.
52. *English Medieval Lapidaries*, p. 20.
53. *ibid.*, pp. 20–1.
54. *ibid.*, p. 41.
55. *ibid.*, p. 21.
56. *ibid.*, p. 41.
57. *ibid.*, p. 41.
58. Arne Zettersten, ed., *A Middle English Lapidary: MS Eng. misc. e. 558* (Lund: C.W.K. Gleerup, 1968), p. 39.
59. Trevisa, *On the Properties of Things*, p. 871.
60. *English Medieval Lapidaries*, p. 121.
61. Zettersten, *A Middle English Lapidary*, p. 25.
62. *A Medieval Book of Magical Stones: The Peterborough Lapidary*, ed. and trans. by Francis Young (Cambridge: Texts in Early Modern Magic, 2016), pp. 38–9.
63. *The Defective Version*, p. 18.
64. See also Scarisbrick, *Rings*, p. 236.
65. *The Defective Version*, p. 20.
66. *ibid.*, p. 115.
67. I diverge here from Greenblatt's characterisation of Mandeville as 'the knight of non-possession': *Marvelous Possessions*, p. 28. For a previous critique of Greenblatt, see Kathleen Biddick, *The Typological Imaginary: Circumcision, Technology, History* (Philadelphia, PA: University of Pennsylvania Press, 2003), p. 32.

68. See Avinoam Shalem, 'Terra Miracula: Blessed Souvenirs from the Holy Land', in *Jerusalem 1000–1400: Every People under Heaven*, ed. Barbara Boem and Melanie Holcomb (New Haven, CT and London: Yale University Press, 2016), pp. 23–5 (p. 24).
69. See Shalem, 'Some Speculations', p. 64.
70. Ashor, *Levant Trade*, p. 211.
71. See J.M. Rogers, 'European Inventories as a Source for the Distribution of Mamluk Enamelled Glass', in *Gilded and Enamelled Glass*, ed. Ward, pp. 69–73.
72. Georgopoulou, 'Orientalism and Crusader Art', pp. 293, 296; see also Ziadeh, *Urban Life*, p. 133.
73. Atil, *Renaissance of Islam*, p. 120.
74. Beaker, glass, 1290–1325, Museum of London, London, Museum Number OST82 [190]<129/1>.
75. Zettersten, *A Middle English Lapidary*, p. 11. Marbode copied extensively from a Greek lapidary attributed to Damigeron: the opening section of his text has become known as the Evax-Damigeron lapidary.
76. Berakhyah ben Natronai Ha-Nakdan, *Sefer Jo'ah ha-aranim (On the Virtue of the Stones): Hebrew Text and English Translation; with a Lexicological Analysis of the Romance Terminology and Source Study*, ed., trans., and annotated by Gerrit Bos and Julia Zwink (Leiden and Boston, MA: Brill, 2010), pp. 4–11.
77. Marbode of Rennes, *De Lapidibus*, pp. 119–29.
78. The Evax-Damigeron lapidary has been transcribed by Joan Evans from Oxford, Bodleian Library, Hatton MS 76, fol. 131, as 'Appendix A' in her *Magical Jewels of the Middle Ages and Renaissance, Especially in England* (Oxford: Clarendon Press, 1922), pp. 194–213. The quotation here is found on p. 195.
79. Oxford, Bodleian Library, Hatton MS 76, fol. 139r.
80. *English Medieval Lapidaries*, p. 30.
81. *Peterborough Lapidary*, ed. and trans. Young, p. 1.
82. Charles Burnett, 'Humanism and Orientalism in the Translations from Arabic to Latin in the Middle Ages', in *Wissen über Grenzen: Arabisches Wissen und lateinisches Mittelalter*, ed. Andreas Speer and Lydia Wegener (Berlin: De Gruyter, 2006), pp. 22–31.
83. *Peterborough Lapidary*, ed. and trans. Young, p. 1.
84. J.E. Holmyard and D.C. Mandeville, *Avicennae de congelatione et conglutinatione lapidum: Being Sections of the Kitâb Al-shifâ': The Latin and Arabic Texts with an English Translation of the Latter and with Critical Notes* (Paris: Geuthner, 1927).
85. See Evans, *Magical Jewels*, pp. 38–42.

86. *Pearl*, ll. 751–2.
87. Marbode of Rennes, *De Lapidibus: Considered as a Medical Treatise; with Text, Commentary and C.W. King's Translation, together with Text and Translation of Marbode's Minor Works on Stones*, ed. John M. Riddle (Wiesbaden: Steiner, 1977), p. 12. For the wider influence of Aristotle, including on medieval representations of stones, see Kellie Robertson, *Nature Speaks: Medieval Literature and Aristotelian Philosophy* (Philadelphia, PA: University of Pennsylvania Press, 2017).
88. Marbode of Rennes, *De Lapidibus*, p. 16.
89. See Avinoam Shalem, 'Jewels and Journeys: The Case of the Medieval Gemstone Called al-Yatima', *Muqarnas* 14 (1997), 42–56 (p. 44).
90. For an English translation, see F. Krenkow, 'The Chapter on Pearls in the Book on Precious Stones by al-Beruni', *Islamic Culture* 16 (1942), 21–36.
91. Shalem, 'Jewels and Journeys', p. 51.
92. *ibid.*, pp. 54–5, n. 85; Donkin, *Beyond Price*, pp. 137–8. Donkin also discusses Arabo-Persian lapidaries (pp. 5–6). The 'balais' ruby derived from Arabic 'balakhsh' and Persian 'Badakhshan'. See 'balas, n.', *OED* [accessed 6 September 2021].
93. Osbern Bokenham, *Legendys of Hooly Wummen*, ed. Mary S. Serjeantson (London: Oxford University Press, 1938), pp. 7–8, ll. 241–2. On Bokenham and relic culture, see Salih, *Imagining the Pagan*, pp. 78–82.
94. Bokenham, *Legendys*, ll. 249–51.
95. *English Medieval Lapidaries*, p. 17.
96. Bokenham, *Legendys*, ll. 285, 305–6, 309.
97. *ibid.*, ll. 610–15.
98. Bokenham's and others' keen defence of relic culture in opposition to idol worship took place against the backdrop of a growing critique of relics. See Robyn Malo, *Relics and Writing in Late Medieval England* (Toronto: University of Toronto Press, 2013), p. 161; Robyn Malo, 'The Pardoner's Relics (And Why They Matter the Most)', *Chaucer Review* 43:1 (2008), 82–102.
99. Bokenham, *Legendys*, ll. 2117–18, 2339–42.
100. The same argument would be used by Protestants against Catholic relics during the iconoclasms of the Reformation. See Alexander Nagel, 'The Afterlife of the Reliquary', in *Treasures of Heaven: Saints, Relics and Devotion in Medieval Europe*, ed. Martina Bagnoli et al. (London: British Museum Press, 2011), pp. 211–22 (p. 212).
101. Bokenham, *Legendys*, ll. 928–9.
102. *ibid.*, l. 245.
103. See Charles Burnett, 'Antioch as a Link between Arabic and Latin Culture in the Twelfth and Thirteenth Centuries', in *Occident et Proche-Orient: contacts scientifiques au temps de Croisades: actes du colloque de Louvain-la-Neuve, 24 et*

25 mars 1997, ed. Isabelle Draelants, Anne Tihon and Baudouin van den Abeele (Turnhout: Brepols, 2000), pp. 1–78.

104. Bokenham, *Legendys*, ll. 1056–7.
105. *ibid.*, ll. 137–41.
106. Bynum writes of reliquaries that 'it mattered that the window was crystal': *Christian Materiality*, p. 28.
107. Bokenham, *Legendys*, l. 145.
108. *ibid.*, ll. 147–49.
109. Sheila Delany, 'Chaucer's Prioress, the Jews and the Muslims', *Medieval Encounters* 5:3 (1999), 198–213 (p. 198).
110. For the Prioress' ruby and lapidaries, see Anthony Bale, *Feeling Persecuted: Christians, Jews, and Images of Violence in the Middle Ages* (London: Reaktion, 2010), p. 85; see also Anthony Bale, *The Jew in the Medieval Book: English Antisemitisms 1350–1500* (Cambridge: Cambridge University Press, 2006), p. 85.
111. *English Medieval Lapidaries*, p. 21.
112. *ibid.*, p. 24. See Strickland, *Saracens, Demons, and Jews.*
113. Malo argues that the ruby 'usurped' Becket, shifting the tenor of the reliquary from relic to treasure. See Malo, *Relics and Writing*, p. 142.
114. Pilgrim badge, mid to late fourteenth century, pewter and lead alloy, Museum of London, London, Museum Number: BC72[55] <1555>.
115. The Centre for Christianity and Culture at York has produced a digital replica of the shrine, c. 1408.
116. Maija Birenbaum, 'Communal Purity and Jewish "Filþe" in *Cleanness*', *Philological Quarterly* 91:3 (Summer 2012), 339–59 (p. 353).
117. *The Siege of Jerusalem*, ed. Ralph Hanna and David Lawton (London: Oxford University Press, 2003), p. 4, l. 50.
118. *ibid.*, ll. 54–83. See Randy P. Schiff, 'The Instructive Other Within: Secularized Jews in *The Siege of Jerusalem*', in *Cultural Diversity in the British Middle Ages: Archipelago, Island, England*, ed. Jeffrey Jerome Cohen (New York: Palgrave Macmillan, 2008), pp. 135–52 (p. 141) for Nathan's 'ethnic opacity'. As Schiff notes, Nathan's name recalls the prophet of the Hebrew Bible. Schiff's article offers an interesting alternative reading of this poem as critiquing Christian imperialism.
119. *The Siege of Jerusalem*, ll. 229–40.
120. 'mammet, n.', *OED* [accessed 6 September 2021].
121. *The Siege of Jerusalem*, l. 296.
122. *ibid.*, ll. 301–2.
123. *ibid.*, l. 305.
124. *ibid.*, l. 324.
125. *ibid.*, l. 438.

126. *ibid.*, l. 473.
127. *ibid.*, l. 476.
128. *ibid.*, l. 484.
129. See Avivah Zornberg, *Moses: A Human Life* (New Haven, CT: Yale University Press, 2016).
130. *The Siege of Jerusalem*, l. 531.
131. *ibid.*, ll. 640–1, 642, 644.
132. *ibid.*, l. 1246.
133. *ibid.*, ll. 1254–9.
134. *ibid.*, ll. 1261–2.
135. *ibid.*, ll. 1263–4.
136. *ibid.*, ll. 1265–7.
137. *ibid.*, ll. 1274–5.
138. *ibid.*, l. 1298.
139. *ibid.*, l. 1301.
140. *ibid.*, ll. 1309–11.
141. *ibid.*, l. 1313.
142. Cambridge, University Library, MS Mm.v.31, fols. 25v–26r.
143. *The Siege of Jerusalem*, l. 1315–16.
144. *ibid.*, l. 1321.
145. Barker, *That Most Precious Merchandise*, p. 10.
146. For the role of Jewish merchants in trade with the Levant, see Ashtor, *Levant Trade*, pp. 33, 44, 51, 85, 238, 355, 504, 505.
147. *Croxton*, ll. 19–20.
148. *ibid.*, l. 194.
149. *ibid.*, ll. 81–4.
150. *ibid.*, l. 85.
151. *ibid.*, ll. 86–92. 'cūriŏus, adj.2', *MED* [accessed 6 September 2021].
152. *Croxton*, l. 822–3.
153. William Shakespeare, *The RSC Shakespeare: William Shakespeare: Complete Works*, ed. Jonathan Bate and Eric Rasmussen (London: Macmillan, 2008), *The Merchant of Venice*, p. 442, III. 1. 57–8. Hereafter cited within the text by line.
154. For the problem of relics as commodities, see Patrick Geary, 'Sacred Commodities: The Circulation of Medieval Relics', in *The Social Life of Things: Commodities in Cultural Perspective*, ed. Arjun Appadurai (Cambridge: Cambridge University Press, 1986), pp. 169–91. For host desecration narratives, see Miri Rubin, *Gentile Tales: The Narrative Assault on Late Medieval Jews* (New Haven, CT and London: Yale University Press, 1999).
155. *Croxton*, l. 69.

156. For Jews in the jewel trade, see Norman A. Stillman, *The Jews of Arab Lands: A History and Source Book* (Philadelphia, PA: The Jewish Publication Society of America, 1979), pp. 207, 289.
157. Ormrod, Story and Tylers, ed., *Migrants*, p. 13.
158. *The Defective Version*, p. 61.
159. *Pearl*, l. 795.
160. *ibid.*, l. 804.
161. *ibid.*, l. 1153.
162. *ibid.*, ll. 1180, 1182.
163. *ibid.*, l. 1187.
164. *The Inventories of Westminster Abbey at the Dissolution*, ed. Mackenzie E. C. Walcott (London: London and Middlesex Archaeological Society, 1872), p. 17.
165. *ibid.*, p. 7.
166. *ibid.*, p. 2.

Part III The Workshop

1. Jenks, *Robert Sturmy's Commercial Expedition*, p. 81.
2. <www.nationalarchives.gov.uk/currency-converter/#currency-result> [accessed 7 September 2021]; Rose, *The Wine Trade*, p. 104; Lisa Jardine, *Worldly Goods: A New History of the Renaissance* (London: Papermac, 1997), p. 114.
3. Jenks, *Robert Sturmy's Commercial Expedition*, pp. 12–15.
4. Charles Singer, *The Earliest Chemical Industry: An Essay in the Historical Relations of Economics and Technology Illustrated from the Alum Trade* (London: The Folio Society, 1948), p. 88.
5. *ibid.*, pp. 95, 117.
6. Ashtor, *Levant Trade*, pp. 6, 108, 130. 194, 331, 334, 440, 480; *Local Port Book of Southampton*, pp. 44, 48, 50, 56, 58, 62, 64, 66, 68, 92, 100, 104.
7. Abulafia, *The Great Sea*, pp. 291–7.
8. See Wallace, *Premodern Places*, pp. 183–4; Abulafia, *The Great Sea*, p. 355; Peter Spufford, *Power and Profit: The Merchant in Medieval Europe* (London: Thames and Hudson, 2002), pp. 338–40; Turner, *Chaucer*, pp. 145–7.
9. *The Libelle of Englyshe Polycye*, ll. 333–6.
10. Spufford, *Power and Profit*, p. 167.
11. Iris Origo, *The Merchant of Prato*: *Francesco di Marco Datini* (London: Jonathan Cape, 1957), pp. 12, 69, 96–7. On Genoese imports of Levantine goods, see Turner, *Chaucer*, p. 156.
12. Wallace, *Premodern Places*, pp. 181–202.

13. Spufford, *Power and Profit*, p. 410. See also Karl Marx, 'The So-Called Primitive Accumulation', in *Capital: A Critical Analysis of Capitalist Production*, ed. Waltraud Falk, Hanna Behrend, Marion Duparré, Hella Hahn, and Frank Zschaler (Berlin and Boston, MA: De Gruyter, 2017), pp. 619–70.
14. *Liber Albus: The White Book of the City of London*, ed. John Carpenter and Richard Whittington, trans. Henry Thomas Riley (London: Richard Griffin, 1872), p. 586.
15. 'Henry VI: November 1450', in *Parliament Rolls of Medieval England*, ed. Chris Given-Wilson et al. (Woodbridge: Boydell, 2005), *British History Online* <www.british-history.ac.uk/no-series/parliament-rolls-medieval/november-1450> [accessed 9 September 2020].
16. Jardine, *Worldly Goods*, p. 116. See also Abulafia, *The Great Sea*, p. 393.
17. Singer, *The Earliest Chemical*, p. 160.

5. Alum / The Demand for Sodomite Salt in England

1. Jenks, *Robert Sturmy's Commercial Expedition*, p. 81.
2. <www.nationalarchives.gov.uk/currency-converter/#currency-result> [accessed 7 September 2021]; Rose, *The Wine Trade*, p. 104; Jardine, *Worldly Goods*, p. 114.
3. See Mary-Jo Arn, 'The Emendation of Wine: Wine Recipes from Beinecke MS 163 ("The Wagstaff Miscellany")', *The Yale University Library Gazette* 64:3/4 (Apr. 1990), 109–23 (p. 118); Rose, *The Wine Trade*, p. 55; J.A. Donkin, *Beyond Price: Pearls and Pearl-Fishing: Origins to the Age of Discoveries* (Philadelphia, PA: American Philosophical Society, 1998), pp. 135, 261.
4. Jones et al., 'The Sugar Industry', p. 594.
5. Genesis 19. 24–6.
6. See James C. Staples, 'Pure Pleasure: *Cleanness* and Fourteenth-Century Sexual Liberation', *Exemplaria* 34:1 (2022), 40–65.
7. *Cleanness*, in *The Poems of the Pearl Manuscript*, ed. Andrew and Waldron, p. 140, ll. 679–80.
8. *ibid.*, ll. 689–90.
9. *ibid.*, l. 772.
10. *ibid.*, ll. 778, 790.
11. *ibid.*, ll. 876, 861–3.
12. *ibid.*, l. 877.
13. *ibid.*, l. 878.
14. *ibid.*, ll. 845–55.
15. *ibid.*, ll. 850–1.
16. *ibid.*, ll. 954–6.
17. *ibid.*, l. 962.

18. *ibid.*, ll. 964, 965, 968.
19. *ibid.*, l. 1005.
20. *ibid.*, ll. 1006–8.
21. Alter, *The Hebrew Bible*, I, p. 63n.
22. *Cleanness*, ll. 984.
23. London, British Library, Harley MS 2838, fol. 34.
24. *Cleanness*, ll. 1020–35.
25. Genesis 14. 10: Alter, *The Hebrew Bible*, I, p. 46.
26. Trevisa, *On the Properties of Things*, pp. 772–3.
27. Isidore of Seville, *The Etymologies of Isidore of Seville*, trans. with intro. and notes by Stephen A. Barney, W.J. Lewis, J.A. Beach, and Oliver Berghof (Cambridge: Cambridge University Press, 2006, repr. 2014), p. 317.
28. 'William Wey's Will', p. 400; Pnina Arad, 'Pilgrimage, Cartography, and Devotion: William Wey's Map of the Holy Land', *Viator* 43 (2012), 301–22. See also P.D.A. Harvey, *Medieval Maps of the Holy Land* (London: British Library, 2012).
29. Compare Cohen, *Stone*, p. 83: 'Geology and Genesis do not offer two versions of the same story'.
30. *Cleanness*, ll. 1036–8.
31. See Liam O. Purdon, 'Sodom and Gomorrah: The Use of Mandeville's *Travels* in *Cleanness*', *Journal of the Rocky Mountain Medieval and Renaissance Association* 9 (1988), 64–9; Daniel W. O'Bryan, 'Sodom and Gomorrah: The Use of the Vulgate in *Cleanness*', *The Journal of Narrative Technique* 12:1 (Winter, 1982), 15–23.
32. John Mandeville, *The voiage and travaile of Sir J. Maundevile, which treateth of the way to Hierusalem; and of marvayles of Inde, with other ilands and countryes. Now publish'd entire from an original MS. In the Cotton library* (London: E. Lumley, 1839), p. 99.
33. *ibid.*, p. 100. The Defective version of the *Travels* records the same passage on asphalt, omitting the previous reference to alum: see *The Defective Version*, p. 41.
34. *The voiage and travaile of Sir J. Maundevile*, p. 100. The actual distance between Jericho and the Dead Sea is approximately six miles. The Dead Sea is about sixty-two miles from Jerusalem.
35. *ibid.*, p. 101.
36. See Anthony Bale, trans., *Sir John Mandeville: The Book of Marvels and Travels* (Oxford: Oxford University Press, 2012), p. 148, n. 51.
37. For more on the medieval category of Sodomy, see Robert Mills, *Seeing Sodomy in the Middle Ages* (Chicago, IL: University of Chicago Press, 2014).
38. Robert J. Blanch and Julian N. Wasserman, *From Pearl to Gawain: forme to fynisment* (Gainesville, FL: University Press of Florida, 1995), pp. 45–64.

39. *ibid.*, p. 62.
40. *Cleanness*, ll. 266, 208.
41. Nicole Chareyron, *Pilgrims to Jerusalem in the Middle Ages*, trans. by Donald Wilson (New York: Columbia University Press, 2005), p. 107.
42. Corrosion at Sodom and Gomorrah, <www.themappamundi.co.uk/mappa-mundi>, 'Depth Changes from Corrosion' [accessed 26 November 2020].
43. Chareyron, *Pilgrims to Jerusalem*, pp. 105–7.
44. *ibid.*, p. 107.
45. London, British Library, Harley MS 658, fol. 39v.
46. 'alembic, n.', *OED* [accessed 6 September 2021].
47. 'arsenic, n.', *OED* [accessed 6 September 2021].
48. Alum was also central in ancient Chinese alchemy, an expansive subject outside the remit of my project. See Tenney L. Davis and Lu-Ch'iang Wu, 'Chinese Alchemy', *The Scientific Monthly* 31:3 (Sept. 1930), 225–35 (p. 231).
49. Thomas Norton, *The Ordinal of Alchemy*, ed. John Reidy (London and New York: Early English Text Society, 1975), p. 9, ll. 148–9.
50. William R. Newman, *The Summa Perfectionis of Pseudo-Geber: A Critical Edition, Translation and Study* (Leiden and New York: Brill, 1991), pp. 227–9.
51. Lee Patterson, 'Perpetual Motion: Alchemy and the Technology of the Self', *SAC* 15 (1993), 25–57 (p. 41).
52. 'gibberish, n. and adj.', *OED* [accessed 6 September 2021].
53. Albertus Magnus, *Book of Minerals*, trans. by Dorothy Wyckoff (Oxford: Clarendon Press, 1967), pp. 237–9.
54. Norton, *The Ordinal*, ll. 1329–30.
55. Albertus Magnus, *Book of Minerals*, pp. 9, 13, 15, 18, 27, 175. See Robert R. Steele, 'Practical Chemistry in the 12th Century, Rhasis *De aluminibus et salibus*', *Isis* 12 (1929), 10–48. See Cohen, *Stone*, p. 217.
56. J.E. Holmyard and D.C Mandeville, *Avicennae de congelatione et conglutinatione lapidum: Being Sections of the Kitâb Al-shifâ': The Latin and Arabic Texts with an English Translation of the Latter and with Critical Notes* (Paris: Geuthner, 1927), p. 36.
57. E.J. Holmyard, ed., *The Works of Geber, Englished by Richard Russell, 1678* (London: J. M. Dent & Sons, 1928), pp. 205–6.
58. Metlitzki, *The Matter of Araby*, pp. 86–8.
59. Mohammed Turāb 'Ali, ed., *Three Arabic Treatises on Alchemy by Muhammed bin Umail, with Excursus and Edition of the Latin Rendering of the Ma al-Waraqi*, by E. Stapleton and M. Hidayat Husain (Calcutta: Memoirs of the Asiatic Society of Bengal, 1933), pp. 39 (Arabic), 180 (Latin corresponding text).

60. *ibid.*, p. 165; for the Arabic version of this passage: p. 28. For other references to alum: pp. 31 (Arabic), 168 (Latin corresponding text).
61. Albertus Magnus, *Book of Minerals*, p. 105.
62. Norton, *The Ordinal*, ll. 1157–8.
63. Raphael Patai, 'Maria the Jewess: Founding Mother of Alchemy', *Ambix* 29:3 (1982), 177–97 (pp. 180–1).
64. See Christine Chism, 'I Demed Hym Som Chanoun for to be', in *Chaucer's Pilgrims: An Historical Guide to the Pilgrims in The Canterbury Tales*, ed. Laura C. Lambdin and Robert T. Lambdin (Westport, CT and London: Greenwood, 1996), pp. 340–56 (p. 348).
65. Turāb 'Ali, *Three Arabic Treatises*, p. 130.
66. *ibid.*, pp. 15, 20, 37, 47, 48, 51, 54, 55, 56, 57, 61, 63, 69, 72, 84, 85, 100, 130, 134, 138; Patai, 'Maria the Jewess', p. 186.
67. *Cleanness*, l. 1018.
68. Trevisa, *On the Properties of Things*, p. 1298.
69. Muhammed Ibn Ishaq Ibn al-Nadīm, *The Fihrist of al-Nadīm: A Tenth-Century Survey of Muslim Culture*, ed. and trans. Bayard Dodge, 2 vols (New York and London: Columbia University Press, 1970), II, p. 844.
70. Raphael Patai, *The Jewish Alchemists: A History and Source Book* (Princeton, NJ: Princeton University Press, 1994), pp. 70–1.
71. Turāb 'Ali, *Three Arabic Treatises*, p. 142; for the Arabic text on which this translation is based, see pp. 48–9; for a medieval Latin version see pp. 192–3.
72. See F. Krenkow, trans., 'The Chapter on Pearls in the Book on Precious Stones by al-Beruni', *Islamic Culture* 16 (1942), 21–36 (p. 30).
73. Cambridge, Trinity College, MS 0.9.29, printed in *The Crafte of Lymmyng and the Maner of Steynyng: Middle English Recipes for Painters, Stainers, Scribes, and Illuminators*, ed. Mark Clarke (Oxford: Oxford University Press, 2016), p. 27.
74. *ibid.*, p. 28.
75. *Cleanness*, ll. 1127–8.
76. Norton, *The Ordinal*, ll. 182, 199, 210–11.
77. Metlitzki, *The Matter of Araby*, p. 88; Turāb 'Ali, *Three Arabic Treatises*, p. 41, ll. 16–17.
78. Turāb 'Ali, *Three Arabic Treatises*, p. 183.
79. George R. Keiser, 'The Conclusion of the Canon's Yeoman's Tale: Readings and (Mis)Readings', *Chaucer Review* 35:1 (2000), 1–21 (p. 2); Alexander N. Gabrovsky, *Chaucer the Alchemist: Physics, Mutability and the Medieval Imagination* (New York: Palgrave Macmillan, 2015).
80. Oxford, Bodleian Library, MS Ashmole 1445, fol. 19v.
81. Isidore, *The Etymologies*, pp. 317–18.
82. For example, see *The Crafte*, p. 91.

83. London, British Library, MS Egerton 2852, printed in *The Crafte*, p. 103.
84. Cambridge, Gonville and Caius College, MS 457/396, printed in *The Crafte*, p. 212.
85. Cambridge, University Library, MS Ee.i.13, printed in *The Crafte*, p. 111.
86. For Syrian gum exports, see Ziadeh, *Urban Life*, p. 140.
87. San Marino, California, Huntington Library, MS HU 1051, printed in *The Crafte*, p. 317.
88. New Haven, Yale, MS R486.M43 1450, printed in *The Crafte*, p. 100.
89. *The Crafte*, pp. 39–40.
90. *ibid.*, p. 42.
91. *ibid.*, p. 12.
92. Trevisa, *On the Properties of Things*, p. 1303.
93. Trevisa cites Aristotle, Ibn Sīnā, and Constantine on this subject. See 'De odoribus', in *On the Properties of Things*, pp. 1296–300.
94. London, British Library, Sloane MS 3548, fol. 25.
95. London, British Library, Egerton MS 747, fol. 9r.
96. *The Cyrurgie*, p. 618.
97. *ibid.*, p. 386.
98. *ibid.*, p. 149.
99. Trevisa, *On the Properties of Things*, p. 875.
100. Ancient Jewish medico-magical recipes record the names of Sodom and Gomorrah, as well as 'Abrasax', the name of the angel who destroyed those cities, in medical amuletic use. The Cairo Genizah also contains medico-magical recipes. See Gideon Bohak, *Ancient Jewish Magic: A History* (Cambridge: Cambridge University Press, 2008), pp. 204–5, 249, 409.
101. *The Cyrurgie*, p. 120.
102. See Violet Moller, *The Map of Knowledge: How Classical Ideas Were Lost and Found: A History in Seven Cities* (London: Picador, 2019), pp. 126–7.
103. *The Cyrurgie*, p. 121.
104. John Arderne, *Treatises of Fistula in Ano: Haemorrhorids, and Clysters: From an Early Fifteenth-Century Manuscript Translation*, ed. D'Arcy Power (London: Oxford University Press, 1910), p. 1.
105. *ibid.*, p. 3
106. *ibid.*, p. 27.
107. Cohen, *Stone*, pp. 232–3.
108. For a recipe for *sanguis veneris*, see Arderne, *Treatises of Fistula in Ano*, p. 90.
109. *ibid.*, p. 28.
110. *ibid.*, p. 22.
111. *The Cyrurgie*, pp. 136–7.
112. *ibid.*, p. 158.

113. Paracelsus, *Four Treatises of Theophrastus von Hohenheim, Called Paracelsus*, ed. Henry E. Siegerist, trans. with introductory essays by C. Lilian Temkin, George Rosen, Gregory Zilboorg, and Henry E. Sigerist (Baltimore, MD and London: Johns Hopkins Press, 1941, repr. 1996), p. 56.
114. *ibid.*, p. 63.
115. *ibid.*, pp. 69, 77.
116. *ibid.*, p. 102.
117. Oxford, Bodleian Library, MS Tanner 407: see *Crafte*, pp. lxxvii, xciv.
118. London, British Library, MS Harley 2390, fol. 75r.
119. *The Crafte*, p. 55.
120. *ibid.*, p. 66.
121. *ibid.*, p. 129.
122. See Daniel Wakelin, *Designing English: Early Literature on the Page* (Oxford: Bodleian Library, 2017).
123. Cambridge, University Library, MS Dd.v.76, printed in *The Crafte*, p. 217.
124. London, British Library, MS Harley 2252, fol. 144v.
125. London, British Library, MS Sloane 122, fol. 93r.
126. Cambridge, University Library, MS Dd.v.76, printed in *The Crafte*, p. 219.
127. San Marino, California, Huntington Library, MS HU 1051, printed in *The Crafte*, p. 315.
128. Kristie Macrakis, *Prisoners, Lovers, and Spies: The Story of Invisible Ink from Herodotus to Al-Qaeda* (New Haven, CT: Yale University Press, 2014), pp. 14, 25.
129. Chaucer, p. 361, ll. 1119–25.
130. *ibid.*, ll. 1140–5.
131. Kathy Cawsey, '"Alum de glas" or "Alymed glass"?: Manuscript Reading in Book III of *The House of Fame*', *University of Toronto Quarterly* 73:4 (2004), 972–9.
132. *Cleanness*, l. 966.
133. Zygmunt Bauman, *Liquid Modernity* (Cambridge: Polity Press, 2000).

6. Coda: The English Market as the Temple of Jerusalem

1. See Jean-François Lyotard, *Libidinal Economy*, trans. Iain Hamilton Grant (London: Bloomsbury Academic, 2015); Noam Yuran, *What Money Wants: An Economy of Desire* (Stanford, CA: Stanford University Press, 2014).
2. For a summary of Max Weber's influential argument as to the relationship between the Reformation and capitalism, see Rey Chow, *The Protestant Ethnic and the Spirit of Capitalism* (New York: Columbia University Press, 2002), pp. 43–7.

3. For an overview, see Peter Spufford, *Money and its Use in Medieval Europe* (Cambridge: Cambridge University Press, 2009).
4. Jenks, *Robert Sturmy's Commercial Expedition*, p. 81.
5. Jere L. Bacharach, 'The Dinar Versus the Ducat', *IJMES* 4:1 (Jan. 1973), 77–96. For the use of ashrafis in international trade, see Ashtor, *Levant Trade*, pp. 280, 290, 371.
6. Philipp Robinson Rössner, 'From the Black Death to the New World (c.1350–1500)', in *Money and Coinage*, ed. Naismith, pp. 151–76 (p. 156); Gaspar Feliu, 'Money and Currency', trans. Ramon Pujol Gorné, in *Money and Coinage*, ed. Naismith, pp. 21–40 (p. 22).
7. 'salū, n. 1.(b)', *MED*.
8. Compare Richard T. Gray, 'Buying into Signs: Money and Semiosis in Eighteenth-Century German Language Theory,' in *The New Economic Criticism*, ed. Mark Woodmansee and Martha Osteen (London: Routledge, 1999), pp. 95–113.
9. The existence of market value as a sign potentially entirely independent of a metallic referent is noted with fascination in Mandeville's *Travels*, in the appearance of paper money at the court of the Great Khan: *The voiage and travaile of Sir J. Maundevile*, p. 239. See Greenblatt, *Marvelous Possessions*, p. 37.
10. Marc Shell, *Art and Money* (Chicago, IL and London: University of Chicago Press, 1995), p. 15.
11. Spufford, *Money*, p. 2. See also Frederic Lane and Reinhold C. Mueller, *Money and Banking in Medieval and Renaissance Venice: Volume I: Coins and Moneys of Account* (Baltimore, MD: Johns Hopkins University Press, 1985); Marc Shell, 'The Issue of Representation', in *New Economic Criticism*, ed. Woodmansee and Osteen, pp. 53–74.
12. Jacques Le Goff, *Money and the Middle Ages: An Essay in Historical Anthropology*, trans. Jean Birrell (Cambridge: Polity Press, 2012), p. 38.
13. Esther Leslie, *Liquid Crystals: The Science and Art of a Fluid Form* (London: Reaktion, 2016), p. 61.
14. Ward, *Elizabeth de Burgh*, p. 142.
15. Feliu, 'Money and Currency', p. 25.
16. Karl Marx, *Capital: A Critical Analysis of Capitalist Production*, ed. Waltraud Falk, Hanna Behrend, Marion Duparré, Hella Hahn, and Frank Zschaler (Berlin and Boston, MA: De Gruyter, 2017), I, p. 115.
17. For alchemy and economic language, see Peggy A. Knapp, 'The Work of Alchemy', *JMEMS* 30:3 (Fall 2000), 575–99. Marx makes extensive use of alchemy as a metaphor for capital. See Marx, *Capital*, I, pp. 81–126.
18. Robert Epstein argues that although alchemy features as a metaphor for the economy in both Marx and medieval literature, Marxist readings of medieval

literature tend to elide the alterity of pre-capitalist economic imaginations: see 'Dismal Science: Chaucer and Gower on Alchemy and Economy', *SAC* 36 (2014), 209–38.

19. Jacques Derrida, *Spectres of Marx: The State of the Debt, the Work of Mourning, and the New International*, trans. by Peggy Kamuf (London: Routledge, 1994), p. 150.
20. Matthew 21. 12–13.
21. London, British Library, Egerton MS 3277, fol. 130v. See also Shell, *Art and Money*, p. 38.
22. See J.A. Burrow, 'Lady Mede and the Power of Money', *Medium Aevum* 74:1 (2005), 113–18.
23. William Langland, *Piers Plowman: A Parallel-Text Edition of the A, B, C and Z Versions. Vol. 1. Text*, ed. A.V.C. Schmidt (London and New York: Longman, 1995), p. 625, B 16. 127–37.
24. 'chaungen v.', *MED.*
25. Langland, *Piers Plowman*, 16. 149.
26. Ruddock, *Italian Merchants*, pp. 174–5.

Conclusion: Christopher Columbus in Chios

1. Greenblatt, *Marvelous Possessions*, p. 61; Jardine, *Worldly Goods*, p. 81; Fernandez-Arresto, *Before Columbus*, pp. 105–18.
2. Christopher Columbus, *A Synoptic Edition of the Log of Columbus' First Voyage*, ed. Francesca Lardicci et al. (Turnhout: Brepols, 1999), p. 37.
3. *Select Letters of Christopher Columbus with Other Original Documents Relating to His Four Voyages to the New World*, ed. R.H. Major (Farnham: Taylor & Francis, 2010), p. 15.
4. Paul Freedman, 'Mastic: A Mediterranean Luxury Product', *Mediterranean Historical Review* 26:01 (2011), 99–113 (p. 102).
5. Valerie Flint, *The Imaginative Landscape of Christopher Columbus* (Princeton, NJ: Princeton University Press, 1992).
6. Nabil Matar argues that taking Columbus' 1492 voyage as a period marker for English literature erases the complexity of sixteenth-century relations between England and the Ottomans – he proposes a significantly later period boundary of 1655, the colonisation of Jamaica: see *Turks, Moors and Englishmen*, pp. 10–11.
7. Douglas Hunter, *The Race to the New World: Christopher Columbus, John Cabot, and a Lost History of Discovery* (New York: Palgrave Macmillan, 2011).
8. Hew Locke, *The Wine Dark Sea*. Selection of up to thirty-four boats, ranging from 23 to 183 cms in length, mixed media.

Epilogue: The Verdict of the Trials of the Genoese

1. England's Immigrants 1330–1550 (http://www.englandsimmigrants.com, version 1.0, 18 July 2023). www.englandsimmigrants.com/search/results?col1=name&col2=nationality&col3=date&col4=origin&col5=residence&documentStartDateDecade_untouched_facet=1450%20-%201459&endDate=1600&keyword=genoese&page=1&startDate=1300
2. Jenks, *Robert Sturmy's Commercial Expedition*, p. 76.
3. W.M. Ormrod, Bart Lambert and Jonathan Mackman, eds., *Immigrant England, 1300–1550* (Manchester: Manchester University Press, 2018), p. 4.
4. For more, see: Ki-ch'ang Kim, *Aliens in Medieval Law: The Origins of Modern Citizenship* (Cambridge: Cambridge University Press, 2000); J. Susanne Jenks, 'Justice for Strangers: The Experience of Alien Merchants in Medieval English Law Courts', in *The Medieval Merchant: Proceedings of the 2012 Harlaxton Symposium*, ed. Caroline M. Barron and Anne F. Sutton (Donington: Shaun Tyas, 2014), pp. 166–82.
5. Bart Lambert and W.M. Ormrod, 'The State and the Immigrant: Negotiating Nationalities in Later Medieval England', in *Migrants in Medieval England*, ed. Ormrod, Story, and Tylers, pp. 298–325 (p. 303).
6. See Kathy Lavezzo, ed., *Imagining a Medieval English Nation* (Minneapolis, MN: University of Minnesota Press, 2003).
7. 1905 Aliens Act, United Kingdom. Available at: <www.legislation.gov.uk/ukpga/Edw7/5/13/contents/enacted>.
8. Lambert and Ormrod, 'The State', p. 307
9. W.M. Ormrod, Nicola McDonald and Craig Taylor, eds., *Resident Aliens in Medieval England* (Turnhout: Brepols, 2017) p. 8.
10. Ormrod, Lambert, and Mackman, *Immigrant England*, p. 8.
11. <www.nationalarchives.gov.uk/currency-converter/#currency-result> [accessed 15 August 2025].
12. Zygmunt Bauman, *Modernity and the Holocaust* (Cambridge: Polity, 1989), p. 56.
13. See the special issue: Henghameh Saroukhani and John McLeod, eds., *Windrush: Writing the Scandal*, *Wasafiri* 114 (2023).
14. Jenks, *Robert Sturmy's Commercial Expedition*, p. 74.
15. *ibid.*, p. 75.
16. See Daniel Boyarin, *The No-State Solution: A Jewish Manifesto* (New Haven, CT: Yale University Press, 2023), p. 33.
17. Jenks, *Robert Sturmy's Commercial Expedition*, p. 75.
18. *ibid.*, pp. 75–6.
19. *ibid.*, p. 76.

20. Sarah Rees Jones, 'English Towns in the Later Middle Ages: The Rules and Realities of Population Mobility', in *Migrants in Medieval England*, ed. Ormrod, Story and Tylers, pp. 265–97 (p. 288).
21. *ibid.*, p. 294.
22. See Bhanu Kapil, *How to Wash a Heart* (Liverpool: Pavilion, 2020).
23. Jenks, *Robert Sturmy's Commercial Expedition*, p. 77.
24. 'Citisein, n.', 3(a), *MED*.
25. Jenks, *Robert Sturmy's Commercial Expedition*, p. 4.
26. *Calendar of the Patent Rolls Preserved in the Public Record Office. Henry VI, 1452–1461.* TannerRitchie Publishing, 2013. *ProQuest Ebook Central*, https://ebookcentral.proquest.com/lib/CAM/detail.action?docID=3410311, p. 517.

Select Bibliography

Abu-Lughod, Janet, *Before European Hegemony: The World System, A.D. 1250–1350* (New York and Oxford: Oxford University Press, 1991)

Abulafia, David, *The Great Sea: A Human History of the Mediterranean* (London: Penguin, 2014)

Akbari, Suzanne Conklin, *Idols in the East: European Representations of Islam and the Orient, 1100–1450* (Ithaca, NY and London: Cornell University Press, 2009)

Alter, Robert, trans., *The Hebrew Bible: A Translation with Commentary*, 3 vols. (New York: Norton, 2019)

Appadurai, Arjun, ed., *The Social Life of Things: Commodities in Cultural Perspective* (Cambridge: Cambridge University Press, 1986)

Ashtor, Eliyahu, *Levant Trade in the Later Middle Ages* (Princeton, NJ: Princeton University Press, 1983)

Atiya, Aziz, *The Crusade in the Later Middle Ages* (London: Methuen, 1938)

Bagnoli, Martina, et al., eds., *Treasures of Heaven: Saints, Relics and Devotion in Medieval Europe* (London: British Museum Press, 2011)

Bale, Anthony, trans. and ed., *Sir John Mandeville: The Book of Marvels and Travels* (Oxford: Oxford University Press, 2012)

Bale, Anthony, and Sebastian Sobecki, eds., *Medieval English Travel: A Critical Anthology* (Oxford: Oxford University Press, 2019)

Barker, Hannah, *That Most Precious Merchandise: The Mediterranean Trade in Black Sea Slaves, 1260–1500* (Philadelphia, PA: University of Pennsylvania Press, 2019)

Biddick, Kathleen, *The Typological Imaginary: Circumcision, Technology, History* (Philadelphia, PA: University of Pennsylvania Press, 2003)

Blazwick, Iwona, and Carolyn Christov-Barkargiev, eds., *Michael Rakowitz* (London: Silvana Editoriale, 2019)

Boem, Barbara, and Melanie Holcomb, eds., *Jerusalem, 1000–1400: Every People under Heaven* (New Haven, CT and London: Yale University Press, 2016)

Burnett, Charles, *The Introduction of Arabic Learning into England* (London: British Library, 1998)

Bynum, Caroline Walker, *Christian Materiality: An Essay on Religion in Late Medieval Europe* (New York: Zone Books, 2011)

Camille, Michel, *The Gothic Idol: Ideology and Image-Making in Medieval Art* (Cambridge: Cambridge University Press, 1989)

Chareyron, Nicole, *Pilgrims to Jerusalem in the Middle Ages*, trans. by Donald Wilson (New York: Columbia University Press, 2005)

Cohen, Jeffrey Jerome, ed., *The Postcolonial Middle Ages* (New York and Houndmills: Palgrave, 2001)

Stone: An Ecology of the Inhuman (Minneapolis, MN: University of Minnesota Press, 2015)

Dinshaw, Carolyn, *Getting Medieval: Sexual Communities, Pre- and Postmodern* (Durham, NC and London: Duke University Press, 1999)

Dyer, Christopher, *Standards of Living in the Later Middle Ages: Social Change in England c.1200–1520* (Cambridge: Cambridge University Press, 1989)

Fernandez-Arresto, Felipe, *Before Columbus: Exploration and Colonization from the Mediterranean to the Atlantic (1229–1492)* (Basingstoke: Macmillan Education, 1987)

Freedman, Paul, *Out of the East: Spices and the Medieval Imagination* (New Haven, CT and London: Yale University Press, 2008)

Gilroy, Paul, *Postcolonial Melancholia* (New York: Columbia University Press, 2004)

Glissant, Édouard, *Poetics of Relation*, trans. Betsy Wing (Ann Arbor, MI: University of Michigan Press, 1997)

Goldberg, Jessica, *Trade and Institutions in the Medieval Mediterranean: The Geniza Merchants and their Business World* (Cambridge and New York: Cambridge University Press, 2012)

Gutas, Dimitri, *Greek Thought, Arab Culture: The Graeco-Arabic Translation Movement in Baghdad and Early 'Abbasid Society (2nd–4th/8th–10th Centuries)* (London and New York: Routledge, 1998)

Heng, Geraldine, *The Invention of Race in the European Middle Ages* (Cambridge: Cambridge University Press, 2018)

Jagot, Shazia, 'Chaucer and Ibn al-Haytham (Alhacen): *Perspectiva*, Arabic Mathematics, and Acts of Looking', *SAC* 44 (2022), 27–61

Khanmohamadi, Shirin, *In Light of Another's Word: European Ethnography in the Middle Ages* (Philadelphia, PA: University of Pennsylvania Press, 2014)

Kholeif, Omar, ed., *Michael Rakowitz: Backstroke of the West* (Chicago, IL: Museum of Contemporary Art Chicago and DelMonico Books, 2017)

Lambourn, Elizabeth, *Abraham's Luggage: A Social Life of Things in the Medieval Indian Ocean World* (Cambridge: Cambridge University Press, 2018)

Lavezzo, Kathy, *Angels on the Edge of the World: Geography, Literature and English Community, 1000–1534* (Ithaca, NY and London: Cornell University Press, 2006)

Le Goff, Jacques, *Money and the Middle Ages: An Essay in Historical Anthropology*, trans. Jean Birrell (Cambridge: Polity Press, 2012)

Metlitzki, Dorothee, *The Matter of Araby in Medieval England* (New Haven, CT and London: Yale University Press, 1977)

Mills, Robert, *Seeing Sodomy in the Middle Ages* (Chicago, IL: University of Chicago Press, 2014)

Nagel, Alexander, and Christopher Wood, *Anachronic Renaissance* (New York: Zone Books, 2010)

Rubin, Miri, *Corpus Christi: The Eucharist in Late Medieval Culture* (Cambridge: Cambridge University Press, 1991)

Shalem, Avinoam, 'The Otherness in the Focus of Interest: Or, if only the Other Could Speak', in *Islamic Artefacts in the Mediterranean World: Trade, Gift Exchange and Artistic Transfer*, ed. C.S. Arcangeli and G. Wolf (Venice: Marsilio, 2010), pp. 183–94

ed., *Constructing the Image of Muhammed in Europe* (Berlin: De Gruyter, 2013)

Shohat, Ella, *On the Arab-Jew, Palestine and Other Displacements* (London: Pluto Press, 2017)

Sobecki, Sebastian, ed., *The Sea and Englishness in the Middle Ages: Maritime Narratives, Identity and Culture* (Woodbridge: Brewer, 2011)

Turner, Marion, *Chaucer: A European Life* (Princeton, NJ and Oxford: Princeton University Press, 2019)

Wallace, David, ed., *Europe: A Literary History, 1348–1418*, 2 vols. (Oxford: Oxford University Press, 2016)

Wharton, Annabel, *Selling Jerusalem: Relics, Replicas, Theme Parks* (Chicago, IL and London: University of Chicago Press, 2006)

Whitaker, Cord J., *Black Metaphors: How Modern Racism Emerged from Medieval Race-Thinking* (Philadelphia, PA: Unviersity of Pennsylvania Press, 2019)

Wintroub, Michael, *The Voyage of Thought: Navigating Knowledge across the Sixteenth-Century World* (Cambridge: Cambridge University Press, 2017)

Ziadeh, Nicola, *Urban Life in Syria under the Early Mamluks* (Beirut: The American Press, 1953)

Index

Page numbers in *italics* refer to content in figures.